Conservation, Sustainability, and Environmental Justice in India

Environment and Society

Series Editor: Douglas Vakoch

As scholars examine the environmental challenges facing humanity, they increasingly recognize that solutions require a focus on the human causes and consequences of these threats, and not merely a focus on the scientific and technical issues. To meet this need, the Environment and Society series explores a broad range of topics in environmental studies from the perspectives of the social sciences and humanities. Books in this series help the reader understand contemporary environmental concerns while offering concrete steps to address these problems.

Books in this series include both monographs and edited volumes that are grounded in the realities of ecological issues identified by the natural sciences. Our authors and contributors come from disciplines including but not limited to anthropology, architecture, area studies, communication studies, economics, ethics, gender studies, geography, history, law, pedagogy, philosophy, political science, psychology, religious studies, sociology, and theology. To foster a constructive dialogue between these researchers and environmental scientists, the Environment and Society series publishes work that is relevant to those engaged in environmental studies while also being of interest to scholars from the author's primary discipline.

Titles in the Series

Conservation, Sustainability, and Environmental Justice in India edited by Alok Gupta
Secular Discourse on Sin in the Anthropocene: What's Wrong with the World? by Ernst M. Conradie
Environment, Social Justice, and the Media in the Age of Anthropocene, edited by Elizabeth G. Dobbins, Maria Lucia Piga, and Luigi Manca
Global Perspectives on Eco-Aesthetics and Eco-Ethics: A Green Critique, edited by Krishanu Maiti and Soumyadeep Chakraborty
Australian Wetland Cultures: Swamp Thinking, edited by John Charles Ryan and Li Chen
Motor Vehicles, the Environment, and the Human Condition: Driving to Extinction, by Hans A. Baer

Conservation, Sustainability, and Environmental Justice in India

Edited by
Alok Gupta

LEXINGTON BOOKS
Lanham • Boulder • New York • London

Published by Lexington Books
An imprint of The Rowman & Littlefield Publishing Group, Inc.
4501 Forbes Boulevard, Suite 200, Lanham, Maryland 20706
www.rowman.com

6 Tinworth Street, London SE11 5AL, United Kingdom

British Library Cataloguing in Publication Information Available

Library of Congress Control Number: 2020944430

ISBN 978-1-7936-1454-4 (cloth)
ISBN 978-1-7936-1455-1 (electronic)

Contents

Preface

It is a fact that today mankind is facing the worst environmental crisis caused by the disturbances in the balance of nature due to cutting down of forests and trees, indiscriminate conversion of grasslands into areas of habitation, leveling and tunneling of mountains, and changes in landscapes. All these man-made activities have destroyed ecosystems, generated chemical and radioactive pollution, and produced nonbiodegradable matter. This has also led to the possibility of greenhouse gases warming up the planet and damaging the ozone layer, which in turn would affect life on earth. Environmental destruction and pollution are seriously threatening human life, health, and livelihood.

Increase in deserts; shrinking of forests; alarming pollution of water, air, and land; extinction of endangered species; and indiscriminate use and exhaustion of natural resources are major problems every nation is facing. Environment protection and preservation has become a global concern. If the quality of life of the present generation has to be ensured and if the future generations have to be saved from an environmental catastrophe, the nature's gift to us in the form of flora and fauna has to be preserved in their natural forms.

A proper balance between development activities and environmental protection is the need of hour, and the solution lies in sustainable development. The object of environmental law is to preserve and protect the nature. But the law alone cannot tackle the problem of pollution. There has to be awareness about the problem, and sustained efforts are required to tackle it. Every nation will have to evolve devices and strategies on these lines for the maintenance of environmental safety and achievement of sustainable development. There is also a need for the active participation of the judiciary in protecting the environment with special reference to public interest "environmental" litigation.

This book contains twenty chapters that discuss various aspects of the conservation and legal dimensions of environment, contributed by faculty, research scholars, academicians, and educationists.

I am indebted to all the authors for reposing their confidence by sending their contributions. My thanks are due to Dr. Douglas Vakoch, president, METI (Messaging Extraterrestrial Intelligence), and Ms. Mikayla Mislak, assistant editor, and Mr. Michael Gibson, senior acquisitions editor, Lexington Books, who worked with keen interest and devotion to ensure timely publication of the book. I am also thankful to my wife, Neetu, and daughter, Anisha, for their support and encouragement.

I hope the book will be immensely useful to academicians, environmentalists, policy planners, scholars, researchers, and students of environmental sciences and law. It focuses on various new aspects and answers several questions on the topics covered. Finally, I hope the book will help in identifying new issues to address on the academic front.

Dr. Alok Gupta

Chapter 1

Environment Protection Laws and Sustainable Development in India

Amit Dhall

INTRODUCTION

The concept behind the term "environment" is very comprehensive and includes the external conditions, resources, stimuli, and so on with which an organism interacts. The consciousness and thought for the environment covers several environmental issues such as pollution of water, air, and soil; land degradation; depletion of natural resources; and the need for urbanization and industrialization. The laws concerning the environment are very vital in protecting natural resources. Environmental laws must be effectively enforced to gain benefits from the optimum use of scarce resources. Laws serve as a valued instrument for educating masses about their responsibility and help in maintaining a healthy environment.

According to the Preamble of the United Nations Declaration on Human Environment, adopted in Stockholm in June 1972, "Man is both creature and molder of his environment, which gives him physical substance and affords him the opportunity for intellectual, moral, social and spiritual growth."

Our environment is obviously at risk from a variety of sources, mostly human sources. There is a need to modify human behavior toward environmentally benign practices and away from environmentally damaging ones. In order to tackle this problem, it is important that we develop strategies. In very broad terms, techniques for modifying human behavior can be thought of as falling into two types: disincentives and incentives. Law is important as it creates a framework within which incentives and disincentives can operate. Environmental law is a frame of law, which is a structure of complex and intertwining statutes, common law, treaties, conventions, regulations, and policies that seek to protect the natural environment, which may be affected, impacted, or endangered by human activities.

Some environmental laws regulate the quantity and nature of impacts of human activities. Setting allowable levels of pollution or requiring permits for potentially harmful activities is a restrictive law. Environmental laws are preventive in nature when they seek to assess the possible impacts before the human activities can happen. Nowadays, environmental law is rapidly becoming an important and specialized branch of law. While the questions that are addressed by environmental law are practical in nature, the remedies of these issues are mainly procedural in nature. Recently, environmental law has become a critical means of promoting sustainable development. Policies and notions such as the precautionary principle, public participation, environmental justice, and the "polluter pays" principle have led to many environmental law transformations. Some of these innovations are eco-taxes, tradable emission allowances, and voluntary standards such as ISO 14000 and negotiated arrangements.

CONSTITUTIONAL AND LEGISLATIVE PROVISIONS FOR ENVIRONMENTAL PROTECTION

The Directive Principles of State Policy enshrined under Part IV of the Constitution of India are the active responsibilities of the state, acting as prescriptions for the guidance of the government. The Constitution under Article 37 of Part IV limits the application of the Directive Principles by declaring that these principles shall not be enforceable by the judiciary. Article 48A provides for protection and improvement of the environment and safeguarding of forests and wildlife. The state shall endeavor to protect and improve the environment and to safeguard the forests and wildlife of the country.

The preservation of the environment from pollution—caused by smoke, industrial waste, and deadly exhaust fumes from motorcars and other combustion engines—is necessary to prevent the damage to the health and well-being of the people. Also, the preservation of wildlife is looked upon as necessary for the preservation of ecological balance. Under Article 48A of the Constitution, it has been rightly emphasized that the state should try not only to protect but rather to improve the environment. Articles 39(e), 47, and 48A of the Directive Principles of State Policy have a definite bearing on environmental issues. Article 49 provides for the obligation of the state to protect monuments, places, and objects of national importance. Further, Article 51(c) directs the state to foster respect for international law and treaty obligations in the dealings with one another.

The Constitution under Article 51A specifies ten fundamental duties. Article 51A(g) states that it shall be the duty of every citizen of India to protect and have compassion for living creatures. Justice Ranganath Mishra has observed: "Preservation of environment and keeping the ecological balance unaffected is a task which not only Government but also every citizen must undertake. It is a social obligation and let us remind every citizen that it is his fundamental duty as enshrined in Article 51A(g)of the Constitution."[1]

It is both a constitutional pointer to the state and a constitutional duty of the citizens not only to protect but also to improve the environment and to preserve and safeguard the forests, flora and fauna, rivers and lakes, and all other water resources of the country. The neglect or failure to abide by the pointer or to perform the duty is nothing short of a betrayal of the fundamental law that the state and, indeed, every Indian, high or low, is bound to uphold and maintain.[2]

The fundamental right to wholesome environment as given under Article 21 provides that no person shall be deprived of his life or personal liberty except according to procedure established by law. Article 32, through remedies for enforcement of rights, provides the right to move the Supreme Court by appropriate proceedings for the enforcement of the rights. The Supreme Court has the power to issue directions or orders, including writs, in the nature of habeas corpus, mandamus, prohibition, quo warranto, and certiorari, whichever may be appropriate, for the enforcement of any of these rights. The Constitution, under Article 19(1)(g), guarantees to all citizens of India the right to practice any profession or to carry out any occupation, business, or trade. This freedom, however, is not unrestrained. In case trade and business interests are affected by the action of governmental agencies in the name of environmental protection, the aggrieved industrialist may resort to Article 19. The judiciary needs to balance environmental interests with the fundamental right to carry on any occupation, trade, or business guaranteed by Article 19(1)(g) of the Constitution of India. The Constitution, under Article 48A, provides a set of Directive Principles of State Policy for the protection and improvement of environment and safeguarding of forests and wildlife. The state shall endeavor to protect and improve the environment and to safeguard the forests and wildlife of the country. Article 49 states that it shall be the obligation of the state to protect every monument or place or object of artistic or historic interest, declared by or under law made by Parliament to be of national importance, from spoliation, disfigurement, destruction, removal, disposal, or export, as the case may be. Article 51A(g) states that it shall be the duty of every citizen of India to protect and improve the natural environment, including forests, lakes, rivers, and wild life, and to have compassion for living creatures.

The Environment (Protection) Act was enacted in the year 1986 with the main objective of ensuring the protection and improvement of environment and matters connected therewith. The law governs the air and water quality, and dictates the ways in which the disposal of waste and hazardous materials can legally take place. Individuals or corporations can be found guilty of environmental crimes. The chief feature of environmental law is the necessity for an interdisciplinary approach owing to the complexity of the matter. In order to prepare appropriate modern legal rules, legal research should be undertaken in the fields of legal necessity and comparative regulation.

The Indian Penal Code (IPC) of 1860 contains elaborate provisions defining the crime of public nuisance. Section 277 deals with offences of the fouling of water of a public spring or reservoir. Whoever voluntarily corrupts or fouls the water of any public spring or reservoir, so as to render it less fit for the purpose for which it is ordinarily used, shall be punished with imprisonment of either description for a term which may extend to three months, or with fine which may extend to five hundred rupees, or with both. Section 278 provides punishment for making atmosphere noxious to the health of a community.

These provisions have direct relevance to environmental protection as they seek to prevent water and air pollution through a penal strategy. However, their effective application toward achieving this objective is doubtful, because the technicalities of Indian criminal law require a complete satisfaction of the ingredients of the offence as stipulated in the penal provisions.

JUDICIAL ACTIVISM

The role played by judicial activism has made its impact felt more in the area of environmental protection than in any other field. *Municipal council, Ratlam v. Vardhichand*[3] is a signpost. The Supreme Court identified the responsibilities of local bodies toward the protection of environment and developed the law of public nuisance in the Code of Criminal Procedure as a potent instrument for the enforcement of their duties.

Under the English law, "a person who for his own purposes brings on his own land and collects and keeps there anything likely to do mischief if it escapes, must keep it in at his peril, and, if he does not do so, is prima facie answerable for all the damage which is the natural consequence of its escape" as laid down by the landmark judgment in *Ryland v. Fletcher.*[4] In India, the rule was evolved in *M C Mehta v. Union of India,*[5] which was popularly known as the Oleum gas leak case. The indirect approval of the right to a humane and healthy environment by the Supreme Court continued further in the Oleum gas leak case.[6] Life cannot be possible without clean drinking water; therefore, the right to clean water is one of the attributes of the right to life in Article 21 of the Constitution.[7]

In *V. Lakshmipathy v. State of Karnataka,*[8] the High Court of Karnataka held that once a development plan had earmarked an area for residential purpose, the land was bound to be put to such use only. The Supreme Court has recognized another aspect of the right to life, that is, right to livelihood enshrined under Article 21 of the Constitution, viz. the right to livelihood. The right to livelihood has been recognized by the Supreme Court in the case of *Olga Tellis v. Bombay Municipal Corporation.*[9] The Court issued directions to the municipal corporation to provide alternative sites or accommodation to the slum and pavement dwellers near their original sites, as well as to provide amenities to slum dwellers. The Constitution, under Article 14, guarantees to every person the right to not be denied equality before the law or equal protection under the laws. The right may be invoked to challenge governmental sanction of projects having an adverse impact on the natural environment and where such sanctions involve arbitrary consideration. In *Indian Council for Enviro-Legal Action v. Union of India*,[10] the court observed, "We are of the opinion that any principle evolved in this behalf should be simple, practical and suited to the conditions obtaining in this country."

The court ruled that "Once the activity carried on is hazardous or inherently dangerous, the person carrying on such activity is liable to make good the loss caused to any other person by his activity irrespective of the fact whether he took reasonable care while carrying on his activity. The rule is premised upon the very nature of the activity carried on."

The control of environment degradation in India is sought through Environment (Protection) Act 1986, the Factories (Amendment) Act 1987, the Public Liability Insurance Act, 1991 (PLIA), and other strict legislations. In 1992, the UN Conference on Environment and Development was held in Rio de Janeiro; it provided a further shot, as did environmental litigation and activism. The most recent law in the field of "accident" law is the National Environmental Tribunal Act, 1995 (NETA). The PLIA deals with interim compensation, and the NETA provides guidelines to adjudicate all claims arising out of "accidents." These acts provide for no-fault liability, making the "owner" liable for paying compensation assessed under legislations and acts.

The right to wholesome environment is a fundamental right protected under Article 21 of the Indian Constitution. But the issue relates to the protection of the environment in the present times when almost all the countries in Southeast Asia are still developing economies. Since development comes through industrialization, which itself is a factor behind the degradation of environment, a need is felt for sustainable development—that is, there must be balance between development and ecosystem. The notion of sustainable development had evolved in 1972 in the Stockholm Declaration. It had been stated in the declaration that "Man has the fundamental right to freedom, equality and adequate conditions of life, in an environment of a quality that permits a life of dignity and well-being and he bears a solemn responsibility to protect and improve the environment for present and future generation." The idea was given a definite shape in a report, titled the Brundtland Report, by the World Commission on Environment, which was known as

"Our Common Future". The world commission was chaired by Ms. G. H. Brundtland who defined sustainable development as "development that meets the needs of the present without compromising he ability of the future generations to meet their own needs."

Some basic principles described in the Brundtland Report are as follows:

1. Intergenerational Equity: It provides every generation the right to get benefits from natural resources. Principle 3 of the Rio declaration states that the right to development must be fulfilled so as to equitably meet developmental and environmental needs of present and future generations. The sole object behind the principle is to ensure that the present generation should not abuse the nonrenewable resources such that it deprives the future generations of their advantages.
2. The Precautionary Principle: It states that the environmental measures by the state government and the local authority must anticipate, prevent, and attack the causes of environmental degradation. In case of threats of serious and irreversible damage, lack of scientific certainty should not be used as a reason for postponing measures to prevent environmental dilapidation. Also, the onus of proof is on the actor or the developer to prove that his action is environment friendly. Principle 15 of the Rio declaration states that "In order to protect the environment, the precautionary approach shall be widely applied by States according to their capabilities. Where there are threats of serious or irreversible damage, lack of full scientific certainty shall not be used as a reason for postponing cost-effective measures to prevent environmental degradation."
3. Polluter Pays Principle: According to Principle 16 of the Rio declaration, "National authorities should endeavor to promote the internalization of environmental costs and the use of economic instruments, taking into account the approach that the polluter should, in principle, bear the cost of pollution, with due regard to the public interest and without distorting international trade and investment." This principle makes the polluter liable not only for compensation to the victims but also for the cost of restoring the environmental degradation.

SUSTAINABLE DEVELOPMENT AND CONSERVATION OF BIODIVERSITY

Sustainable development can be achieved only by protecting the environment. The environment degradation resulting from industrial pollution, deforestation, and depletion of ozone layer causes global warming. Greenhouse gases cause environment disturbances and negatively affect the climate, creating an adverse impact on health human. The need to achieve sustainable development has been long felt. This can be achieved through the conservation of biodiversity, protection of wetlands, control of environmental pollution, and maintenance of ecological balance. The effect of global warming is that there is a gradual increase in the average temperature of the Earth's atmosphere and its oceans. The climate changes due to global warming cause extinction of species and destroy their habitats. The chances for ecosystems to adapt naturally are fading, and this is one of the greatest threats to the planet. Climate changes have increased the occurrences of natural disasters such as droughts, cyclones, and floods.

In the year 1988, the National Forest Policy was introduced with a focus on ensuring environmental stability, restoring the ecological balance, and preserving forests to meet the need for fuelwood, fodder, and small timber for rural and tribal people while recognizing the need to actively involve local people in the management of forests. The document on Indian National Forest Policy, 2009 stresses the need to combine India's efforts toward forest conservation with sustainable forest organization.

Wetlands have the characteristics of both wet and dry environments, and show immense diversity based on their genesis, geographical location, hydrological regimes, and substrate aspects. These characteristics include the most productive life support. India is a signatory to the Ramsar Convention on Wetlands and the Convention on Biological Diversity (CBD). The former, signed in Ramsar, Iran, in 1971, is an intergovernmental treaty that provides a framework for national action and international cooperation for the conservation and wise use of wetlands and their resources. This convention is the only global environment treaty dealing with a particular ecosystem. Governments that have joined the convention have expressed their willingness to make a commitment for helping to reverse the history of wetland loss and degradation. In addition, many wetlands are international systems across the boundaries of two or more countries, or are part of river basins that are spread across more than one country. Wetlands are complex ecosystems and encompass a wide range of inland, coastal and marine habitats, floodplains, swamps, marshes, fishponds, and tidal marshes. Wetlands can be natural or man-made. They are essential to the survival of natural biodiversity and have immense socioeconomic and ecological importance for human beings.

The conservation of biodiversity is extremely pertinent to human existence. The Parliament of India enacted the Biological Diversity Act in 2002 for the preservation of biological diversity in India. It provides a mechanism for the equitable sharing of benefits arising from the use of traditional biological resources and knowledge. The objective of this legislation is to meet the obligations under CBD, to which India is a signatory. The National Biodiversity Authority (NBA) was established in 2003 as a statutory, autonomous body to perform facilitative, regulatory, and advisory functions for the Government of India on issues of conservation, sustainable use of biological resources, and fair and equitable sharing of benefits arising out of the use of biological resources. NBA is also tasked with the duty to implement the Biological Diversity Act. The conservation of wildlife has become an increasingly important practice owing to the negative effects of human activity on wildlife in India. The Wildlife Conservation Act was enacted in 2002 to protect wildlife in India. Wildlife conservation is the essential practice of protecting endangered plant and animal species and their habitats. The introduction of Project Tiger ensured that a feasible population of tigers in India is preserved as a natural heritage for the benefit, education, and enjoyment of people. In February 1992, Project Elephant (PE), a centrally sponsored scheme, was launched to provide financial and technical support to major elephant-bearing states in the country for the protection of elephants and their corridors and habitats in India.

Since the late 1970s, the depletion of ozone has occurred at a steady rate of about 4 percent per decade from the total volume of ozone in the Earth's stratosphere (the ozone layer); moreover, a much larger springtime decrease in stratospheric ozone has occurred over the Earth's polar areas. The ozone depletion has increased with an increase in the emission of pollutants. Chlorofluorocarbons (CFCs) and other contributory substances are referred to as ozone-depleting substances. The ozone layer protects the Earth's inhabitants from the ultraviolet rays of the Sun, and as such the increasing size of the ozone hole is dangerous to their safety.

The environmental impact assessment (EIA) is an assessment of the possible impact that a proposed project may have on the environment, consisting of the environmental, social, and economic aspects. The objective of the assessment is to ensure that before any project is undertaken, a study of the impact of the activities on the environment is undertaken. The International Association for Impact Assessment (IAIA) defines an environmental impact assessment as "the process of identifying, predicting, evaluating and mitigating the biophysical, social, and other relevant effects of development proposals prior to major decisions being taken and commitments made." Such assessments are exclusive as they do not require adherence to a predetermined environmental outcome, but rather they require the decision makers to account for environmental values in their decisions and to justify those decisions in light of detailed environmental studies and public comments on the potential environmental impact.

CONCLUSIONS AND SUGGESTIONS

Environmental issues are best handled with the participation of all concerned citizens at the relevant level. Every individual must have (i) appropriate access to information concerning the environment that is held by public authorities, including information on hazardous materials and activities, in their communities, and (ii) the opportunity to participate in the decision-making process.

Lately, litigation related to environmental pollution has grown at a rapid pace, as businesses come under greater inquiry for their environmental practices and face heavy liabilities. Rapid industrialization has posed serious concern for environment protection. If we follow the developments around the world in the past two decades or so, it is clear that both judicial and legislative processes have applied the yardstick of "strict or absolute liability" to judge the conduct of the polluters. The concept of "environment" can be described as a limited area or the entire planet, even including a part of the outer space that surrounds the Earth. The social mechanism of environmental protection can be characterized by a three-stage approach. At the preliminary stage, the law—mainly national constitutions, laws with a large environmental scope, and major intentional declarations or treaties—defines the environmental values to be protected and preserved. At the second stage, the environmental policy determines the objectives and strategies that should be used in order to ensure that environmental values are respected, taking into account the prevailing economic, cultural, and social conditions. At the third stage, legal instruments are used to achieve the objectives fixed by the environmental policy. The content of such instruments can be economic, educational, political, or social. However, their implementation needs the support of public opinion, the agreement of which was the very basis of the recognition of the environment as a fundamental principle. States must facilitate and encourage public awareness and participation by making information widely available. They should also provide effective access to judicial and administrative proceedings, including redress and remedy against environmental crimes. Environment protection and development are two sides of the same coin. One cannot be sacrificed for the other as both are equally important for ensuring a safe future for the community. Thus, it is the responsibility of the Supreme Court and the high courts to deal with these cases with caution of a high degree. Then only we will achieve our goal of realizing balanced economic growth and a pollution-free, developed country for our next generations. India has had a diverse growth pattern and is among the most rapidly growing economies in the world. The people of India should strive to conserve the ecological character of their country's ecosystems along with the biodiversity of the associated flora and fauna. In addition to government regulations, the development of a better monitoring system is needed to spread and gain from the knowledge about the physical and biological characteristics of wetland resources. A better understanding of environmental dynamics and their controlling processes can be ensured through public awareness and education.

NOTES

1. *Rural Litigation and Entitlement Kendra v. State of U.P.,* AIR 1987 SC 359, 364.
2. *Kinkridevi v. State of Himachal Pradesh,* AIR 1988 HP 4, 8.
3. AIR 1980 SC 1622.
4. (1868) LR 3 HL 330.
5. AIR 1987 SC 1086.
6. *M.C. Mehta v. Union of India,* AIR 1987 SC 965.
7. *Attakoya Thangal v. Union of India* 1990 (1) KLT 580.
8. AIR 1992 Kant 57.
9. AIR 1986 SC 180.
10. *AIR1996SC1446.*

REFERENCES

Bakshi, Upendra, *Environment Protection Act: An Agenda for Implementation,* N.M. Tripathi Pvt. Ltd., Bombay, 1987.

Bakshi, P.M., *The Environment Protection Act, 1986,* Indian Law Institute, New Delhi, 1992.

Baxi, Upendra, *Environment Protection Act: An Agenda for Implementation,* ILI, Delhi, 1987.

Diwan, Paras. and Diwan, Peeyushi, *Environmental Laws- Implementations, Problems and Perspectives,* Deep and Deep Publications Pvt. Ltd., New Delhi, 2002.

Jaiswal, P.S., *The Environment (Protection) Act, 1986, Environmental Law,* Pioneer Publications, Delhi, 2003, pp. 36–75.

Chapter 2

Corporate Social Responsibility

An Effective Tool for Climate Change

Amit M. Bhattacharya

INTRODUCTION

It is a well-known fact that climate change, positive or negative, is attributed to manmade activities. From carbon emission and the consequent depletion of the ozone layer to two deaths per minute in India due to inhalation of poisonous air or consumption of contaminated water or adulterated food, there are many direct manifestations of the illogical and uncontrolled production–consumption human behavior. Comparatively, far less populous industrially developed countries are held responsible for emission of astronomical amounts of carbon, and their reckless consumption patterns are held responsible for global warming. It is true to some extent; however, it is also true that these are the countries that are taking most sincere and effective steps to contain global warming in a time-bound manner. India and other developing countries are in the rat race of imitating the Western pattern of reckless consumption to attain ever higher GDP without any consideration for the consequences of their acts that are endangering the lives of their people and the survival of this planet. Had the people of the developing nations had enormous wealth like the US, the EU, or the oil-rich Middle Eastern countries, the quantum of their carbon footprint would have surpassed that of the developed nations seven decades ago. Surely, a poor person's consumption pattern of things from fuel to food is so limited that they cannot emit the amount of carbon in even 100 years that an affluent person emits it in a day.

Oxfam India has stated that "73 percent of the wealth generated last year went to the richest one percent, while 67 crore Indians who comprise the poorest half of the population saw one percent increase in their wealth" and "it would take 941 years for a minimum wage worker in rural India to earn what the top paid executive at a leading Indian garment company earns in a year."[1] From these analyses, it should be easily understood as to who will possess more and more cars, air conditioners, refrigerators, room heaters, LED TVs, multiple concrete buildings, lawns, luxurious bathtubs, swimming pools, and so on, and what would their contribution to carbon emissions be. Hitting at the gaping inequality in India, the report further states, "In the last 12 months the wealth of this elite group increased by Rs. 20,913 billion. This amount is equivalent to total budget of Central Government in 2017–18" and that "it would take around 17.5 days for the best paid executive at a top Indian garment company to earn what a minimum wage worker in rural India will earn in their lifetime (presuming 50 years at work)." The purpose of mentioning the inequality is that it may give a vague idea that the consumption pattern of the elite class is changing at a rapid pace, thereby adding substantially to the country's carbon footprint and accelerating the climate change. Such Indian elite class can afford to waste Rs. 244 crore worth of food a day while 194 million poor go hungry daily. Food worth Rs. 88,800 crore is wasted in India per year. This food involves a range of energy inputs for activities such as production, processing, distribution, storage, preparation, and waste disposal, and all these processes emit huge amounts of carbon. It is no surprise then that India's rank in the Global Hunger Index is 100 among 119 countries.[2] Further, the cumulative effect of such wasteful behavior attracts attention to a report published with the heading "2019 will see the highest carbon dioxide levels on record"; the report elaborates,

> Carbon dioxide levels in the atmosphere are expected to make one of the biggest rises this year in more than six decades, warn scientists. The build-up of the greenhouse gas could soar because changing weather in the Pacific could reduce the ability of natural "sinks" such as forests or grass-lands to absorb excess carbon. Combined with rising emissions from human activity, such as burning fossil fuels, this implies that experts predict one of the largest rises in atmospheric carbon dioxide in 62 years of measurements.

The report further points out in a nutshell that "weather patterns linked to swings in the Pacific Ocean temperatures affect the absorption of carbon by plants. The tropical pacific is expected to be warmer this year, which means many regions become drier and this limits the growth of plants." It further adds that "2018 was fourth hottest year" and that "the last four years have been the hottest since record-keeping began, with 2018 the fourth warmest on record, according to Berkley Earth. Temp in 2018 was around 1.16 degrees Celsius above the average temp of the second half of the 19th century, from 1850–1900, often used as a pre-industrial baseline for global temp targets."[3]

Hence, imminent danger is looming large on India, and the nation cannot escape its responsibility toward a clarion call for tackling climate change.

Ad hocism and instability are emerging as the new normal in Indian political culture. While this chapter discusses the formulation and strict implementation of policies for arresting and reversing the alarming climate change, it is observed that from 2009 to 2019, no minister in the Ministry of Environment, Forest and Climate Change in India could perform for a full term. The ministry records show the periods of various ministers—Mr. Jairam Ramesh (2009–2011), Ms. Jayanthi Natarajan (2011–2013), Mr. Veerappa Moily (2013–14), Mr. Prakash Javadekar (2014–2016), Mr. Anil Madhav Dave (2016–2017), and Dr. Harsh Vardhan (2017–2019)—who worked as if on a merry-go-round and thus remained utterly ineffective in addressing the interrelated grave challenges of climate change.

GLOBAL CLIMATE CHANGE AND INDIA

Climate change is not at all a new phenomenon, and it has been present since the origin of the Earth. The threat of climate change has emerged because of its accelerated rate and projected negative impacts caused by man-made developmental activities. The Fourth Assessment Report of the Intergovernmental Panel on Climate Change (IPCC) mentions that the adverse impact of human activities on climate and climate systems can no longer be denied. A Government of India report states that "It is no longer the scientific enquiry but the concern now rather is the timing and magnitude of the abrupt changes in the climate."[4]

Although data on climate change and global warming has been presented by the IPCC, Berkeley Earth and the Zurich University of Applied Sciences differ considerably. The difference may be due to the fact that a separate set of parameters for global warming has been considered by the information sources. While Berkley states that "the average temperature comes out to 13.8°C (56.9°F). When subtracting 5.5 ± 1.5°C (9.9 ± 2.7°F) from the 1850–1899 average, the average temperature for the last glacial maximum comes out to 8.3 ± 1.5°C (47.0 ± 2.7°F). This is about 6.7 ± 1.5°C (12.1 ± 2.7°F) colder than the 2013–2017 average." However, the IPCC does not agree with the figures given by Berkeley Earth,[5] and the illustration in figure 2.1 shows the direct impact of climate change on the water level.

India is not an exception that climatic variations will spare its flora, fauna, business, growth, and development, including physical, mental, and sociocultural functioning. The vast Indian peninsula is facing the increasing wrath of nature in the form of extreme weather events since 1980 following the rapid

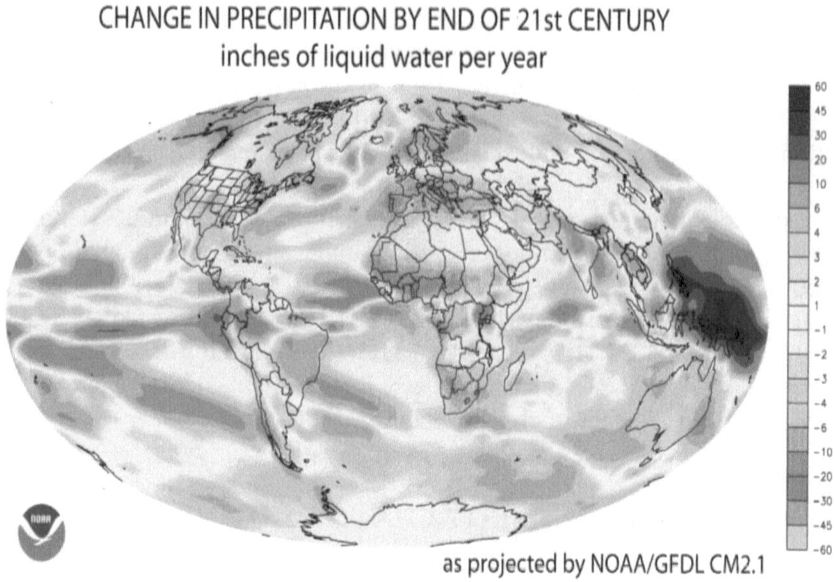

Figure 2.1 Impact of Climate Change on Water Level. *Source:* Geophysical Fluid Dynamics Laboratory report: https://www.gfdl.noaa.gov/global-warming-and-hurricanes/

expansion of growth activities in the country. These events are intensifying with each passing day. Climate is a vital factor in the economic development of India. Its geographical uniqueness endows it with all six climate types, and every aspect of life is largely determined, directly or indirectly, by climatic variations. Comparatively, India contributes less than 10 percent to global carbon emissions. However, it has become imperative that India implements all the measures and options strategically to contain the menace of greenhouse gases (GHGs) to ensure continuous growth and sustainability.

While figures 2.1, 2.2, and 2.3 give India credit for not being critically responsible for GHGs in the global perspective, they may be misleading.

The World Bank provided data for India for the period 1960–2014. The data revealed that the average value of carbon emissions from India was 704,903 kilotons, with a minimum of 120,582 kilotons in 1960 and a maximum of 2,238,377 kilotons in 2014.

Figure 2.4 shows the ever-rising percentage of emissions due to the use of fossil fuels. It is bound to increase in the coming decades because India's efforts to attain higher economic growth rate would definitely boost industrialization and the use of fossil fuels in various ways.

In early 2019, all the metropolitan and major cities in India recorded "Very Poor" air quality, ranging from 353 to 476 parts per million (safe air quality ranges from 75 to 95 parts per million). In particular, people in New Delhi were at great risk in spite of all possible precautions taken to brave the air

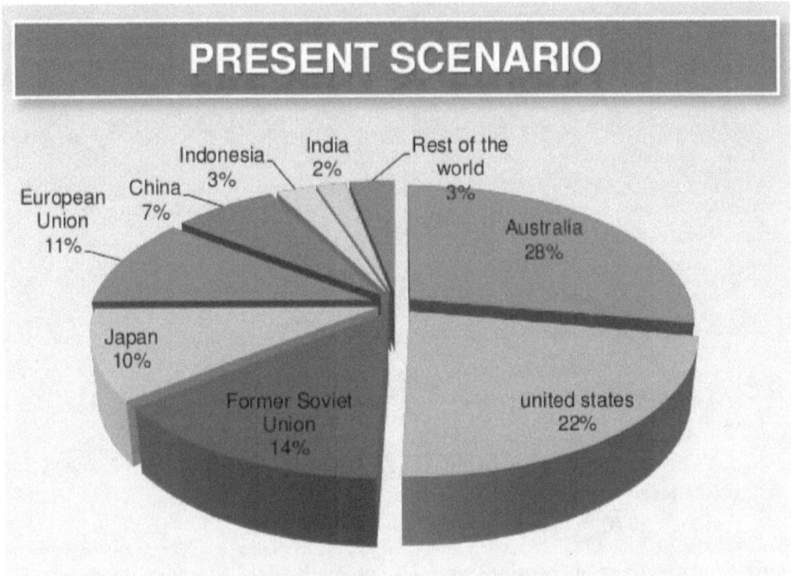

Figure 2.2 Present Scenario of Greenhouse Effect. *Source:* Geophysical Fluid Dynamics Laboratory report: https://www.gfdl.noaa.gov/global-warming-and-hurricanes/

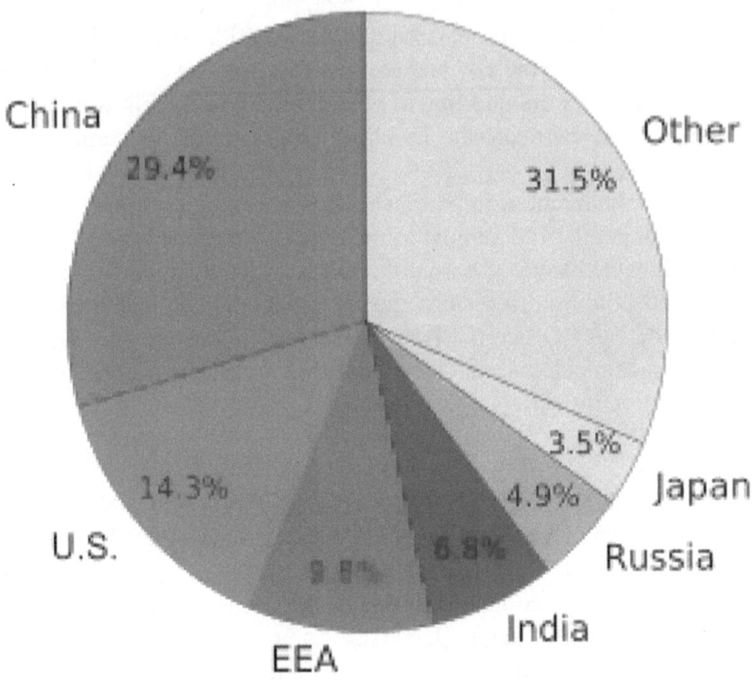

Figure 2.3 Percentage of Carbon Emission. *Source:* Geophysical Fluid Dynamics Laboratory report: https://www.gfdl.noaa.gov/global-warming-and-hurricanes/

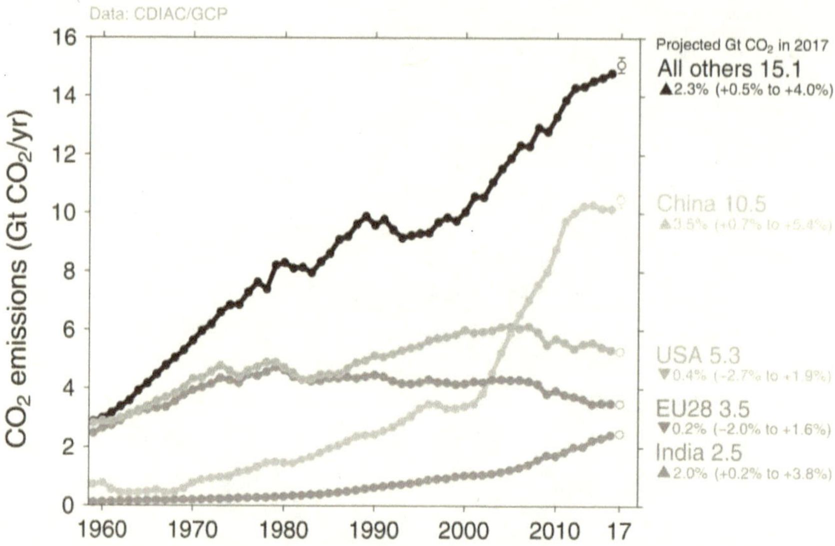

Figure 2.4 Percentage of Emissions from Use of Fossil Fuels. *Source:* Geophysical Fluid Dynamics Laboratory report: https://www.gfdl.noaa.gov/global-warming-and-hurricanes/

pollution. The gravity of the situation can be understood from the fact that a judge of the Supreme Court declared that he would leave New Delhi on the day of his retirement as the city had literally become a gas chamber. Citizens repeatedly asked the valid question of whether the government was indirectly legitimizing "passive euthanasia" by blindly imitating the Western economic growth model.

Realizing the paramount importance for countering the imminent danger of climate change, the Indian government created a framework for statistics relating to climate change. The final shape was given after consulting the key ministries and holding discussions during a national seminar organized by the Central Statistics Office (CSO) in 2013, which was attended by a large number of academicians, researchers, state/UT government representatives, data-producing ministries, and data users.

CARBON EMISSION IN INDIA AND RECENT INITIATIVES OF THE GOVERNMENT

In 2015, the national communication to the United Nations Framework Convention on Climate Change (UNFCCC) mentioned that "energy sector is the biggest greenhouse gas emitter in India" and that "more climate models [are] needed for improving future projections."

The issue of climate change was debated in India for the first time as a political agenda during the Fourth Five Year Plan (1969–1974), and the then-prime minister Indira Gandhi added Article 48A to the Constitution for the creation of a full-fledged ministry for effectively handling the situation. The ministry came into being in 1980 and was reshaped as the Ministry of Environment, Forest and Climate Change (MoEFCC) in 2014. Since 2010, the Government of India has implemented several initiatives to tackle climate change, which are listed in table 2.1.

CORPORATE SOCIAL RESPONSIBILITY FOR ENVIRONMENT PROTECTION

It is a commonplace notion that which cannot be measured cannot be improved. The author made his best efforts to gather data on how much the firms listed herein spent on corporate social responsibility (CSR) activities in 2018–2019 and what impact they created. Even though CSR has been made mandatory, it has been observed that a good number of companies do not report their CSR funding size and the sector-wise projects they support.

Figure 2.5 shows the status of CSR expenses by some of the leading private and public sector companies in India for the fiscal 2013–2014.

The Ministry of Corporate Affairs (MCA) produced a list of 5097 companies and their CSR expenses for 2015–2016. Of such a large list, only 2693 companies showed their interest toward CSR. Among these, 848 companies spent Rs. 0.1 crore only, while 2405 listed and profit-earning companies did not spend any amount on CSR.

The maximum amount on CSR was spent by Reliance Industries Limited (Rs. 652 crore). It was followed by TCS (Rs. 294 crore), ITC (Rs. 247 crore), TISCO (Rs. 204 crore), Wipro (Rs. 156 crore), and HUL (Rs. 92 crore). Similarly, among the state-owned companies, the maximum CSR expenses were incurred by NTPC (Rs. 492 crore), followed by ONGC (Rs. 421 crore), NMDC (Rs. 210 crore), GAIL (Rs. 160 crore), and IOC (Rs. 158 crore).[6]

However impressive these numbers seem to be, it is difficult to say how much resources were actually spent toward climate change issues, owing to lack of authentic data on government portals. Oftentimes, it has been observed that owing to defective interpretation, various public sector enterprises such as railways and banks treat even fulfilling the quota of disabled persons as a CSR activity, while private companies spend huge amounts on awareness programs and on meaningless activities such as "Run for Clean Air" and "March to Save Water," some of which are under the aegis of environment protection.

Table 2.1 Initiatives by the Government of India

S. No.	*Initiative*	*Description*
1	Indian Network for Climate Change Assessment (INCCA)	A network of 120 research institutions with 250 scientists launched in 2010
2	Himalayan Glaciers Monitoring Program	A comprehensive program to scientifically monitor the Himalayan glaciers
3	Launch of an Indian satellite to monitor greenhouse gases (GHGs)	A microsatellite launched by ISRO in 2010 to study aerosols and monitor GHGs
4	Research on India's forest and tree cover as a carbon sink	For estimating the value of India's forests as a carbon sink
5	India's GHG emissions profile	India's GHG Emission Pathways until 2030
6	Expert group on low carbon economy	Group set up to develop a strategy for India as a low carbon economy
7	State action plans on climate change	States finalizing their plans on policy development
8	National Policy on Biofuels	Production and use of biofuels in transport and other applications
9	National Action Plan on Climate Change	National missions on solar energy
10	First National Conference on Green Buildings	Materials and technologies to stimulate a green building sector
11	Thirty "solar cities"	Thirty "solar cities" with an aim of 10% reduction in the projected demand for conventional energy
12	Energy efficiency standards	Energy efficiency ratings made mandatory for appliances
13	Fuel efficiency norms plan	Fuel economy norms for vehicles announced
14	CDM Program India	Indian projects to neutralize 10% of emissions by 2012
15	India to host Rio+20	11th COP of Convention on Biodiversity (CBD) held in India in 2012
16	UN Climate Technology Conference	India successfully hosted a global conference on technology
17	SAARC Environment Conference India	SAARC Summit on the theme of Climate Change International Cooperation
18	India's submissions to the UNFCCC Report	India's twelve proactive submissions to UNFCCC released
19	State of Forests Report 2009	Latest State of Forests Report released
20	Launch of CAMPA	A 2010 document shows continued rise in India's forest cover
21	Green India Mission	New mission under NAPCC to fast-track reforestation
22	Capacity building in forestry schemes	New Rs. 369 crore (USD 80 million) scheme for forest personnel
23	Intensification of forest management	New Rs. 600 crore forestry scheme announced for the management of forests, infrastructure, fires, and so on
24	Inclusion of forestry within MNREGA	India's flagship employment guarantee scheme to fast-track reforestation

SR NO.	COMPANY	REVENUE	AVG PAT	ACTUAL SPEND	2% OF PAT
1	INDIAN OIL CORPORATION	442,459	7,783	83	156
2	RELIANCE INDUSTRIES	368,571	21,138	288	423
3	BHARAT PETROLEUM CORPORATION	223,315	1,438	8	29
4	HINDUSTAN PETRO-LEUM CORPORATION	195,891	1,118	27	22
5	TATA MOTORS	170,678	8,437	15	169
6	OIL & NATURAL GAS CORPORATION	151,121	23,660	121	473
7	STATE BANK OF INDIA	147,197	13,056	71	261
8	TATA STEEL	135,976	3,895	146	78
9	PNB GILTS	104,628	29	NA	1
10	HINDALCO INDUSTRIES	82,549	3,597	28	72
11	COAL INDIA	78,410	11,759	119	235
12	BHARTI AIRTEL	71,506	6,511	33	130
13	MMTC	67,023	129	3	3
14	NTPC	66,366	9,334	49	187
15	LARSEN & TOUBRO	64,960	4,818	70	96
16	ESSAR OIL	63,428	-201	NA	N/A
17	MAHINDRA & MAHINDRA	63,030	2,948	22	59
18	MANGALORE REFINERY & PETROCHEMICALS	57,214	1,066	NA	21
19	TATA CONSULTANCY SERVICES	48,894	8,935	51	179
20	BHARAT HEAVY ELECTRICALS	50,654	5,823	37	116
21	STEEL AUTHORITY OF INDIA	51,428	5,153	61	103
22	GAIL (INDIA)	44,861	3,891	54	78
23	STERLITE INDUSTRIES (INDIA)	43,116	6,831	7	137
24	CHENNAI PETROLEUM CORPORATION	45,397	392	3	8
25	ADANI ENTERPRISES	39,416	1,940	14	39
26	ICICI BANK	37,995	6,366	24	127
27	PUNJAB NATIONAL BANK	37,447	4,460	NA	89
28	WIPRO	37,308	5,152	NA	103
29	MARUTI SUZUKI INDIA	40,050	2,162	12	43
30	JSW STEEL	36,964	1,569	32	31
31	INFOSYS	33,734	7,128	26	143
32	STATE TRADING CORPORATION OF INDIA	30,905	60	NA	1
33	CANARA BANK	30,816	3,313	NA	66
34	BANK OF BARODA	30,488	4,262	NA	85
35	RUCHI SOYA INDUSTRIES	30,332	167	0	3

Figure 2.5 CSR Approaches Adopted by Various Firms in India. *Source:* https://icmai.in/upload/CASB/GN-Treatment-CSR.pdf

Till date, most organizations think that CSR is a trivial issue in comparison to consumer satisfaction. They are unable to grasp that the emissions from their industries are polluting the global environment and endangering the very existence of their consumers.

Previously, governments had relied on compelling legislation and regulations for companies to contribute toward mitigating climate change. However, shrinking government resources, coupled with a disregard for the regulations, have led to the exploration of voluntary and nonregulatory initiatives instead.

THE STERLITE CASE

On March 23, 2018, Thoothukudi (Tamil Nadu) residents woke up to itchy eyes, burning throats, and breathing troubles. Sterlite Industries ran India's biggest copper smelter in that region. The plant was shut on the night of March 21 for routine maintenance. When the repair work was going on, a few people complained of breathing trouble and nausea. The Tamil Nadu Pollution Control Board (TNPCB) accused the factory of releasing sulfur dioxide gases as the levels had gone up to 2939.55 milligram per cubic meter against the prescribed limit of 1250 milligram per cubic meter. Sterlite denied all allegations. The company said it had promptly obtained a "clean chit" from the district environmental engineer (DEE) of TNPCB.

However, the troubles of the local people were enough to fuel their protest against the factory. "The factory was accused of polluting the environment and causing irreparable health hazards. The on-and-off protests that have the backing of political parties, such as V Gopalsamy's Marumalarchi Dravida Munnetra Kazhagam and the Centre of Indian Trade Unions, have caused the factory to shut down five times till 1996."[7] Such frequent shutdowns resulted in huge losses (to the tune of Rs. 50 crore) for each day of closure. In 1998, a petition was filed in the Madras High Court seeking closure of the smelter. The High Court gave an interim order to close the plant in November 1998, but it was opened within a month after Sterlite agreed to put in place measures to stop pollution as suggested by the National Environmental Engineering Research Institute (NEERI).[8]

Sterlite's fiasco is broadly based on four major issues: (1) it was located very close to the sensitive region of Gulf of Munnar, (2) it did not create a sufficient green belt around the factory, (3) deliberations were not held with local residents and their representatives, and (4) pollutants from the factory were seeping into the groundwater. The Madras High Court had imposed a fine of Rs. 100 crore on Sterlite for polluting the water, soil, and air around the plant. Later, it was found that owing to the complete lack of unanimity on the part of the state government officials, the DEE report, and the district collector, Sterlite was given a clean chit. A joint panel—comprising members from Sterlite, TNPCB, and other 20 factory owners from the area—headed by a green tribunal is deliberating upon solutions to the problem. The CEO of Sterlite Mr. Ramnath stated, "This is a welcome move. This should have been done right at the start before taking the drastic step of closing the plant."

Interestingly, sifting through the published records of the Thoothukudi plant, it could not be ascertained how much the company spent through CSR on restoring the air, water, and soil quality of the ecologically extra-sensitive area. There are lakhs of small and big industrial units in India that are constantly polluting the basic elements of life with impunity.

In a previously published book, the author states,

> Although, collectively, all the commercial entities have contributed substantially toward sustainable development and social welfare programs such as, increasing green covers, introduction of more sophisticated technology to reduce Greenhouse Gases emission, increased contribution in health- education, development of rural infrastructure and enabling the youth to live a life of dignity and honor, they have generated a mixed reaction from general public. The cut-throat competition among the private corporate to optimize profits has equally added to deep environmental degradation in many parts of the country. The Comptroller and Auditor General of India, in its report (June 2014), brought out that against the forestlands handed over to development projects, 1,03,381.91 hectares of non-forestlands were to be converted to forests. Out of which only 28,086 hectares were procured and compensatory forestation was carried out over a mere 7,280.84 hectares i.e. just 7% of the land. The report reveals that some of the leading corporate entities of the country were provided large financial and legal gains while distributing government forest lands in violation of Supreme Courts' order and forest laws. The CAG pointed out that it was important to strengthen law enforcement and monitoring mechanism further to control such anomalies in environmental and social responsibility of the corporate.[9]

GOVERNMENT ATTITUDE TOWARD CLIMATE CHANGE

During a question and answer session with school children in September 2014, the prime minister of India Narendra Modi casually brushed aside a question on climate change, saying that climate is not a critical issue but our "inability" to deal with climate is.

Whatever international applause India garnered for its intended contributions to the Paris Agreement as a whole, the real evidence largely contradicts the claims. A CAG audit report highlighted that "total Rs 53,967 crore were collected as Clean Energy Cess from 2010–11 to 2016–17. Against this, only 28.69 per cent or Rs. 15,483 crore had been transferred to the NCEF [National Clean Energy Fund] in the public account, resulting in a shortage of Rs. 38,484 crore (71 per cent). According to a Parliamentary Standing Committee reply, an additional Rs. 29,700 crore is expected to have been collected in 2017–18. A little over one-third of the funds have been transferred to the NCEF and, according to the Parliamentary Standing Committee reply, less than Rs. 7,000 crore has been spent on projects."

According to a news report,[10] "unspent funds amounting to Rs. 56,700 crore would be diverted to compensate for losses incurred during the rollout of the ambitious Goods and Services Tax regime in 2017. This is despite the CAG report stating that such measures were 'not tenable' since the NCEF is a non-lapsable fund,"[11] Thus, it is evident that climate change is still not the top priority for the government, and it seems to transfer its responsibility to the corporate sector.

FACTS AND FUTURE STRATEGY FOR ENVIRONMENT CONSERVATION

Any amount of blame games and fault finding will not help India in any way, and the country has to accept the facts and create a clear-cut strategy that would lead to real efforts. According to the MCA, as of June 30, 2018, "among 'active companies', Maharashtra has the maximum number of active companies (234,151), followed by Delhi (216,286) and West Bengal (1, 34,336)."

The fact is that big industries, owing to their high fossil fuel consumption, CO_2 emissions, and waste generation, have been traditionally labeled as the villains responsible for climate change. Can India afford to shut down all the industries, big or small, for addressing climate change? With its ever-growing population, expanding middle class, and improving conditions for the poor and their rapidly changing consumption patterns, the answer is a big NO.

The MCA analyzed data on the CSR expenditure of all Indian companies in 2014–2015. They found that though the corporates had contributed to only 14 percent (Rs. 1213 crore) of the total CSR spending in India, they have started thinking about emissions and are striving to combat responsibly them.

Based on secondary data, figures 2.4 and 2.5 depict the major variations in the approaches of the top Indian corporations in pursuing their CSR activities.

It is quite an encouraging sign that corporates are sensing large business opportunities and profit augmentation through CSR activities, and they are shifting from statutory philanthropy to responsible business strategies.

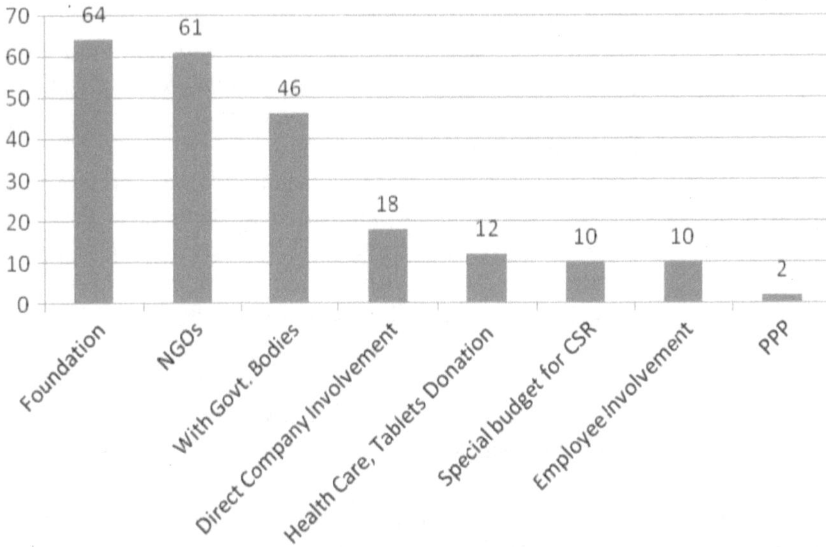

Figure 2.6 Nature of CSR Organisations. *Source:* Ministry of Forest and Climate Change, Govt. of India

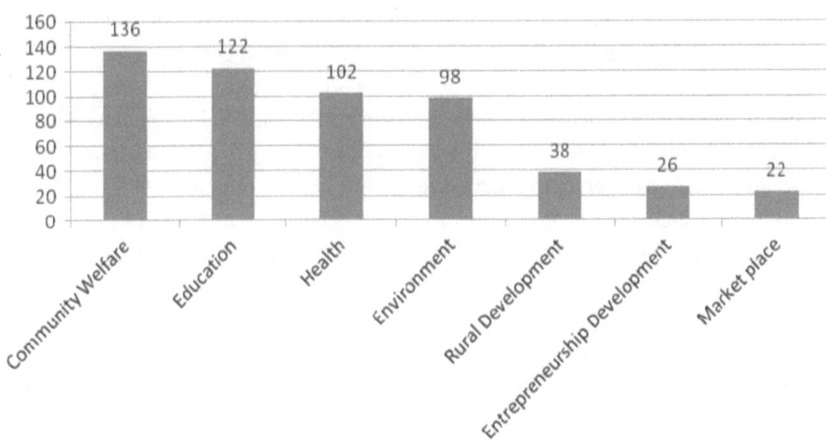

Figure 2.7 Area of Operations. *Source:* Ministry of Forest and Climate Change, Govt. of India

Presently, the most attractive environment-related CSR initiatives are those that have led to the use of renewable energy, ranging from solar street lamps to biomass cook stoves and various rooftop solar installations. Organic farming has become a progressive trend, and extensive commercialization of processed bovine excreta is gradually improving the soil quality. Water-related projects such as rainwater harvesting, watershed development, and ocean water processing are not only helping air, water, and soil conservation but also reducing the dependence on fossil fuel and underground water. Corporates have realized the medium- and long-term benefits of clean air, water, and green energy, and their numerous cascading effects on income generation and socioeconomic development.

Even FMCG companies that procure raw materials from farmers and exploit local water bodies have become motivated to protect the farmers' interests and the sustainability of local resources because resource regeneration has become extremely critical. Similarly, other manufacturing and energy companies, which are considered to be the worst climate offenders, are investing in environment-friendly projects because they have started using biodiesel and various types of agricultural waste as raw materials to supplement their manufacturing and processing units.

For several mammoth companies,

> sustainability has become a way of doing business. ITC's CSR Committee is aptly called the "CSR and Sustainability Committee." Similarly, HUL's projects focus on water stewardship tie-in with Unilever's global focus on addressing water scarcity. Axis Bank spent nearly 28 crore on reducing GHG emissions through the use of renewable energy and optimizing energy efficiency, choosing to concentrate on reducing the company's footprint on the environment.
>
> At the same time, several large companies are starting to work on shared value projects which create value for both the community and for the business. For example, as per their Sustainable Living Plan 2015, HUL has a clear roadmap to source 100 percent of agricultural raw material sustainably by 2020. And their sustainable tea procurement project, carried out as a part of the CSR activities serves a dual purpose—meeting the 2 percent criteria as well as the company's own responsible business targets.[12]

India's development potential is enormous, and if the climatic hazards are not tackled strategically by 2022, the experts' forecast of India's GDP surpassing that of China by 2030 is well-nigh impossible. Such a strategy may be multipronged as detailed below:

- The public–private partnership (PPP) mode should be promoted in every production and processing function, and rigorous monitoring should be conducted keeping in view the escalating social cost factor.
- Corporates should be tasked with developing innovative technologies for production processes and given adequate funds for research and innovation.
- The largest corporate houses should be motivated to establish a network of mega air-purifier system similar to that erected in China, which is the world's largest air-purifier system and has had a visible impact on Beijing's and Shanghai's air quality.

- Electricity generation companies should be given a free hand in installing on- and off-grid solar-powered lighting systems and water conservation projects. They may be encouraged to tie up freely in the countries where they may install such provisions. The world's total electricity requirement has been estimated as 13 terawatt..
- If strategic installations are erected, it may produce 20 terawatt without using any fossil fuel or high-cost nuclear energy, and with zero carbon emission. The map indicates the places worldwide from where maximum solar energy might be tapped.
- With an increase in the disposable income of people, even the third-world countries will witness a car boom. The illustration below gives an idea about the number of cars that will be used by the countries in the coming decades. The future seems promising in that Japanese hybrid cars will ply on Indian roads by 2021, and the government has assured that it will extend incentives to all the hybrid carmakers.[13] For now, the government should statutorily compel automobile companies to attach small air purifiers with every unit so that air polluting and purifying process may occur simultaneously, till electric automobiles replace the CO_2-emitting ones altogether.
- Like the list of goods and services for GST, the government should classify air-, water-, and soil-purifying options and specifically nominate corporate houses to undertake CSR activities for environment protection, so that the efforts for cleansing the environment are carried out systematically and resources are not scattered toward nonpriority activities.
- A clear-cut national policy for the academia–industry link should be created at the earliest, and the stakeholders may be pursued to evolve courses that promote an ecofriendly rational lifestyle and culture. Moreover, a "National R" culture of "Rethink, Reduce, Refuse, Reuse, Recharge, and Restore" should be inculcated in every aspect of civic life.

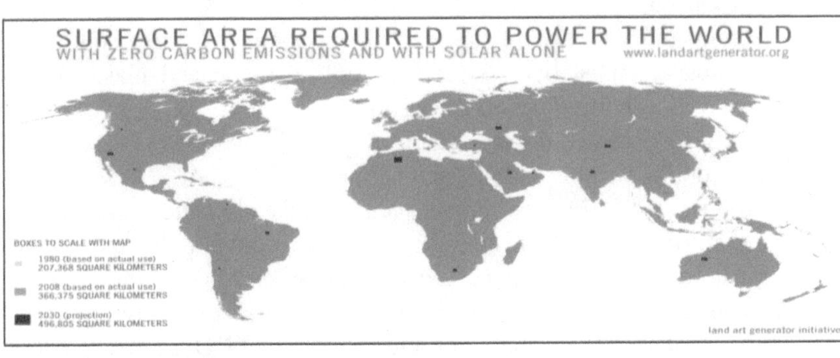

Figure 2.8 Surface Area Required to Power the World. *Source:* Report on 'Sustainable Living Plan 2015', Hindustan Unilever Ltd.

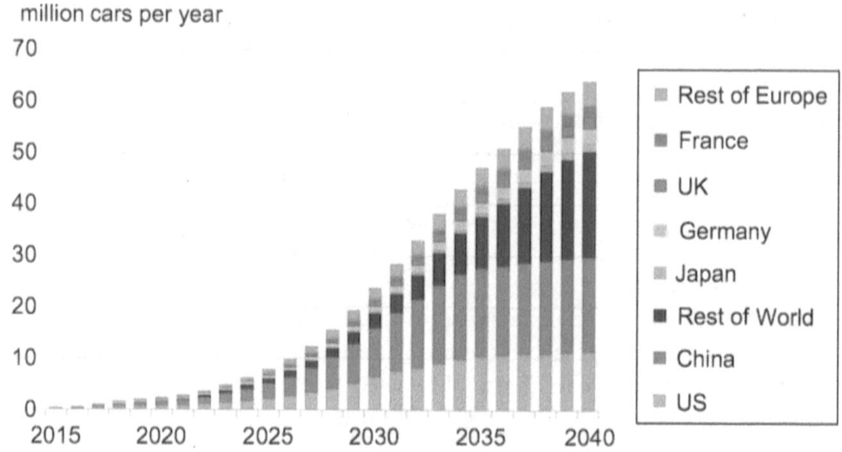

Figure 2.9 Number of Cars to be Used. *Source:* Report on 'Sustainable Living Plan 2015', Hindustan Unilever Ltd.

- A 20-point program (described below), if adopted immediately on a large scale through CSR, may immediately counter the adverse effects of global warming in the Indian peninsula:
    1. Carbon sinks must be created by every large and small religious congregation.
    2. Cheap/subsidized small air purifiers must be kept in every urban home.
    3. Laminated newspaper rolls/sticks must replace the wood, plastic, and metal used for making pencils and pens.
    4. Books/copies and printing paper for computers may be manufactured from biodegradable fiber sheets or recyclable fibers.
    5. All heating and cooling systems must be driven by solar energy.
    6. Solar-energy-driven small cars, bikes, buses, and trains must be introduced..
    7. Laminated bags and boxes made from a mix of waste cotton and newspapers must be produced to replace metal and plastic boxes generally used for household purposes.
    8. Reinforced fibers must be used to replace the wood in making furniture, doors, window panels, and so on.
    9. Production of fringe pollutants such as bidis, cigarettes, and conventional tobacco products must be minimized, and populist movements must be run to mold the behavior of the masses.
    10. Vegetarianism must be promoted to minimize the consumption of nonvegetarian foods that emit huge amounts of CO_2 in their processing, preparing, and storing.

11. Use of mosquito nets must be made convenient and compulsory for households, and regular usage of chemical-based mosquito repellants must be discouraged everywhere.
12. Community laundry systems should be implemented in every area to reduce the unnecessary usage of large volumes of water and draining of detergents into the rivers and in surrounding areas.
13. Air conditioners must be fitted with inbuilt air-purifier systems. Moreover, users must be charged higher tax rates because if they can afford to contribute to air pollution, they must accept the air- and water-purification charges.
14. Existing laws must be enforced stringently for every individual and micro-business units. Moreover, these entities must be pursued to perform one "green job" daily so that it becomes a social habit gradually.
15. Increasing financial inequality is a blatant evidence of poor governance. An affluence line (say, Rs. 100 crore per annum) can be defined similar to the poverty line, and anyone earning above this line should be automatically added to a "National Reserve and Surplus Fund" controlled by the Reserve Bank of India (RBI). All industrialists and businessmen can withdraw from this fund for reinvestment at the rate of 2 per cent per annum without any hassle.
16. Affluent consumption patterns must be discouraged at all levels to contain economic offences, fancifulness, and soaring class feelings and jealousy in the society.
17. Free cycles must be distributed to all citizens, so that they can feel proud in cycling for short distances. Paid community bus services must be promoted, comprising of executive and nonexecutive classes at cheap rates, so that the use of personal vehicles will be discouraged for at least four days in a week.
18. The carpooling system of South Korea and Japan must be implemented so that office goers will be compelled to pool with others instead of using personal vehicles. Electric cars, buses, trains, and two-wheelers must be promoted within three years. Concrete should be used for making only main roads, and rest of the service lanes and narrow lanes should be covered with fly-ash-based pavers. Moreover, all buildings should be constructed using fly-ash bricks and blocks insulated with *bari-chuna* and white color only to reflect the heat of the Sun. Roofs and exterior walls of the buildings must be covered with white paints only to reduce the internal temperature of the buildings.
19. People should be continuously reoriented to avoid three C's—collection (of goods more than their needs), comparison (with

anyone), and conflict (again, with anyone)—and taught that neither is frugality an indication of poverty or backwardness nor is leading a simple life qualitatively and elegantly a signal of wretched financial condition.

20. Right from childhood, everyone should be taught that their frugality will ensure the sustainability of Mother Earth and that it will be their real contribution to mankind.

CONCLUSIONS

It is peculiar that the whole world is not only horrified with the pace and ill effects of global warming but also suggesting ever-increasing awkwardly scientific solutions to counter the issue. Recently, an engineering team at Harvard University claimed that it might bring down the heat of the sunrays by repeating volcano explosions. Even more peculiarly, their research efforts are financially supported by the Bill Gates Foundation. The geo-engineers feel that minute particles from a volcanic eruption would rise to the stratosphere and would create an artificial canopy that would reduce the heat factor by more than 1.5 degree Celsius within a short period. They got the idea from the eruption of Mount Pinatubo in 1991 that spewed more than 2 crore tons of sulfur dioxide in the stratosphere and brought down the Earth's temperature by 0.5 degree Celsius for 18 months. Similarly, other scientists at Yale University are seriously thinking of shifting the Earth from its orbit by controlling the force of the comets. Dr. Rebecca Roche, a philosopher at London University, has suggested that the coming human generations may be dwarfed through genetic engineering so that their consumption level decreases by 90% and they never indulge in nonvegetarian foods. While some genetic engineers are looking for increasing the canopy areas of trees, Professor Claus Lefner in the Geophysics Department at Columbia University has suggested creating artificial trees that can absorb huge amounts of carbon in comparison to natural sinks.[14] Everyone knows that the problem of uncontrolled carbon emissions and global warming is a manifestation of the wrong side of the human perception. Still, global intellectuals and institutions are suggesting unnatural and deadly solutions to tackle it, when the most effective solution is hidden in the contentment of human beings. Finland has been ranked the happiest country in the world in spite of being a highly developed industrialized economy. The Government of India must create an environment of cooperation with the corporates to turn the negatives of climate change to positives. Stopping carbon emissions is impossible with the existing growth model, but it can be slowed down to a large extent through various innovative ways and means, thereby expanding the possibility of sustainability. After all, India has to accept that GNH (gross national happiness) is far more important than GDP (gross domestic product).

NOTES

1. Fifteen Shocking Facts about Inequality in India, by Oxfam India, 24 January 2018, https://www.oxfamindia.org/.
2. ET Bureau Updated: 08 January 2018.
3. Times of India Supplement dated: 29 January 2019, www.toistudent.com.
4. India Ministry of Statistics and Programme Implementation Government of India Central Statistical Office Social Statistics Division New Delhi www.mospi .gov.in.
5. Wikipedia.
6. An Assessment of CSR Expenditure of 5097 Companies for the year 2015–16 who have filed their Annual Financial Statements till 31 December 2016 with MCA.
7. 'Sterlite's Pollution Problem', *Business Standard*, 25 March 2018.
8. 'Participation of Corporate Sector in Socio-Economic Development in India' by Dr. A. M. Bhattacharya in edited book, published by CRIID, Chandigarh in 2016.
9. 'Participation of Corporate Sector in Socio-Economic Development in India' by Dr. A. M. Bhattacharya in edited book, published by CRIID, Chandigarh in 2016.
10. https://scroll.in/article/844528/india-diverts-rs-56700-crore-from-the-fight -against-climate-change-to-goods-and-service-tax-regime.
11. 'Is the Modi Government Serious About Climate Change?' by Shreeshan Venkatesh, Down to Earth Last Updated: Sunday 27 May 2018.
12. 'CSR and Sustainable Development: Do Indian Companies Care about the Environment?' by Indra Saha, published in L*ivemint,* 05 January 2017.
13. 'Japanese Hybrid Cars to Hit Indian Roads in 2021', by Malyaban Ghosh in *Livemint*, 04 February, 2019.
14. 'Global Warming Se Bachao KIi Jugat' by Mukul Vyas in Aha! Zindagi, p. 31, January 2019..

Chapter 3

Sustainable Development in India

Environment vs Development

Abdul Jabbar Haque

INTRODUCTION

Environment problems are a burning issue nowadays, with environment protection becoming a global issue. Industrialization, urbanization, population explosion, poverty, overexploitation of resources, depletion of traditional resources of energy and raw materials, and so on are some of the factors that have contributed to environmental deterioration globally.

The term "sustainable development" was first used during the Cocoyoc Declaration on Environment and Development in the early 1970s. Since then, it has become the trademark of international organizations dedicated to achieving environmentally benign or beneficial development.[1]

Sustainable development comprises sustainability and development; while "sustainability" connotes continuation, "development" simply means change. The conceptual framework of sustainable development, though still passing through the requirement phase, has succeeded in stimulating efforts to find common solutions through collective efforts for a common secured and better future.

Development is a perpetual process enabling humans to expand or realize their potential to achieve a greater or better state. Following the first United Nations Conference on Human Environment in 1972, importance was laid on development not merely as betterment in the quality of life but with an added dimension of sustainability of such betterment. The concept of sustainable development has acquired dimensions in terms of economic growth, social and cultural growth, scientific growth, and environment protection.

Development is a continuous process, and its every step influences the next step. Therefore, the foundation of sustainable development will be laid like a process of changing the current development process from environmentally unsound to sustainable.

In developing countries such as India, the exploitation of natural resources is essential for economic progress through industrial development. While international and national laws and policies have already provided various guidelines—legal or executive—the concept of sustainable development still requires special attention and emphasis to bring awareness among industrialists and others engaged in the exploitation of natural and man-made resources for economic progress.

Under Article 21 of the Constitution of India, it is the basic right of every human being to live in a healthy environment. The crying need of the hour is sustainable development.

ORIGIN AND CONCEPT OF SUSTAINABLE DEVELOPMENT

The term sustainability originates from the Latin word *sustinere*, which means "to hold up," "to endure." *Webster's New Collegiate Dictionary* describes sustainability as "to give support" or "to keep up."

Sustainable development means an integration of development and environmental imperatives. To be sustainable, development must possess both economic and ecological sustainability. It indicates the way in which development planning should be approached.[2]

According to Goodland and Ladac, sustainable development is a pattern of social and structural economic benefits available in the present without jeopardizing the likely potential for similar benefits in the future.[3]

Sustainable development is not a new concept. The doctrine had come to be known as early as in 1972 in the Stockholm Declaration. It had been stated in the declaration that[4]

> Man has the fundamental right to freedom, equality and adequate conditions of life, in an environment of a quality that permits a life of dignity and wellbeing and he bears a solemn responsibility to protect and improve the environment for present and future generation.

Sustainable development has been defined in many ways, but the most frequently quoted definition is from "Our Common Future," also known as the Brundtland Report. The concept had been further discussed under Agenda 21 of the United Nations Conference on Environment and Development held in June 1992 in Rio de Janeiro, Brazil. The commission, which was chaired by the then Norway Prime Minister, Ms. G. H. Brundtland, defined sustainable development as[5]: "Sustainable development is development that meets the needs of the present without compromising the ability of future generations to meet their own needs." It contains within it two key concepts:

- The concept of needs, in particular the essential needs of the world's poor, to which overriding priority should be given
- The idea of limitations imposed by the state of technology and social organization on the environment's ability to meet present and future needs

At present, the most accepted definition of sustainable development is this: "Sustainable development is the pivot that connects the two wheels of progress, that is, economic development and environmental protection."

OBJECTIVES OF SUSTAINABLE DEVELOPMENT

Sustainable development focuses on three things:

(i) To follow a path of development that does not impair or damage the environment
(ii) To use renewable natural resources in such a way that their rate of regeneration is always greater than their rate of use
(iii) To use nonrenewable resources in a sparing and responsible manner, and ceaselessly work to find substitutes for them[6]

PRINCIPLES OF SUSTAINABLE DEVELOPMENT

The concept of sustainable development has grown since its inception at the international forum, and it has assumed different dimensions in the form of economic growth, development, and environmental protection. The environment and development are a means and not ends in themselves. The environment and development are for people; people are not for environmental and development. Some of the basic principles of sustainable development as described in the Brundtland Report are as follows:

1. Intergenerational Equity
2. Use and Conservation of Natural Resources
3. Environmental Protection
4. The Precautionary Principle
5. The Polluter Pays Principle
6. Obligation to Assist and Cooperate

7. Eradication of Poverty
8. Financial Assistance to Developing Countries

INTERGENERATIONAL EQUITY

The theme of intergenerational equity is the right of every generation of human beings to get benefit from cultural and natural resources. Intergenerational equity requires conserving the diversity and quality of biological and renewable resources such as forests, water, and soils.[7]

Principle 3 of the Rio Declaration, 1992 states that: "The right to development must be fulfilled so as to equitably meet developmental and environmental needs of present and future generations."[8]

The natural resources, land, air, and water on the Earth cannot be exhausted by the present generation to meet their needs. It is the obligation of the present generation to leave these resources in adequate amounts for the next generation too.

USE AND CONSERVATION OF NATURAL RESOURCES

In order to meet humanity's needs in a sustainable manner, it is absolutely necessary to use the Earth's natural resources carefully and to conserve and enhance them. It is our moral obligation to other livings beings and generations that the resources must be conserved and enhanced to meet the needs of the world's growing population.[9]

Principle 23 of the Rio Declaration, 1992 states that the environment and natural resources of people under oppression, domination, and occupation shall be protected.[10]

Similarly,

> principle 8 of the Rio Declaration, 1992 states that to achieve sustainable development and a high quality of life for all people, states should reduce and eliminate unsustainable patterns of production and consumption. Thus, use and conservation of natural resources is an essential principle of sustainable development.[11]

ENVIRONMENTAL PROTECTION

The protection of the environment is an essential part of sustainable development. Without adequate environment protection, development is undermined. Further, without development, resources will be inadequate for the necessary investments, and environmental protection is bound to fail. Strong environment policies complement and reinforce sustainable development.

In the case of *Citizen, Consumer and Civic Action Group v. Union of India*,[12] the Supreme Court observed that while the courts have social accountability in the matter of protection of environment, there should be a proper balance between environmental protection and development activities, which are essential for progress. There can be no dispute that the society has to prosper, but it shall not be at the expense of the environment. In a similar vein, the environment shall have to be protected, but not at the cost of the development of the society. Both development and environment shall coexist and go hand in hand. Therefore, a balance has to be struck and administrative actions ought to proceed in accordance therewith, and not de-hors the same.

THE PRECAUTIONARY PRINCIPLE

The main purpose of the precautionary principle is to ensure that a substance or activity posing a threat to the environment is prevented from adversely affecting the environment, even if there is no conclusive scientific proof of linking that particular substance or activity to environmental damage. The words "substance" and "activity" imply substance and activities introduced as a result of human intervention.[13]

In the case of *Vellore Citizen's Welfare Forum v. Union of India*,[14] popularly known as the Tamil Nadu Tanneries case, the Supreme Court expressed the view that the precautionary principle and the polluter pays principle are essential features of sustainable development and that they have been accepted as part of the law of the land. The court had no hesitation in holding that the precautionary principle and the polluter pays principle are part of the environmental law of the country. The court also observed that even otherwise, these principles are accepted as part of the customary international law, and hence, there should be no difficulty in accepting them as part of our domestic law.

In the context of the municipal law, the precautionary principle means[15]

1. Environmental measures by the state government and the local authorities must anticipate, prevent, and attack the causes of environmental degradation.
2. Where there are threats of serious and irreversible damage, lack of scientific certainty should not be used as a reason for postponing measures to prevent environmental degradation.
3. The onus of proof is on the actor or the developer/industrialist to show that their action is environmentally benign.

THE POLLUTER PAYS PRINCIPLE

As interpreted by the Supreme Court of India, the polluter pays principle means that the absolute liability for harm to the environment extends not only to compensate the victims of pollution but also recover the cost of restoring the environmental degradation. Thus, it includes environmental costs as well as direct costs to people or property. Remediation of the damaged environment is part of the process of sustainable development, and as such the polluter is liable to not only pay damages to the individual sufferers but also pay the cost of reversing the damaged ecology.[16]

The polluter pays principle is an environmental policy principle that requires that the costs of pollution be borne by those who cause it. This principle is normally implemented through two different policy approaches: command and control and market-based. Command-and-control approaches include performance and technology standards, such as environmental regulations in the production of a given polluting technology. Market-based instruments include pollution or eco taxes, tradable pollution permits, and product labelling.[17]

Despite the difficulties inherent in defining the principle, the European Community has accepted it as a fundamental part of its strategy on environmental matters. The Environment Action Programmes have laid down certain basic principles of the European Community environmental policy. The most important are set out in Article 130R(2):[18]

(a) Preventive action is to be preferred to remedial measures.
(b) Environmental damage should be rectified at the source.
(c) The polluter should pay for the costs of the measures taken to protect the environment.
(d) Environmental policies should form a component of the European Community's other policies.

Principle 16 of the Rio Declaration, 1992 provides that national authorities should endeavor to promote the internationalization of environmental costs and the use of economic instruments, taking into account the approach that the polluter should, in principle, bear the cost of pollution with due regard to the public interest and without distorting international trade and investment.[19]

OBLIGATION TO ASSIST AND COOPERATE

Environmental problems are not the problems of an individual or of one country. They are global problems and can be tackled only with the assistance and cooperation of all.

Principle 9 of the Rio Declaration, 1992 provides that the states should cooperate to strengthen indigenous capacity building for sustainable development by improving scientific understanding through exchanges of scientific and technological knowledge, and by enhancing the development, adaptation, diffusion, and transfer of technologies, including new and innovative technologies.[20]

Further, principle 10 of the Rio Declaration, 1992 provides that environmental issues are best handled with the participation of all concerned citizens, at the relevant level.[21]

Similarly, principle 12 of the Rio Declaration provides that the states should cooperate to promote a supportive and open international economic system that would lead to economic growth and sustainable development in all countries, to better address the problems of environmental degradation.[22]

Finally, principle 27 of the Rio Declaration, 1992 expects the people and the states to cooperate in good faith and in a spirit of partnership in the further development of international law in the field of sustainable development.[23]

Thus, the obligation to assist and cooperate is one of the important principles of sustainable development.

ERADICATION OF POVERTY

Sustainable development has to address the problems of a large number of people who live in absolute poverty and who cannot satisfy even their basic needs. At the Stockholm Conference, 1972, the former Prime Minister of India Mrs. Indira Gandhi said, "Of all pollutants we face, the worst is poverty." The G.H. Brundtland Report has rightly pointed out that poverty reduces people's capacity to use resources in a sustainable manner, and hence, it intensifies pressure on the environment. Most of the developing countries are under the stress of poverty.[24]

The United Nations Conference on Environment and Development, that is, Earth Summit, 1992, has brought about a leap in public awareness about key environment and development issues, and rightly projected that the elimination of poverty is a must for sustainable development, particularly in developing countries. The key to achieve sustainability is to break the vicious cycle of poverty.[25]

FINANCIAL ASSISTANCE TO DEVELOPING COUNTRIES

Developing countries face poverty as the worst pollutant. The people in developing countries strain their natural resources and overexploit them to meet their basic needs. Moreover, these countries do not have the finances and modern technology to follow the path of sustainable development.[26]

Therefore, financial assistance and transfer of technology from developed countries to developing ones is a must if we want to achieve the goals of sustainable development and environmental protection.

ENVIRONMENT VS DEVELOPMENT

Every state has sovereignty in its own territories. It has the right to development. This right to development has been recognized by the United Nations General Assembly on December 4, 1986, in the "Declaration on the Right to Development." This declaration stated that the right to development of a sovereign state is a necessary right to protect human rights.

Right to wholesome environment is a fundamental right under Article 21 of the Constitution of India. The Supreme Court has interpreted that the right to life and personal liberty includes the right to a wholesome environment.[27]

Threats to the global environment have the potential to open our eyes and make us accept that the protection of environment is an essential feature of sustainable development. It is a known fact that without adequate environmental protection, development is undermined. Since progress of mankind and pollution of environment go side by side as an interdependent phenomenon, modern thinking is geared toward drawing up a line of control around both these contingencies, whereby the degree of exploitation of natural resources as well as the degree of economic development should be maintained at such a rate that will ensure sustenance to both the generation and future generations in a wholesome environment.

To ensure the balance between sustainable development and the environment, the Indian judiciary has made judicial contributions in various ways.

SUSTAINABLE DEVELOPMENT AND THE ROLE OF JUDICIARY IN INDIA

Justice is one of the primary needs of a civilized society. Law changes according to the changes in the needs and aspirations of people. Laws enacted by the Parliament and state legislatures are not able to ensure complete justice in all cases in our society. The judges of the Supreme Court and high courts, with their extraordinary legal acumen and innovative vision, have endeavored to fill up the blank spaces between various laws by pronouncing their interpretations of laws to meet the concurrent needs and situations of the people. The Supreme Court has laid down several new legal principles to keep alive and active the system of justice in order to ensure protection of human rights and social justice. Thus, in India, there has been regular development of the law regarding the protection of the environment. India has enacted various laws from time to time for the protection of the environment. At the same time, the judiciary plays an important role in not only protecting the environment but also promoting sustainable development.

It should be remembered that most of the environmental cases have come before the courts through public interest litigations (PILs) under either Article 32 or Article 226 of the Constitution of India.

The first case on which the apex court had applied the doctrine of sustainable development was *Vellore Citizen Welfare Forum v. Union of India.*[28] The Supreme Court held that the remediation of the damaged environment is part of the process of sustainable development, and as such, the polluter is liable to pay damages to the individual sufferers as well as the cost of reversing the damaged ecology.

But even before the Vellore Citizens case, the Supreme Court had tried in many cases to keep the balance between ecology and development.

In the case of *Rural Litigation and Entitlement Kendra, Dehradun v. State of Uttar Pradesh*,[29] popularly known as the Doon Valley case, the Supreme Court directed to totally stop the operation of mining in certain areas on the grounds of environmental protection.

In the case of *Subhas Kumar v. State of Bihar*,[30] the Supreme Court stated that pollution-free air and water, and a life free from diseases are guaranteed under Article 21 of the Constitution of India.

In the case of *Tarun Bhagat Singh v. Union of India*,[31] the Supreme Court issued directions that no mining work or operation could be continued within the protected area.

But it would be unwise to hold that the courts always favor the environment without giving any significance to the development aspect when a dispute arises between environment and development.

In the case of *B. L. Wadhera v. Union of India*,[32] the Supreme Court held that pollution-free water and air is a fundamental right under Article 21 of the Constitution of India.

In the case of *F. K. Hussain v. Union of India*,[33] the Supreme Court held that the right to sweet water and the right to free air are attributes of the right to life under Article 21 of the Constitution of India, for those are the basic elements that sustain life itself.

In the case of *Calcutta Youth Front v. State of West Bengal*,[34] the Supreme Court contended that there must be a balance between ecology and development. Development is necessary for the human society. At the same time, no one should cause any harm or injury to the environment.

In the case of *M. C. Mehta v. Union of India*,[35] popularly known as the Taj Trapezium case, the Supreme Court issued directions for shifting of 292 industries from the Taj Trapezium or to close them.

In the case of *Indian Council for Enviro-Legal Action v. Union of India*,[36] the Supreme Court cautioned the industries discharging inherently dangerous oleum and H acid. The court held that such type of pollution infringes on the right to wholesome environment and ultimately the right to life.

In the case of *M. C. Mehta v. Union of India*,[37] the Supreme Court issued directions for the closing of mechanical stone crushing activities in and around New Delhi, which was declared by World Health Organization (WHO) as the third most polluted city in the world. However, the court realized the importance of stone crushing and issued directions for allotment of sites in a new "crushing zone" set up at village Pali in the state of Haryana.

Thus, it is quite obvious that the courts give equal importance to both ecology and development while dealing with the cases of environmental degradation.

In the case of *Kinkri Devi v. State*,[38] the high court of Himachal Pradesh relied on the Doon Valley case and pointed out that if a just balance is not struck between development and environment by proper tapping of natural resources, there will be violation of Articles 14, 21, 48A, and 51A(g) of the Constitution of India. It was further observed by the court that tapping has to be done with care so that ecology and environment may not be affected in any serious way.

In the case *of Ishwar Singh v. State of Haryana*,[39] the high court issued directions for closing down those stone crushing units that were not situated within the identified zone.

In the case of *V. Lakshmipathy v. State*,[40] the Karnataka high court in a public interest litigation directed the municipal corporation to shut down industries set up in a residential area. The court also observed that land earmarked for residential purposes should not be used for setting up industries.

In the case of *M. L. Sud v. Union of India*,[41] the Supreme Court issued necessary directions to the concerned authorities for maintaining the city.

In the case of *Ajay Singh Rawat v. Union of India*,[42] the Supreme Court issued certain directions regarding preventive and remedial measures to be taken on a war footing so that Nainital may regain its unsoiled beauty and attract tourists. It was directed that sewage water has to be prevented at any cost from entering lakes. The court also suggested that multistoried group housing and commercial complexes should be banned in the town area of Nainital. The court further directed that the offence of illegal felling of trees was required to be made cognizable and vehicular traffic on the Mall Road had to be reduced.

In the case of *People United for Better Living in Calcutta v. State of West Bengal*,[43] the Calcutta high court held that it is the duty of the court to find a balance between development programs and the environment. The court highlighted the importance of wetlands and the part they play in the proper maintenance of environmental equilibrium in the city of Kolkata. It was further held that wetlands are important for the maintenance of environmental equilibrium and necessary to preserve the environment.

CONCLUSION AND RECOMMENDATIONS

Environment and development are two sides of the same coin. Any one of these cannot be sacrificed for the other. On the contrary, both are equally important for our better future. Thus, the responsibility lies on the Supreme Court and various high courts in India to deal with environmental cases with a high degree of caution. Then only we will achieve our goal of securing a pollution-free developed country for our future generations.

In spite of various provisions in the Constitution, legislative enactments, decisions, and monitoring by courts, the situation is not encouraging and conducive for the protection and preservation of the environment. This is because many provisions in Air Act, Water Act, Environment Protection Act, and Factories Act are not being applied and implemented in their true spirit to regulate the pollution caused by industries and to fix individual and collective liability. The strict application of the provisions of these acts in their true spirit is what is required urgently for ensuring the very existence of society and mankind.

In India, sustainable development is rooted in the firm realization that the bounties of nature are drying up. It is both a challenge and an opportunity. Sustainable development can only be pursued if the population size and growth are in harmony with the changing productive potential of the ecosystems. It is also concluded that in a democratic polity, community participation is a must if tangible results are expected for environmental protection.

Educational institutions, pollution control boards, NGOs, and gram panchayats can play a vital role in imparting environmental education by conducting awareness programs for achieving the goal of sustainable development, but judicial intervention has to be improved. Though efforts are being made to improve judicial intervention, they are still not enough to mitigate environmental pollution. A few suggestions and recommendations for controlling environmental pollution and strengthen the concept of sustainable development are presented here:

1. People who violate the provisions of various enactments relating to environment must be fined heavy penalties. Wherever desirable, industrialists or managers should be made personally liable for the violation of environmental laws.

2. Special environmental courts must be established to try cases relating to the violation of environmental laws. Such courts must be assisted by experts having special knowledge and experience in the field of environmental protection.
3. The Supreme Court should liberally interpret Article 21 of the Constitution of India and declare the right to have unplugged environment as a fundamental right.
4. Courts should rule in favor of providing damages for the violation of the right to life and personal liberty on account of environmental pollution.
5. The ever-increasing population makes excessive demands of environmental utilization, which results in its degradation. The state should take all required measures to control population growth.
6. For controlling pollution, industrial and town planning should be given due importance—new industries should be located such that residential areas are not affected by them.
7. Sometimes, aggrieved parties are unable to approach the court for enforcing their right to have a clean environment. Therefore, courts should encourage PILs to deal with the problem of environmental pollution.
8. Legal aid clinics or cells should educate people about their rights and duties to achieve the goal of protecting and improving the environment by preventing pollution. These clinics or cells should also take up environmental issues before the courts to ensure a pollution-free environment.
9. Whoever fails to preserve and protect the environment as provided in Article 51A(g) of the Constitution of India must be awarded severe punishment under the law.
10. Since industries are the major contributors to pollution in our country, they should be classified into three categories: (a) less polluting, (b) moderately polluting, and (c) highly polluting. Accordingly, necessary control should be exercised over these industries while granting consent by respective state pollution control boards.
11. The right to pure drinking water and air are part of the right to life guaranteed under Article 21 of the Constitution of India, but none of these are available to us and our lives are going to be shorter than our elders'. Hence, this right should supersede any other right.
12. Last but not least, the ozone layer, which is in the upper atmosphere, is already under threat, as reported widely. It needs immediate protection with the common interests of countries acknowledging the issue. Otherwise, the whole human race is going to be extinct in a few decades.

NOTES

1. Dr. P. S. Jaswal, *Environmental Law,* Pioneer Publications, Delhi, 2006, p. 87
2. Ibid.
3. S. M. Todiwala, Sustainable Development: Need of the Hour, p. 47 (*Law Profiles: A Monthly Legal Journal in English;* Volume 3, Issue 9; September 2012.
4. Ibid.
5. Dr. J. J. R. Upadhyaya, *Environmental Law*, p. 127 (Allahabad: Central Law Agency, 2011).
6. Supra Note 4.
7. Shyam Divan & Armin Rosencranz, *Environmental Law and Policy in India,* Oxford University Press, New Delhi, 2011, p. 585.
8. Supra Note 6.
9. Supra Note 2, p. 109.
10. Ibid.
11. Ibid.
12. AIR 2002 Mad. 298.
13. Supra Note 2, p. 110.
14. [(1995) 5 SCC 647].
15. Sustainable Development and Role of Judiciary, *available at:* http://www.legalserviceindia.com/articles/sustainable development and judiciary.htm (Last Visited on April 1, 2017).
16. Supra Note 6, p. 141.
17. Environment and Sustainable Development: A Study of Judicial Role in Realising Sustainable Development, *available at:* http://www.legalservicesindia.com/article/article/environment-and-sustainable-development-1853-1.html (Last Visited on April 1, 2017).
18. Simon Ball and Struat Bell, *Environmental Law*, pp. 97–98 (Blackstone Press Ltd., 1991).
19. Supra Note 6, p. 141.
20. Ibid.
21. Ibid.
22. Ibid.
23. Ibid.
24. Supra Note 2, p. 116.
25. Ibid.
26. Ibid.
27. *Rural Litigation and Entitlement Kendra, Dehradun -vs- State of Uttar Pradesh, AIR 1988 SC 2187.*
28. (1996) 5 SCC 647.
29. AIR 1989 SC 594.
30. AIR 1991 SC 420.
31. 1992 Supp. (2) SCC 448.
32. AIR 1996 SC 2969.

33. AIR 1990 Ker 321.
34. AIR 1998 SC 436.
35. [(1997) 2 SCC 353].
36. AIR 1996 SC 1446.
37. (1992) 3 SCC 256.
38. AIR 1988 H.P. 4.
39. AIR 1996 P & H 30.
40. AIR 1992 Kant. 57.
41. 1992 Supp. (2) SCC 123.
42. (1995) 3 SCC 266.
43. AIR 1993 Cal. 215.

Chapter 4

Corporate Initiative of Green Marketing in India

A Sustainable Approach

Alok Gupta

INTRODUCTION

The green marketing process started in the 1980s as part of the corporate social responsibility of the corporate sector. In simple terms, green marketing refers to the process of selling products and/or services based on their environmental benefits that may be environmentally friendly in themselves or produced in an environmentally friendly way.

Green marketing being a very wide field of study and having a wide subject area, there does not exist a standard definition for it. However, various experts and associations have tried defining it. As per the American Market Association, there are three ways of defining green marketing:

1. Retailing Definition: Green marketing is the marketing of products that are presumed to be environmentally safe.
2. Social Marketing Definition: Green marketing is the development and marketing of products designed to minimize negative effects on the physical environment or to improve its quality.
3. Environmental Definition: Green marketing constitutes the efforts by organizations to produce, promote, package, and reclaim products in a manner that they are sensitive or responsive to ecological concerns.

REVIEW OF LITERATURE

A number of studies have been conducted by scholars emphasizing green marketing. A few of them are discussed here.

Kotlar and Keller[1] emphasized the relevance of green marketing and environmental friendly strategies. Ginsberg[2] proposed different models to develop a strategy that includes the green marketing grid and green marketing matrix. Chaudhary and Bhattacharya[3] stated that the clean development mechanism established under the Kyoto protocol has the potential to assist developing countries in achieving sustainable development by promoting environment friendly investment in business. Uberoi[4] emphasized that environmental problems cannot be tackled without a sound proactive policy by the government. Akhileshwar Singh Arora[5] emphasized that green marketing assumes even more importance and relevance in developing countries such as India, which should be path breakers and trendsetters for all others to follow. Neeraj Kumar Sharma[6] pointed out that the concept of green marketing is still in its infancy stage and a lot of research is required to fully explore its potential. B. Nandini[7] emphasized that green marketing has become an important aspect as a key strategy for sustainable development.

INTERNATIONAL CONVENTIONS ON ENVIRONMENTAL LAW

a. Stockholm Conference on Human Environment, 1972

The United Nations Conference on the Human Environment, which took place in Stockholm, Sweden in 1972, was the first conference focusing on human environment. The conference agreed upon a declaration with 26 principles concerning the environment and development, an action plan with 109 recommendations, and a resolution.

b. World Commission on Environment and Development, 1987

The World Commission on Environment and Development, also known as the Brundtland Commission, was instrumental in developing the theme of sustainable development, as well as in uniting countries to pursue sustainable development together.

c. Earth Summit, 1992

The United Nations Conference on Environment and Development took place in Rio de Janeiro in 1992. It was instrumental in taking up several initiatives, some of which include a global conference on small island developing states, a convention to combat desertification, and an agreement on highly migratory and straddling fish stocks. The importance of the summit can be gauged from the fact that the outcomes of this summit have been published in three volumes consisting of resolutions adopted by the conference, proceedings of the conference, and statements made by heads of state or governments at the summit.

d. World Summit on Sustainable Development, 2002

The World Summit on Sustainable Development included the Johannesburg Declaration on Sustainable Development and the implementation plan for the summit itself. This plan included poverty eradication measures; sustainable development initiatives by small developing island states and other geographic regions such as the Asia-Pacific, Latin America and the Caribbean, and West Asia; and an institutional framework to be adopted by the UN institutions for achieving the various goals of sustainable development.

e. UN Conference on Sustainable Development, 2012

The UN Conference on Sustainable Development was held in Rio de Janeiro in 2012. The outcome document of this conference was titled "The Future We Want." The document consisted some common visions that the UN expected to achieve in the nearby future, including among others eradicating poverty; mainstreaming sustainable development by interlinking it with economic, social, and environmental aspects in order to achieve sustainable development in all dimensions; accelerating the commitment to achieve internationally agreed developmental goals including the Millennium Development Goals by 2015; taking urgent action to achieve sustainable development; and reaffirming commitment to strengthen international cooperation to address persistent challenges to sustainable development for all.

SIGNIFICANCE OF GREEN MARKETING

Green marketing is significant and has increased importance today because of a simple reason, which is the basic definition of economics. According to it, economics is the study of how people use their limited resources to try to satisfy unlimited wants. Thus, mankind has limited resources on the earth, with which they must attempt to provide for the world's unlimited wants. As organizations face limited natural resources, they must develop new or alternative ways of satisfying these unlimited wants. Ultimately, green marketing looks at how marketing activities utilize these limited resources while satisfying the wants of consumers, both individuals and industries, as well as achieving the selling organization's objectives.

1. Green marketing provides avenues for sustained long-term growth and profitability of companies.
2. It helps in saving resources by curtailing extra costs in packaging and delivering.

3. It helps companies to market their products and services, with the companies keeping in view environmental aspects and trying to access new markets and enjoy a competitive advantage.
4. It gives a sense of responsibility toward reducing environmental degradation while working in an environmentally friendly way.
5. Lastly and most importantly, it promotes corporate social responsibility.

INITIATIVES TAKEN BY INDIAN COMPANIES TOWARD GREEN MARKETING

The Indian corporate sector has taken many initiatives toward sustainable development. It has been claimed that green policies/products are profitable and reduce costs; moreover, green firms can shape future regulations and reap first-mover advantages. There are numerous examples of firms that have strived to become more environmentally responsible while serving to better satisfy their consumers' needs. Moreover, their activities also help them to improve their revenues and profits in various ways.

- Unilever's Surf Excel detergent emphasized reducing water consumption while cleaning clothes.
- Lifebuoy (an Indian soap brand from Unilever) ran an advertising campaign that encouraged children to keep their streets clean and not worry about germs as Lifebuoy protected them.
- The Indian outlets of McDonald's restaurant uses napkins and bags made of recycled paper.
- Coca-Cola pumped syrup directly from tanks instead of plastic containers, which saved 68 million pounds per year.
- The Badarpur Thermal Power Station of NTPC in Delhi utilized coal ash for making bricks.
- The Barauni Oil Refinery of Indian Oil Company took steps for restricting the use of air and water pollutants.
- CNG was introduced for all motor vehicles in public transport systems in Delhi to curb pollution.
- HCL created an eco-safe Environment Management Policy.
- HP promised to cut its global energy use by 20 percent by the year 2010.
- HP announced plans to deliver energy-efficient products and services.
- E-commerce businesses such as Flipkart, Amazon, ShopClues, and many more offered a web tool that allowed customers to replace similar items in their shopping carts with greener products.

- The refrigerator industry has shifted from chlorofluorocarbons (CFCs) to more environmentally friendly gases.
- Plantation and cultivation activities taken up by many national and international firms are examples of socially responsible activities contributing to environment preservation.
- Philips introduced compact fluorescent lamps (CFLs) that are more energy efficient than other bulbs.
- Maruti Suzuki implemented plans to make its supply chain green.
- Amway claims that its products are environmentally friendly.
- ITC's Social and Farm Forestry initiative has greened over 80,000 hectares of land, creating an estimated 35 million person days of employment among the disadvantaged section of society.
- ITC's Sustainable Community Development initiatives include women empowerment, supplementary education, and integrated animal husbandry programs.
- All environment, health, and safety management systems in ITC conform to the best international standards.
- The Supreme Court of India forced a shift to alternative fuels. In 2002, a directive was issued to completely adopt CNG in all public transport systems to curb pollution.
- In India, the green building movement was spearheaded by the Confederation of Indian industry (CII) and resulted in the Godrej Green Business Center.
- The recycling of used products minimizes waste.
- Tata Steel, HLL, Jindal Vijayanagar Steels, Essar Power, and Gujarat Fluorochemicals Ltd. got clearance to undertake specifically designed projects in order to gain benefits from carbon trading (Kyoto Protocol).
- Plantation and cultivation activities taken up by Intel India are an example of socially responsible firms contributing to environment preservation.
- ITC's Bhadrachalam paper unit has invested Rs. 500 crore on technology that makes the unit chlorine free.
- At Jubilant Organosys's Distillery in Gajraula, treated wastewater is piped to farmers and CO_2 is sold to cola majors.
- Atlas Copco in India claims to use safer compressor condensate disposal practices, including a step that removes oil from the water that is discharged into rivers.
- Kirloskar Copeland Limited (KLC) claims to have introduced an eco-friendly gas compressor. For achieving better living standards in society and a sustainable economy, many other firms are contributing to environment conservation directly and indirectly.

HOW TO MAKE GREEN MARKETING EFFECTIVE?

1. It should be ensured that green marketing strategies should not be misleading to customers and should adhere to all regulations or laws dealing with environmental marketing.
2. Companies should consider the possible negative effects any new product on the environment and minimize them at the beginning itself.
3. Firms using green marketing strategies must ensure that they are doing what they claim to do in their green marketing campaigns.
4. Companies can leverage ecofriendly packaging as part of their advertising programs to help attract new environmentally conscious customers.
5. Companies should create awareness among consumers about the benefits of green products.
6. The need to recycle waste goods

CHALLENGES OF GREEN MARKETING

1. It needs to be implemented from a long-term perspective, and investors and consumers need to be educated about the benefits of green marketing.
2. Transparency is required in disclosing information to realize an environmentally friendly economy.
3. Appropriate long-term investments need to be planned for adopting green marketing methods.

CONCLUSIONS

Green marketing is an important method for protecting the environment. In India, environmental problems are increasing because of rapid economic development, high population growth, and rapid industrialization that put a lot of strain on the environment, infrastructure, and other resources in the country. Green marketing should be adopted to improve environmental and social dimensions attached to it. The corporate sector needs to change their mindset from adopting traditional marketing strategies to green ones with investments in technology and methods through research and development. Green strategies include ecofriendly product design, ecofriendly labelling, ecofriendly packaging, etc. to have a positive impact on the environment. To conclude, it is essential to view green marketing and the concept behind it as a means to achieve sustainable development. Using environmentally friendly ways to make products and selling them in ecofriendly ways link, in a way, the marketing economics of products with sustainable development.

As the UN has rightly stated, without interlinking all fields it is not possible to achieve overall sustainable development globally. Green marketing as a concept has the potential to help realize the goals of the UN to achieve global sustainable development by applying ecofriendly ways to make products as well as to market them to create awareness among consumers. Green marketing helps the corporate sector to think of ways to make products or invest in projects or activities that do not harm the environment, are in sync with their surrounding environment, and do not need to change the original environment.

NOTES

1. Kotlar, P. & Keller, K. Marketing Management, 2010.
2. Ginsberg, M. & Bloom, N. Choosing the Right Green Marketing Strategy, MIT Sloan Management Review, Vol. 46, No. 1, 2004, pp. 79–88.
3. Chaudhary, R. & Bhattacharya, V. Clean Development Mechanism: Strategy for Sustainability and Economic Growth, Indian journal of Environmental Protection, Vol. 27, No. 10, 2007, pp. 919–922.
4. Uberoi, K., Environmental Management, Excel Books, Delhi, 2007.
5. Singh, Akhileshwar Singh, Green Marketing in India: New Hopes, Challenges and Opportunities, Journal of Advances and Scholarly Researches in Allied Education, Vol. IX, No. XVII, January 2015.
6. Sharma, Neeraj Kumar, Industry Initiative for Green Marketing in India, Business and Economics Journal, Vol. 7, No. 1, 2015.
7. Nandini, B., Green Marketing: A Way to Sustainable Development, AIJRRLSJM, Vol. 1, No. 5, 2016.

REFERENCES

Aparna Choudhary and Samir Gokarn, Green Marketing: A Means for Sustainable Development, RW-JASC 2013; 4(3): 26, 27.

Charter, Green Marketing: A Responsible Approach to Business (1992).

Coddington, Green Marketing: Positive Strategies for Reaching the Green Consumer (1993).

Govind Rathod, Green Marketing in India: Emerging Opportunities and Challenge, Asian Journal of Management Sciences 2014; 2(3): 111–115.

Gurmeet Singh, Evolution and Practice of Green Marketing by Various Companies in India. International Journal of Management and Social Sciences Research 2013; 2(7): 49–56.

Jacob Cherian and Jolly Jacob, Green Marketing: A study of Consumers' Attitude towards Environment Friendly Products, Asian Social Science 2012; 8(12): 117–126.

Jaya Tiwari, Green Marketing in India: An Overview. IOSR Journal of Business and Management, 1(6): 33–40, 2014.

Michael J. Polonsky, An Introduction to Green Marketing, Electronic Green Journal 1(2): 3, 1994

Jacquelyn A. Ottman, The New Rules of Green Marketing, J. Ottman Consulting, Inc., UK, 2011.

Reeta Arora, Green Marketing: Emerging Opportunities and Challenges, International Journal of Research in Management, Economics & Commerce 2014; 4(4): 11–24.

Yasmin Begum R, Nadaf & Shamshuddin M, Nadaf. Green Marketing: Challenges and Strategies for Indian Companies in 21st Century. Impact: International Journal of Research in Business Management 2014; 2(5): 91–10.

Chapter 5

Save Environment, Save Society

Toward Sustainable Development

Urmil Vats

INTRODUCTION

Sustainable development has been defined in many ways, but the most frequently quoted definition is from "Our Common Future," also known as the Brundtland Report:

"Sustainable development is development that meets the needs of the present without compromising the ability of future generations to meet their own needs."

Sustainable development is a strategy by which communities seek to accommodate economic development approaches that also benefit the local environment and quality of life. It has become an important guide to many communities that have discovered that traditional approaches to planning and development are creating, rather than solving, societal and environmental problems. Where traditional approaches can lead to congestion, sprawl, pollution, and resource overconsumption, sustainable development offers real, lasting solutions that will strengthen our future.

Sustainable development provides a framework under which communities can use resources efficiently, create efficient infrastructures, protect and enhance their quality of life, and create new businesses to strengthen their economies. It can help us create healthy communities that can sustain our generation as well as the subsequent generations.

Sustainable development is not a new concept. Rather, it is the latest expression of a long-standing ethic involving people's relations with the environment and the current generation's responsibilities toward future generations. For a community to be truly sustainable, it must adopt a three-pronged approach that considers economic, environmental, and cultural resources. Communities must consider these needs in the short term as well as the long term.

DEFINITIONS OF SUSTAINABLE DEVELOPMENT

Some common definitions of sustainable development are given below:

- "Sustainable development meets the needs of the present without compromising the ability of future generations to meet their own needs."[1]
- "Then I say the earth belongs to each . . . generation during its course, fully and in its own right, no generation can contract debts greater than may be paid during the course of its own existence."[2]
- "Sustainability refers to the ability of a society, ecosystem, or any such ongoing system to continue functioning into the indefinite future without being forced into decline through exhaustion of key resources."[3]
- "Sustainability is the [emerging] doctrine that economic growth and development must take place, and be maintained over time, within the limits set by ecology in the broadest sense—by the interrelations of human beings and their works, the, biosphere and the physical and chemical laws that govern it. . . . It follows that environmental protection and economic development are complementary rather than antagonistic processes."[4]
- A sustainable community effort consists of a long-term, integrated, systems approach to developing and achieving a healthy community by jointly addressing economic, environmental, and social issues. Fostering a strong sense of community and building partnership and consensus among key stakeholders are also important elements of such efforts.

  The focus and scale of sustainability efforts depend on local conditions, including resources, politics, individual actions, and the unique features of the community. The sustainable communities approach has been applied to issues as varied as urban sprawl, inner-city and brownfield redevelopment, economic development and growth, ecosystem management, agriculture, biodiversity, green buildings, energy conservation, watershed management, and pollution prevention. Many of these issues and other community problems cannot easily be addressed by traditional approaches within our society. "Many people feel it is better to address such problems through a more collaborative and holistic systems approach because such problems are diffuse, multidisciplinary, multiagency, multi-stakeholder and multisector in nature."[5]

Sustainable development can be thought of as a process requiring simultaneous progress in four dimensions—economic, human, environmental, and technological. The close "links between these different dimensions and actions in one area can reinforce goals in another," for example, "it cannot neglect environmental constraints or be" based on "the destruction of natural resources. It cannot succeed without the parallel development of human resources; and it will require transformation of the existing industrial base and the development and diffusion of more earth-friendly technologies."[6]

Sustainable development also means that the following principles should underlie the activities undertaken within these four dimensions:

- The principle of intergeneral justice or futurity
- Equal access to the world's material and energy
- Diversity of social and ecological systems leading to the strengthening of local cultures and stability
- Participation by citizens

SUSTAINABLE DEVELOPMENT THROUGH EDUCATION

We need to identify and develop educational programs that focus on the causes rather than just the symptoms of the environmental crisis. It is imperative, therefore, that we become acquainted with the global environmental crises such as the greenhouse effect, risks to ozone layer, acid rain, pollution of world's oceans, desertification, loss of tropical forests, and soil loss, particularly the environmental problems of third-world countries such as "hazardous products and technologies, the green revolution, destructive fishing techniques, destruction of mangrove forests, and energy mega-projects." In India, we face the dual problem of population growth and poverty. To these, we can trace the all our major environmental problems such as the denudation of forests, overgrazing, sewage pollution, malnutrition, and communicable diseases. Simultaneously, in some parts of the country, the environmental problems due to industrial pollution and urban congestion can be clearly discerned.

Population has exploded, physical resources are being depleted, and technological growth has been phenomenal, resulting in unprecedented water and noise pollution, land destruction, and accumulation of pesticide residues. We have started to realize and are rather haunted by the feeling that the world is moving ahead toward a disaster, or perhaps we might have reached the brink and might soon destroy ourselves. It is, therefore, extremely urgent that we diagnose this malady and adopt preventive and curative measures.

Environmental education deals with understanding human beings' relationship with natural and man-made surroundings. It involves understanding the relationship of population, pollution, resource allocation and depletion, conservation, transportation, technology, and urban and rural planning with the total environment. Moreover, environmental education involves recognizing values and clarifying concepts to develop skills and attitudes necessary to understand and appreciate the interrelatedness among human beings, their culture, and their biophysical surroundings. Therefore, it is essential to include environmental education in the school curriculum right from primary to university level.

The importance of environmental education is also reflected in the National Policy on Education (1986), which states, "There is a paramount need to create a consciousness of the environment. It must permeate all ages and all sections of society, beginning with the child. Environment consciousness should inform teaching in schools and colleges. This aspect should be integrated in the entire educational process."[7]

Most people recognize the urgent need for environmental education, but only some have clear ideas about what needs to be done, and very few have the actual experience of the knowledge about the course that needs to be taught. The primary objective of environmental education is that individuals and social groups should acquire awareness and knowledge; develop attitudes, skills, and abilities; and participate in solving real-life environmental problems. The ultimate goal of successful educational environment programs is to foster a valuing approach and responsible action through modified attitudes and lifestyles.

Environmental education should he taught to students to help them recognize that they are a part of an interdependent human and natural web. Students can emerge as a new generation educated to question prevalent attitudes and values; to seek a balance between the lifestyles our society takes for granted and an ecologically sound environment; to protect and respect diversity wherever it occurs in natural and human communities; to live in conformity with an ethic that sees people as part of the natural world—not its masters—and to care so much about the world they have inherited that they are willing to work together to pass it on to future generations a little better than they found it. The perspective should be integrated, interdisciplinary, and holistic in character. Obviously, the approach has to be bottom-up, that is, from the primary stage itself.[8]

NEED FOR ENVIRONMENTAL EDUCATION AT PRIMARY STAGE

Providing environmental education is indeed very important for children at the primary stage because, first, awareness and observation of the environment and nature is developed at this stage. The bond of appreciation would get strengthened as the child grows. Second, primary education constitutes a broad base of the educational pyramid in many developing countries. It has been conjectured that for a sizeable proportion of the children, primary education may be the only formal education that they might have. Many of the children may drop out of school and go back into the larger society. If education, by and large, is to prepare people for purposeful living, there is a need to introduce the study of environment or ecology in the primary education cycle. This calls for careful planning and implementation of a more functional primary environmental curriculum that concentrates on the needs of the majority who terminate their education at primary level, while bearing in mind the needs of those who graduate to the secondary cycle. Therefore, there is a need for environmental education at primary stage, to give practical skills that would make and relate better to the social and economic realities of the country rather than the largely academic education. Strong emphasis should also be placed on the importance of teaching ethics. However, at the primary stage the emphasis should be mostly (75%) on building up awareness, followed by real-life situations (20%) and conservation (55%). This would prepare the children to understand the subtleties of sustainable development. Here, the attempt is only to sensitize the child about environment right from the early stage.

The National Policy on Education (1986) has also emphasized the importance of environmental education to begin with the child, that is, from the primary school stage itself.

ENVIRONMENTAL EDUCATION

Environmental education is education through environment, about environment, and for environment. It is both a style and subject matter of education. In so far as the style is concerned, it means using environment as a teaching–learning aid and as an approach to education. In so far as the subject matter or content is concerned, it means teaching about the components and constituents of the environment. In so far as the teaching for environment is concerned, it means controlling the environment, and establishing proper ecological equilibrium, which entails proper use and conservation of resources and also involves control of environmental pollution. It also includes proper environmental planning so that environment is not only functionally useful but is also aesthetically enjoyable. This aspect would include horticultural planning, rural planning, and urban planning.

This definition of environmental education appears at first to be simplistic and superficial, but actually it is very comprehensive and deep, for it denotes that environmental education is a medium and process of education and that it covers human beings' relationship with their natural as well as social and man-made environments. Environmental education is multidisciplinary in character and its quintessence is a commitment on the part of one and all—all of us inhabiting this planet Earth—to prevent deterioration of air, water, land, and physical and social environment, including interrelations among people and among peoples so that a nuclear war, a chemical warfare, or any other cataclysm generated by humans may not destroy the world. Further, environmental education should be a lifelong process and should not only aim at merely imparting knowledge and understanding of the total environment and of the methods and their application for improving our near and distant surroundings, but it should also aim at inculcating skills, attitudes, and values necessary to understand, appreciate, and improve our biosphere and troposphere.

> To create an awareness and an understanding of the evolving social and physical environment as a whole, its natural, manmade, cultural, spiritual resource, together with the rational use and conservation of these resources for development.

The aforesaid quotation would remain incomplete unless the definition formulated at the Tbilsi Conference, which was held at Georgia in the erstwhile USSR in October 1977 under the auspices of UNESCO and UNEP (United Nations Environment Programme), is also reproduced. The Tbilsi Conference resolved that environmental education involves

1. Awareness: To help social groups and individuals so as to have an awareness of and sensitivity to the total environment and its allied problems.
2. Knowledge: To help social groups and individuals so as to gain a variety of experiences in and get a basic understanding of the environment and its associated problems.
3. Attitude: To help social groups and individuals achieve a set of values and feelings of concern for the environment and the motivation for actively participating in environmental improvement and protection.
4. Skill: To help social groups and individuals so as to acquire skills for identifying and solving environmental problems.
5. Evaluation ability: To help individuals and social groups so as to evaluate environmental measures and education programs in terms of ecological, economic, social, aesthetic, and educational factors.
6. Participation: To give social groups and individuals an opportunity so as to be actively involved at all levels in working toward the resolution of environmental problems.[9]

ENVIRONMENTAL EDUCATION—GUIDING PRINCIPLES

The guiding principles of environmental education are as follows:

- The environment has to be considered in its totality—natural and built, technological and social, economic, political, moral, cultural, historical, and aesthetic aspects.

- Environmental education should be a continuous life process that begins at the preschool level and continues through all formal and nonformal stages.
- Environmental education should be interdisciplinary in its approach. The specific contents of each discipline should play a specific role in making possible a holistic and balanced perspective.
- Environmental education should emphasize active participation in preventing and solving environmental problems
- Environmental education should examine major environmental issues from local, national, regional, and international points of view so that learners get insights into environmental conditions in other geographical areas.
- Environmental education should focus on current and potential environmental situations while taking into consideration the historical perspective.
- Environmental education should explicitly regard environmental aspects in plans for development and growth.
- Environmental education should emphasize the complexity of environmental problems and thereby the need to develop critical thinking and problem-solving skills.
- Environmental education should be able to promote the value and necessity of local, national, and international cooperation in the prevention and solution of environmental problems.
- Environmental education should use a diverse learning environment and a broad array of educational approaches with due stress on practical activities and first-hand experience.
- Environmental education should help learners to find out the symptoms and the real causes of environmental problems.
- Environmental education should be able to relate environmental sensitivity, knowledge, problem-solving, and values clarification in every grade, laying special emphasis on environmental sensitivity to the learners' own community.[10]

INDIA AND SUSTAINABLE DEVELOPMENT

The concept of sustainable development as an ideology has been a part of traditional ethos in India. Traditional knowledge has always emphasized the value of being frugal and leaving enough for society. The religious texts also reinforce these values.

Historically, nature was both revered and feared in India. Wilderness (forests, lakes, rivers, grassland, coasts, and deserts) was considered variously to be the abode of the gods, of the souls of ancestors, or of evil demons and spirits. Similarly, species of plants and animals were considered sacred and worthy of respect and protection. Across the country, there were thousands of sacred sites and groves where nature was allowed to remain and evolve relatively undisturbed. Even today, after a hundred years of attack, some of the best conserved areas in India are those that were protected by traditional communities as sacred sites.[11]

Traditional values regarding nature still survive in various parts of India, especially in rural areas and tribal belts. However, the control of communities over nature has almost disappeared. Most of the forests and other wild areas now belong to the government. Therefore, new methods and safeguards have to be evolved to ensure that these areas are properly conserved.

Indications of the current levels of the environmental crisis in India are given below:

- As against the requirement of a 33 percent forest cover, only a little over 10 percent of the land area of India is covered by forests.
- The industrial wood demand on India's forests is almost three times their annual increment rate.
- The load of livestock on India's forests is calculated to be about three times its carrying capacity.
- India's forests are among the least productive in Asia, their average annual productivity of less than one cubic meter per hectare being about a fourth of the Asian average.
- Fuel wood extraction from the forests is calculated to be almost thrice the sustainable levels.
- India has among the lowest per capita availability of forests in the world, less than 0.1 hectare per head.
- The annual loss of top soil, by erosion, is estimated to be over 6000 million tons.
- The tendency of industrial development to expand production and consumption is incompatible with the finite nature of the planet. Soon the limits of expansion will be reached. Sustainability and industrialism are mutually exclusive.[12]
- Industrial development cannot answer the environmental problems; they can provide temporary success but they cannot provide lasting solutions.

At a philosophical level, the ecological movement can be divided into two broad streams. The first school is known as "Light Anthropocentrists," who believe that humans provide the sole criterion that determines both what is valuable and of what value.[13] The other school is known as "Biocentralists" or "Deep Ecologists," who do not give primary value to the human individual but to the ecosphere as a whole of which humans are a part. The latter school is "ecocentric" as opposed to "anthropocentric" like the first school. Apart from these two schools, there is a radical wing of ecologists for whom nature is more important than human beings. Critics call them "eco-fascists."[14]

As per the theory propagated by James Robertson, the concept of work will also significantly change in the SHE economy. The present formal are:

- Over a third of India's land is affected by soil erosion.
- The area prone to flooding has more than tripled in the last 40 years, from 19 million hectares to over 60 million hectares. Ironically, nearly half the districts in India have suffered from both floods and droughts.
- There is rapid degradation and loss of grasslands, deserts, coasts, rivers, and marine ecosystems, and related species.
- Riverine and marine fisheries are being severely impacted because of the destruction of large areas and high levels of water pollution.
- Recent data suggests that a third of the entire riverine length in the country (about 6000 kilometers) has moderate to severe pollution.
- According to the Central Pollution Control Board, over 5 million liters of liquid effluents a day flow untreated from polluting industries into our water bodies. Similarly, 17 million liters of untreated liquid effluents flow from urban areas into our water bodies every day.
- According to WHO estimates, over 20 percent of all communicable diseases in India are due to poor water quality. The proportion is much higher in terms of infant mortality.
- A large proportion of Indian cities have unhealthy levels of air pollution, especially in terms of total suspended particulates.
- A World Bank study of thirty-six major cities in India estimated that, annually, there are over 40,000 premature deaths and nearly two crore cases of hospital admissions and sickness requiring medical treatment due to air pollution. The poorer inhabitants of these cities, given their lower standard of living, nutrition, and health, are more susceptible to negative health impacts from air pollution.[15]

The rich–poor divide is also apparent in the area of sustainable development. Nature and natural resources are increasingly being cornered by the rich, who can overconsume and overpollute the environment while sitting in the artificial safety of air purifiers in their homes, offices, and cars. The poor, who, for their sheer survival, need access to nature and natural resources, are increasingly being elbowed out from the list of mainstream contenders for the use of natural resources. This is forcing the poor to commit ecological suicide by overusing the few resources allowed to them. It is also allowing the rich to destroy the remaining resources as they seek increasingly opulent lifestyles.

In this context, the rise of the Green Movement and a realization of the disastrous consequences of indiscriminate development at the international level led to a change in the attitude of governments. The Government of India is signatory to various UN conventions on the environments such as the Rio

Earth Summit, 1992; Johannesburg Summit on Sustainable Development, 2002; UN Conference on Sustainable Development, 2012; UN Sustainable Development Summit, 2015; and World Sustainable Development Summit, 2018. The summits and conventions at the global level have sensitized governments the world over on the issue of sustainable development, and India is no exception. However, it is just the beginning as India with its subcontinental landmass also poses environmental problems of a great magnitude. Second, as has been reiterated at the Johannesburg Summit, issues like environment and sustainable development cannot be handled exclusively by the governments. The role of NGOs and larger civil society is, if not more, equally important in bringing about a paradigm shift. There are several issues on which the government, the NGOs, and the civil society can concentrate to create a more sustainable development paradigm.[16]

CONCLUSIONS

The ultimate goal of successful environmental education programs is to foster a valuing approach and responsible action, both individually through modified attitudes and lifestyles and collectively through community action and political process. Effective programs should build an awareness and an appreciation of the natural world we are striving to protect as well as of the specific hazards threatening the world. It is our collective responsibility to think constructively to save the environment.

NOTES

1. "Sustainability and Sustainable Development," Circular Ecology, Retrieved 2018.
2. Robert Gilman, President of Context Institute.
3. United Nations World Commission on Environment and Development Thomas Jefferson, 6 September, 1789.
4. D. Ruckelshaus, "Toward a Sustainable World," Scientific American, September 1989.
5. E. Lachman, Critical Technologies Institute, "Linking Sustainable Community Activities to Pollution Prevention: A Sourcebook," April 1997.
6. (World Resources Institute, Environmental Education Project, and Teacher's Guide)
7. Ibid.
8. Dr. Haseen Taj – Current Challenges in Education, Neelkamal New Delhi, 2008.
9. Ibid.
10. Ibid.

11. Shekhar Singh, "Caring For the Earth: Conserving Our Environment while Meeting Our Economic Needs," paper presented at the refresher course on Human Rights, Gender & Environment, organized by CPDHE, Delhi university, October 4–25, 2004.

12. Porritt, Seeing Green: The Politics of Ecology Explained, Oxford, Blackwell, 1984, p. 49.

13. Andrew Vincent, Modern Political Ideologies, Oxford Blackwell, 1992, pp. 224–225.

14. Ibid.

15. Ibid.

16. James Robertson, Future Work, Temple Smith.

Chapter 6

Resolving Water Pollution and Legal Personality to Rivers

Kriti Parashar

INTRODUCTION

Environmental degradation is a contemporary problem that finds its presence in several areas. One such area is the alteration of the land surface by humans in terms of on-site impacts as well as off-site effects, notably rivers.[1] With more than 260 international river basins covering 45 percent of the Earth's land surface and with freshwater sources, water is humanity's most valuable natural resource. Both environmental degradation and climate change have negatively affected water resources, especially the rivers around the world. Changes in the river behavior have also affected daily human activities such as farming owing to the high amount of water flow that rapidly changes or even the severe erosion of riverbanks. For example, a survey conducted in the Indian city of Shantipur (West Bengal) found that 90.13 percent of respondents had lost their land because of riverbank erosion over the past forty years.[2]

The United Nations Food and Agricultural Organization (FAO) has counted more than 3600 treaties on international water issues between the years 805 and 1984. Further, it has been counted that there are around 300 international treaties on non-navigational issues of water management, flood control, hydropower projects, and allocations for consumptive or nonconsumptive uses of international rivers since 1945.[3] This is in exclusion to the various national regimes of riverbed management and water pollution policies. However, even with such an extensive framework, many rivers are drying up, water temperature is rising, and species in rivers are dying. This chapter seeks to study the interrelation between climate change and rivers, and to explore whether granting a legal personality to rivers could be a solution to checking the negative impact of environment degradation and climate change on rivers.

CLIMATIC CHANGE AND IMPACT ON RIVERS

The impact of climate change on rivers can be viewed as a "feast-or-famine" case. On the one hand, we have increased water flow due to glaciers melting and increased rainfall due to changing precipitation patterns. On the other hand, it is a famine from the perspective of changing long-term precipitation patterns, severe storms, and evaporation attributed to overall warming, which has parallel impact on the quality of river water. Extreme rainfall events lead to a lot of runoff because the soil simply is not able to absorb the precipitation at the rate it is falling. In urban, suburban, and agricultural areas, this runoff will pick up pollutants from the landscape and carry them to nearby rivers and other waterways. In Bolivia, this situation was a significant contributor to the complete disappearance of the nation's second-largest lake, Lake Poopó. The scientists studying Arctic river ice revealed what is being described as "the first case of large-scale river reorganization as a result of human-caused climate change."[4] These are just a few examples of the major changes happening to rivers and streams all over the world as temperatures rise and precipitation patterns change.

Another impact of climate change on rivers is the displacement of cold-water species. As air temperatures rise, so do water temperatures—particularly in shallow stretches of rivers and surface waters of lakes. Streams and lakes may become unsuitable for cold-water fish but support species that thrive in warmer waters. Some warm-water species are already moving to waters at higher latitudes and altitudes. In a study, the potential impact of climate change on the hydrology of a west-flowing-river basin, i.e., Gurupura basin, was analyzed. The temperature was found to be increasing at the rate of 0.10 degrees Celsius per decade. The study suggested that a decrease in rainfall and river flow induced additional stresses on water resources of the basin and may require various adaptation strategies to sustain it with climate change. The results would serve as preliminary guideline for sustainable water resources management of the basin.[5]

Climate change has also created "dead zones" in rivers. In a warming climate, a warmer upper layer in deep lakes slows down air exchange—a process that normally adds oxygen to the water. This, in turn, often creates large "dead zones"—areas depleted of oxygen and unable to support life. Persistent dead zones can produce toxic algal blooms, foul-smelling drinking water, and massive fish kills.[6] For example, in 2010, a study by a team of Cardiff University scientists found that salmon and trout populations in the River Wye and its tributaries fell significantly between 1985 and 2004, and suggested warmer water and lower river levels (correlated with changing climate) were to blame.[7] Thus, there is sufficient evidence to suggest that climate change threatens to fundamentally alter where and when water is available across the nation. How far our legal system is ready to tackle these changes is a pertinent question of concern. The first part of the chapter studies of the pre-environmental degradation approach to rivers. The second part discusses the new rights-based approach to nature and rivers. The next part discusses the developments around the world and in India. The chapter concludes by giving suggestions on implementing the regime.

PRE-DEGRADATION APPROACH TO RIGHTS TO RIVERS

Traditions and cultures around the world have always lived in harmony with nature. Christianity, Islam, Hinduism, Chinese, and African cultures have worshipped trees, plants, rivers, and animals as gods and goddesses. Rivers in these cultures have received prominent respect for being the source of life and supporting life of the whole community. Water bodies have been considered as deities and are often personified. River Lourdes among Catholic Romans, Jordan River in Christianity, the Zamzam Well in Islam, majority of rivers in Hinduism, "Hapi" the Nile God in Africa, and the Yellow River (Huang He) in China are examples of water bodies that have been assigned the status of deities and been culturally important for centuries.

The relationship of the present legal system with rivers and other natural water bodies has not remained this direct. Rivers are protected under the environment protection law, water pollution is made punishable, and municipalities have been assigned their duties to maintain them. What is pertinent is that the legal system does not directly recognize rivers; it gives them status through individuals. The rights of humans to have a healthy environment including clean water is being enforced by the courts, and it is through this right that rivers exist for the courts and the legal system. A direct relationship with these life-giving water bodies by establishing them as a legal person is a distant idea at present. The next sections explore the viability of this idea for our legal system to ensure not only human rights to individuals but also rights to these water bodies on which human civilization largely depends.

PROTECTING ENVIRONMENT THROUGH RIGHTS TO NATURE

Law has treated nature as property subject to ownership. Christopher D. Stone in his book *Should Trees Have Standing?* has remarked, "Until a rightless thing receives its rights, we cannot see it as anything but a thing for the use of 'us'—those who are holding rights the time."[8] Peter Singer writes with regard to animal rights, "The fact is, that each time there is a movement to confer rights onto some new 'entity,' the proposal is bound to sound odd or frightening or laughable."[9] Assigning rights to nature would acknowledge that they are not just resources to be used but also life forms which have the right to exist, persist, maintain, and regenerate. Rivers being part of the ecosystem would also be granted these rights. However, only few scholars agree on the matter of granting rights to natural bodies.

Rodrick Frazier Nash's *The Rights of Nature*, Christopher Stone's *Should Trees Have Standing?*, David R. Boyd's *The Rights of Nature: A Legal Revolution That Could Change the World*, and *The Rights of Nature* by the Council of Canadians are pertinent works advocating the idea that nature could be assigned rights. The Pachamama Alliance of the Global Alliance for the Rights of Nature and the first Global Tribunal on the Rights of Nature in 2013 are also some such developments.

Apart from the writings of these scholars, there is at least one reported decision of the Supreme Court of the United States, penned by the great environmentalist Justice William O. Douglas, suggesting that United States' trees and rivers deserve the legal status given to individual citizens, private corporations, and even ships to bring a lawsuit. Justice Douglas forcefully asserted that "the voice of the existing beneficiaries of these environmental wonders should be heard."[10] Recently, while interpreting animal rights in the case of *Animal Welfare Board of India v. A. Nagaraja*,[11] the Supreme Court of India remarked that "Article 21 of the Constitution, while safeguarding the rights of humans, protects life and the word 'life' has been given an expanded definition and any disturbance from the basic environment which includes all forms of life, including animal life."

Such an expansive interpretation of Article 21 would also grant a constitutional standing to rivers being a form of life. The Indian Supreme Court has also expanded the locus standi requirements for filing a case on anyone's behalf a decade ago saying that the same can be done "in the service of the poor, oppressed and voiceless."[12] Being voiceless, nature makes both the state and public its trustee.

Developments like this imply that the groundwork for assigning rights and duties to rivers is being laid; it is only up to the legislators and the legal system in the country to move ahead and implement the idea. Eric O Donnel, in this regard, remarks, "There is still a big question about whether these types of legal rights are relevant or appropriate for nature at all. But what is clear from the experience of applying this concept to other non-human entities is that these legal rights don't mean much if they can't be enforced."[13] Begonia Filgueria, an environmental lawyer, put forth a question: "It took until 1998 for the United Kingdom Parliament to incorporate human rights directly into the domestic legal system. In light of the dangers posed by climate change, is it time to go one step further and grant rights to the Earth herself?"[14] The Community Environmental Legal Defense Fund (CELDF), a pertinent body associated with environmental agendas and rights of nature, has remarked the following:[15]

> Many nations have expanded their body of legal rights to recognize a human right to a healthy environment, including Spain, France, Portugal, Greece, and Finland. However, as global warming accelerates and ecosystems are pushed to collapse, we are finding that the human right to a healthy environment cannot be achieved without securing rights of the environment itself. This means recognizing in law the right of nature to be healthy and thrive.

In light of these questions being asked time and again, does it make sense—legally, philosophically, or ethically—for rivers to be relegated to the property status, when ships and corporations can sue and be sued in the courts of law? If a legal fiction can come to the aid of inanimate companies, why cannot a natural fact be taken notice of to assist rivers?[16] Hence, it is about time that theories of legal personality be made flexible enough to the idea of assigning personality to rivers.

DEVELOPMENT OF RIVERS AS LEGAL PERSONALITY AROUND THE WORLD

In the past year, three rivers around the world have been identified as legal persons: first, the Whanganui River was granted personality by legislators in New Zealand under a new legislation. The legislation emerged as a result of the Māori tribe's efforts and negotiations to protect the river with which they had special relationship under their culture. The other two are Rivers Ganga and Yamuna in India which were identified as persons by Uttarakhand High Court. One of the Uttarakhand High Court orders has been stayed and the issue is pending to be finally decided before the Supreme Court of India. Joerg Mueller in this regard says,

> Granting legal rights to New Zealand's Whanganui River catchment (Te Awa Tupua) has taken eight years of careful negotiation. In contrast, almost overnight, the High Court in India had ruled that the Ganga and Yamuna Rivers will be treated as minors under the law, and will be represented by three people—the director general of Namami Gange project, the Uttarakhand chief secretary, and the advocate general—who will act as guardians for the river.

Studying the contrasting setups in these two and other different countries, we see how rivers around the world can be made legal persons.

New Zealand

In New Zealand, the Whanganui River Claims Settlement Act, 2017 grants Whanganui River personhood. Section 14 of the act declares Te Awa Tupua (Whanganui River) to be a legal person as follows:

1. Te Awa Tupua is a legal person and has all the rights, powers, duties, and liabilities of a legal person.
2. The rights, powers, and duties of Te Awa Tupua must be exercised or performed, and responsibility for its liabilities must be taken, by Te Pou Tupua on behalf of, and in the name of, Te Awa Tupua, in the manner provided for in this Part and in Ruruku Whakatupua—Te Mana o Te Awa Tupua.

The act defines liabilities of the river as "debts, charges, duties, and other obligations, whether present, future, actual, contingent, payable, or to be observed or performed in New Zealand or elsewhere." Section 25 of the act makes the river a single person for the purpose of tax treatment and not separate from its representative body and beneficiaries.[17] Schedule 5 of the act specifies that liabilities of the river exclude the following:

a. remediation of any historical contaminated site on the relevant land if the contamination was caused at any period when the land was held by the Crown;
b. an existing structure on the bed of the Whanganui River if the structure was established before the date on which the relevant land vested;
c. an existing activity (whether authorized under a consent or designation, as a permitted activity, or by or under any legislation) if the activity was authorized before the date on which the relevant land vested; and
d. public access to, and use of, the Whanganui River, including for navigation.

On and from the date on which land vests in Te Awa Tupua by section 41(1) or under Section 53(3) or 55(3)(a), the Crown retains

a. any existing liabilities it may have in relation to the land arising from
    i. a historical contaminated site if the contamination was caused while the Crown held the relevant land;

   ii. an existing structure on the bed of the Whanganui River if the structure was established before the date on which the relevant land vested;
   iii. an existing activity, whether authorized under a consent, under a designation, as a permitted activity, or by or under legislation, if the activity was authorized before the date on which the relevant land vested;
   iv. plants that are attached to the bed of the Whanganui River, together with the biosecurity risks associated with those plants; and

b. any other liability arising from landowner functions performed or decisions made by the Crown before the date on which the relevant land vests.

Schedule 7 of the act provides certain customary activities that would be permitted by an authorized notice of the board. The trustees are only permitted to authorize certain activities when they do not cause significant adverse impact to the river. Thus, we can say that the act comprehensively provides the rights and liabilities of the river. Exclusion in the liabilities of the Crown with regard to the river limit the lacuna that could have arisen from making the river an entity in the eyes of law. Similar provisions can be taken as a framework for other countries thinking to grant river bodies rights and duties.

Ecuador

The constitution of Ecuador mandates that nature has the right to exist, maintain, and regenerate. Preamble to the constitution states that "Celebrating nature, the Pacha Mama (Mother Earth), of which we are a part and which is vital to our existence." Article 71 of the constitution states that

> Nature, or Pacha Mama, where life is reproduced and occurs, has the right to integral respect for its existence and for the maintenance and regeneration of its life cycles, structure, functions and evolutionary processes. All persons, communities, peoples and nations can call upon public authorities to enforce the rights of nature. To enforce and interpret these rights, the principles set forth in the Constitution shall be observed, as appropriate. The State shall give incentives to natural persons and legal entities and to communities to protect nature and to promote respect for all the elements comprising an ecosystem.

Article 72 gives nature the right to be restored. It provides that "this restoration shall be apart from the obligation of the State and natural persons or legal entities to compensate individuals and communities that depend on affected natural systems." Based on such a setup, rivers have also received rights. This has opened the door for many environmental advocates. Vilcabamba

River had half receded from its basin, when a lawsuit was brought by Mr. R. F. Wheeler and Mr. E. G. Huddle in the name of the river as a plaintiff. The plaintiff, i.e., the Vilcabamba River, was contending its right to thrive and exist which was hampered by a construction project of the government. In 2011, the provincial court ruled in favor of the river. It granted a constitutional injunction to the plaintiff river stating that[18]

- The suitability and efficacy of the constitutional injunction as the only way to remedy in an immediate manner the environmental damage focusing on the undeniable, elemental, and essential importance of nature, and taking into account the evident process of degradation;
- That, based on the precautionary principle, until it is objectively demonstrated that the probability of certain danger that a project undertaken in an established area does not produce contamination or lead to environmental damage, it is the responsibility of the constitutional judges to incline toward the immediate protection and the legal tutelage of the rights of nature, doing what is necessary to prevent contamination or call for remedy. Note that we consider in relation to the environment that one act not only under the certainty of damage but its probability;
- The recognition of the importance of nature, raising the issue that damages to nature are generational damages, defined as such for their magnitude that impact not only the present generation but also future ones;
- That, using the principle of inversion of the burden of proof, the plaintiffs should not have to prove the existence damages but that the provincial government of Loja, as the entity that administers the activity and as the defendant, had to have provided certain proof that the widening the road would not affect the environment; and
- That the argument of the provincial government that the population needs roads does not apply because there is no collision of constitutional rights of the population, nor is there any sacrifice of them, because the case does not question the widening of the Vilcabamba–Quinara road, but the respect for the constitutional rights of nature.

This case marked the first time that a court upheld the constitutional rights of a river. This judgment is a remarkable example of how granting rights to a river could open up the door for several litigations which are avoided owing to a lack of locus standi. The court had shifted the burden of proof not on the representatives of the river to prove damage but on the state to prove that its activities were not violative of the rights of the river. Granting rights to river in the constitution itself has taken the river on the highest pedestal, thus protecting it from damage due to overexploitation.

Bolivia

The Bolivian "Framework Law of Mother Earth and Integral Development for Living Well" has established judicial character to Mother Earth. Article 7 of the law enumerates seven rights to which Mother Earth is entitled:[19]

To life: It is the right to the maintenance of the integrity of life systems and natural processes which sustain them, as well as the capacities and conditions for their renewal.

To the Diversity of Life: It is the right to the preservation of the differentiation and variety of the beings that comprise Mother Earth, without being genetically altered, nor artificially modified in their structure, in such a manner that threatens their existence, functioning, and future potential.

To water: It is the right of the preservation of the quality and composition of water to sustain life systems and their protection with regards to contamination, for renewal of the life of Mother Earth and all its components.

To clean air: It is the right of the preservation of the quality and composition of air to sustain life systems and their protection with regards to contamination, for renewal of the life of Mother Earth and all its components.

To equilibrium: It is the right to maintenance or restoration of the interrelation, interdependence, ability to complement, and functionality of the components of Mother Earth, in a balanced manner for the continuation of its cycles and the renewal of its vital processes.

To restoration: It is the right to the effective and opportune restoration of life systems affected by direct or indirect human activities.

To live free of contamination: It is the right for preservation of Mother Earth and any of its components with regards to toxic and radioactive waste generated by human activities.

The original law was adopted in December 2010 and its successor—Framework Law of Mother Earth and Integral Development for Living Well—was passed in October 2012.[20] This law also makes a specific mention to water bodies' right not to be contaminated and to sustain life systems. Even though the framework has not yet received implementation on the practical front, it is nevertheless a positive step in granting rights to rivers.

India

Granting a river rights in India might seem an ambiguous concept, but the truth is we have already traveled in that direction a certain distance—whether through a constitutional mandate under directive principles and fundamental duties, or statutory rights, or in the form of judicial pronouncements. Article

51A(g) of the Constitution of India casts a fundamental duty on every citizen "to protect and improve the natural environment including forests, lakes, rivers and wild life, and to have compassion for living creatures."[21] There are also comprehensive provisions for interstate river disputes under our Constitution.[22] It also guarantees cities the right to decide and implement their environmental policies. This was done through the 74th Constitutional Amendment.[23]

The Indian Penal Code, 1860 punishes "whoever voluntarily corrupts or fouls the water of any public spring or reservoir, so as to render it less fit for the purposes for which it is ordinarily used."[24] Similarly, the Water Act, 1974 also provides for similar protection to water bodies. The act is comprehensive in its coverage, applying to "streams (including those temporarily dry), inland waters (whether natural or artificial), subterranean waters, and sea or tidal waters." The act protects the rivers by establishing state and central boards[25] which can sue and be sued on behalf of the river.[26] We can say that in India there is already a setup no matter how slow in implementation toward giving environmental bodies a standing.

The most pertinent development in India, however, was the Uttarakhand High Court's judgment on March 20, 2017 that held Rivers Ganga and Yamuna to be legal persons. In *Mohd Salim v. State of Uttarakhand & Ors*,[27] a local resident Mohammed Salim had filed a petition asking the high court to direct the government of the state of Uttarakhand to remove illegal construction along the banks of the River Yamuna and to manage water resources properly.[28] The court while holding them to be legal persons held that

> To protect the recognition and the faith of society, Rivers Ganges and Yamuna are required to be declared as the legal/living persons. This would support and assist both the life and natural resources and health and well-being of the entire community. Rivers Ganges and Yamuna are breathing, living and sustaining the communities from mountains to sea.

The court remarked, "We may, therefore, define a person for the purpose of jurisprudence as any entity (not necessarily a human being) to which rights or duties may be attributed." The court finally declared:

> Accordingly, while exercising the parens patrie jurisdiction, the Rivers Ganga and Yamuna, all their tributaries, streams, every natural water flowing with flow continuously or intermittently these rivers are declared as juristic/legal persons/living entities having the status of a legal person with all corresponding rights, duties and liabilities of a living person in order to preserve and conserve Rivers Ganga and Yamuna. The Director of Namami Gange, the Chief Secretary of the State of Uttarakhand and the Advocate General of the State of Uttarakhand

are hereby declared in loco parentis as the human face to protect, conserve and preserve the Rivers Ganga and Yamuna and their tributaries. These Officers are bound to uphold the status of the Rivers Ganges and Yamuna and also promote the health and well-being of these rivers.

This judgment now stands stayed via an order of the Supreme Court on July 7, 2017.[29] The stay order came upon hearing a special leave petition of the state of Uttarakhand against the verdict. The one sentence order reads: "In the meantime, the operation of the impugned order shall remain stayed." In light of this order, it is rather ambiguous to say where India stands in terms of giving personality to rivers. One thing is, however, certain that acceptance of personality to rivers has found its establishment in India. It is only awaited if this would be accepted by the Supreme Court, and most importantly, how would it be incorporated and implemented in the Indian legal system.

A lawyer at the Indian Supreme Court in his remark has criticized the idea of rivers being persons as follows:[30]

> If a farmer pumps water onto his land from the river, is he violating the "person" of the river? What happens in the case of a flood, will the authorities in loco parentis compensate the people harmed? In the case of temples and their trusts, there are rights and responsibilities, but in this case there are only rights. A religious trust can both sue, and be sued. Who is going to sue a river, if it runs dry, if it is polluted, if it floods?

These questions can only be answered by a comprehensive legislation like National Ganga River Rights Act as has been done by New Zealand by environmentalists, and nature rights activists in India could specify the details associated with personhood at best.

Shyam Krishnakumar in his article says[31]

> These verdicts represent a shift from a view that sees nature as a resource to one that considers it an entity with fundamental rights. Environmental laws only focus on regulating exploitation. But this is now changing, with calls for the inherent rights of nature to be recognised, both in India and around the world. It may no longer be necessary to prove in court that polluting the Ganges actually harms humans. Contamination on its own could be enough to make the case that it violates the river's "right to life."

This shift would provide several reliefs in putting constraints on polluting developmental activities. The burden of proof is always on the prosecution to prove that a river was being polluted or a pond put with sewage; they inherently have no rights. Further, even if the pollution to the river is proved, the polluter would just be punished and the river as a whole would not get any benefit, rights, or compensation to prevent its damage. Even if the polluter is made to pay a fine, the amount of the fine is never equivalent to the amount of damage. Christopher Stone writes in this regard that "there are threefold problems with natural bodies—they have no standing in their own right, their unique damages do not count in the award and they are not always beneficiaries of their award."[32] These can be solved by giving rights to rivers.

IMPACT ON WATER POLLUTION—RIGHTS AND DUTIES OF RIVERS

Having studied the developments regarding rivers as legal persons, we also need to know the implications of making rivers legal persons. Suppose a river is made a legal person in the eyes of law. What would it imply in terms of its rights and duties? Making rivers legal persons like mosques, idols, companies, and trust would imply the following:

1. Appointment of guardians for the rivers as their representatives and beneficiaries
2. Giving them locus standi to file a case on behalf of the rivers
3. Making the representatives of the rivers accountable in cases brought against the rivers

Most of the above implications regarding the personhood of a river can be easily addressed by appointing a government body as its representative. The problem arises when the rights and duties are to be enforced by and against private persons. Can a private person be sued to ensure the river's right to flow freely? On a positive side, this would make industries disposing effluents and citizens polluting the river accountable to one single entity as compared to the idea of an "abstract state." Begonia Filgueira says, "This will put an end to much of the legal standing issues that NGOs come across when trying to stand in and defend nature from overexploitation or damage."[33] The guardianship approach also provides rivers with supervision like bankruptcy provides to an endangered corporation. The guardian[34] knows that the lawn needs water or the smog is destroying the forest reserve.

Since such a body would be representative of the river, so the compensation received can be used for restoring balance in the river directly. This would ensure transparency in river management. However, when activities like dams and irrigation projects would come in conflict with the river, would they still be violating the river's right to flow freely or not to be polluted?

Perhaps the river's right would become subservient to the "public purpose" then. What would constitute public purpose then is an important agenda. Development activities conflicting with the rights of rivers can often be protected under this garb. It is, therefore, necessary that while granting personhood to rivers, we should also carve out exceptions to their rights when they come in conflict with public purpose or development agendas.

Another area in which making rivers legal persons would be problematic is implementing duties. Floods and displacement are caused by rivers. A citizen can claim compensation from the representatives of the river body. To avoid these situations, the river body can be assigned imperfect rights. According to Salmond, "a perfect right is one which corresponds to a perfect duty. A perfect duty is one which is not merely recognized by law but also enforced by law." Those rights and duties which, though recognized by law, are not perfect in nature are called imperfect rights. An example of such an imperfect right is a claim barred by the lapse of time. In such a case, the limitation does not extinguish the right but bars the remedy only. Assigning such nature of rights to rivers can make them immune to such force majeure situations.

CONCLUSIONS

Rivers are each day being affected by sewage disposal, rising temperatures, chemical effluents, changing precipitation, and so on. This negative impact is directly affecting humans as rivers are drying up and the water stress on them is increasing. Irrigation, agricultural produce, land use changes, and so on are directly impacted. In this light, it is time that the idea that rivers be made legal persons be given serious thought by environmentalists, legislators, and judiciary alike. Keeping in mind the benefits associated with granting rights to rivers, the deficiencies in the idea are merely lacunas that can be covered by a well-drafted legislation, policy, or judicial pronouncement. Broader locus standi, better river management, assignment of direct responsibility, compensation to restore pollution caused by industries, and so on are few of the plausible advantages of this idea. It not only strengthens the existing environmental legislations but also empowers the doctrines such as public trust, polluter pays, and sustainable development at the practical level. It is time that we moved from the gray area lying between worshipping rivers in our religions to using them as property for our benefit. It is time we clarify in our mind as well as in legislations and doctrines that rivers, the very source around which human civilizations have flourished, should neither be worshipped, used, nor protected. They need to be assigned their true status as a person as did our ancestors when they paid obeisance to them as deities.

NOTES

1. Robin F. Warner, 'Impacts of Environmental Degradation on Rivers', *Available at:* https://doi.org/10.1080/00049189108703016 (Visited on 27/02/2019).

2. Awang Nasrizal Awang Ali and others, 'Environmental Degradation: A Review on the Potential Impact of River Morphology', *Available at:* https://www.matec-conferences.org/articles/matecconf/pdf/2017/17/matecconf_iscee2017_04001.pdf (Visited on 27/02/2019).

3. Thomas Bernauer, International River Management, *Available at:* http://www.ib.usp.br/limnologia/textos/Explaining%20Success%20and%20Failure%20in%20International%20River%20Management.pdf (Visited on 27/02/2019).

4. 'Climate Reality Project', *Available at:* https://www.climaterealityproject.org/sites/climaterealityproject.org/files/Soil%20Health%20and%20Climate%20Change.pdf (Visited on 27/02/2019).

5. T. M. Sharannya, Amogh Mudbhatkal and A. Mahesha, 'Assessing climate change impacts on river hydrology – A case study in the Western Ghats of India', *Journal of Earth Systematic Science*, 127 (2018).

6. *Available at:* http://www.climatehotmap.org/global-warming-effects/lakes-and-rivers.html (Visited on 27/02/2019).

7. 'Climate Change' Danger to Salmon and Trout in Wye', BBC News, 17 May 2010.

8. Christopher D. Stone, 'Should Trees have Standing? Toward Legal Rights for Natural Objects', 1, *California Law Review*, 59, 1985.

9. Peter Singer, *Animal Liberation* (Harper Perennial Modern Classics, Reissue edition, February 24, 2009).

10. *Sierra Cluv* v. *Morton*, 405 U.S. 727 (1972).

11. (2014)7SCC547, 2014 (5) SCJ 614.

12. *Subhash Kumar* v. *State of Bihar*, A.I.R. 1991 S.C. 420, para. 7.

13. Erin O Donnel, '3 Rivers just became legal persons', *Available at:* https://www.livescience.com/58398-3-rivers-just-became-legal-persons.html (Visited on 20/06/2018).

14. *Available at:* https://ukhumanrightsblog.com/2011/06/02/and-about-time-for-rights-to-nature-by-begonia-filgueira/ (Visited on 20/06/2018).

15. 'Rights of Nature', *Available at:* https://celdf.org/rights/rights-of-nature/ (Visited on 20/06/2018).

16. Raju Moray, 'Fundamental Rights for Animals: An Idea Whose Time has Come', 10, *Lawyers Collective,* 26 (January–February, 1995).

17. Section 25 of the Act states that "(1) Te Awa Tupua and Te Pou Tupua are deemed to be the same person for the purposes of the Inland Revenue Acts and the liabilities and obligations placed on a person under those Acts."

18. Natalia Greene, 'The first successful case of the rights of nature implementation in Ecuador', *Available at:* http://therightsofnature.org/first-ron-case-ecuador/ (Visited on 21/06/2018).

19. 'Framework Law of Mother Earth and Integral Development for Living Well', *Available at:* http://www.ftierra.org/ft/index.php?option=com_content&view=article&id=4288:rair&catid=152:cc&Itemid=210 (Visited on 21/06/2018).

20. Law of the Rights of Mother Earth, *Available at:* http://www.worldfuturefund.org/Projects/Indicators/motherearthbolivia.html (Visited on 21/06/2018).

21. The late T. K. Tope was of the view that with the inclusion of the chapter on fundamental duties by the 42nd Amendment, the Constitution has accepted the concept of "unenumerated rights." Accordingly, the rights of animals/living creatures fall within the category of unenumerated rights which are crying out for enumeration by our Supreme Court.

22. Article 262 confers exclusive power on the Parliament to enact a law providing for the adjudication of any dispute or complaint with respect to the use, distribution, or control of waters of, or in, any interstate river or river valley.

23. 'For the love of Ganga', *Available at:* http://www.blueplanetjournal.com/ecology/for-the-love-of-ganga-science-religion-and-a-clean-conscience.htmlhttp://www.blueplanetjournal.com/ecology/for-the-love-of-ganga-science-religion-and-a-clean-conscience.html (Visited on 30/12/2014).

24. S. 277 India Penal Code.

25. S. 3(3), 4(3) of the Act.

26. S. 3(2)(d), 4(2)(d) of the Act.

27. WPPIL No. 126 of 2014.

28. Vrinda Narain, 'Indian Court Recognizes Rivers as Legal Entities', Int'l J. Const. L. Blog, June 13, 2017, at: http://www.iconnectblog.com/2017/06/indian-court-recognizes-rivers-as-legal-entities (Visited on 21/06/2018).

29. Special Leave Petition No. 16879/2017.

30. *Available at:* https://scroll.in/article/833069/a-court-naming-ganga-and-yamuna-as-legal-entities-could-invite-a-river-of-problems (Visited on 21/06/2018).

31. *Available at:* https://www.bbc.com/news/world-asia-india-39488527 (Visited on 21/06/2018).

32. Supra note 8 at16.

33. Begonia Filgueira, 'About time to give rights to nature?', *Available at:* https://ukhumanrightsblog.com/2011/06/02/and-about-time-for-rights-to-nature-by-begonia-filgueira/ (Visited on 25/06/2018).

34. Water control boards or pollution control boards are guardians of these natural bodies this way.

Chapter 7

Sustainable Development

Growth of Indian Environmental Jurisprudence and the Social Responsibility of Corporates toward the Environment

Vatsala Sood

INTRODUCTION

Environment is the wellspring of life on Earth like water, air, soil, and so on, and determines the presence, development, and improvement of humanity and all its activities. The concept of ecological protection and preservation is not new. It has been intrinsic to many ancient civilizations. Ancient Indian texts highlight that it is the dharma of each individual in the society to protect nature. The term "nature" includes land, water, trees, and animals which are of great importance to us. In the Atharva Veda, the ancient Hindu seers stated, "What of thee I dig out let that quickly grow over."[1]

Environmental protection and sustainable development of the material resources represent, currently, a common preoccupation of all the nations of the world, a global objective. To this end, a series of international provisions with universal vocation have been adopted by means of collaboration and cooperation among nations. The international measures regarding environmental protection have been provided for, stated, or recognized at the level of international general or conventional law.

Sustainable development has to be taken into consideration in establishing the line of action at the level of the whole communitarian process, establishing exigencies regarding information about long- and short-term objectives that are looked after in all five domains that have an impact on the environment. Durable development or a durable way of life means a general assembly of human activities and the biosphere, taken into consideration in their dynamic form.

These relations have to allow the continuity of human life, the satisfaction of each individual's own needs, and the development of a variety of cultures, but in such a way that the changes made depending on the nature of the human activity comply with certain limits such that the biophysical context is not harmed.[2] According to the Brundtland Commission Report, 1987 (titled "Our Common Future,"), "Sustainable development is development that meets the needs of the present, without compromising the ability of future generations to meet their own needs."[3]

Sustainable development has three goals: to minimize the depletion of natural resources, to promote development without causing harm to the environment, and to make use of environmentally friendly practices.

RIO EARTH SUMMIT AND ITS ROLE IN DEVELOPING ENVIRONMENTAL JURISPRUDENCE IN INDIA

Earth Summit 1992 was the United Nations Conference on Environment and Development (UNCED), commonly known as the Rio Summit or Rio Conference. It was a major UN conference held in Rio de Janeiro from June 3 to June 14, 1992. It was attended by the representatives of 172countries. The aim was to reconcile worldwide development with the protection of the environment. By means of treaties and other documents signed at the conference, most of the world's nations nominally committed themselves to the pursuit of economic development in ways that would protect the Earth's environment and nonrenewable resources.[4]

The Rio Declaration on Environment and Development, 1992 builds on the principles of sustainable development, intergenerational equity, and sovereign rights mentioned in the Stockholm Declaration, as well as expands the concept of sustainable development and reaffirms, among others, the importance and centrality of the precautionary principle, the polluter pays principle, and environmental impact assessments.

PRECAUTIONARY PRINCIPLE AND POLLUTER PAYS PRINCIPLE

The Convention on Biological Diversity (CBD), 1992 is a binding treaty requiring nations to take inventories of their plants and wild animals and protect the endangered species. The United Nations Framework Convention on Climate Change (UNFCCC), or Global Warming Convention, is a binding treaty that requires nations to reduce their emission of carbon dioxide, methane, and other gases thought to be responsible for global warming. The treaty stopped short of setting binding targets for emission reductions, however. The CBD had three main goals: (1) the conservation of biological diversity, (2) the sustainable use of its components, and (3) the fair and equitable sharing of the benefits arising from the use of genetic resources.

Such targets were eventually established in an amendment to the UNFCCC, the Kyoto Protocol (1997), which was eventually superseded by the Paris Agreement on Climate Change (2015). The Rio Declaration laid down twenty-seven broad, nonbinding principles for environmentally sound development. The objective of the UNFCC was the stabilization of greenhouse gas concentrations in the atmosphere at a level that would prevent dangerous anthropogenic interference with the Earth's climate system.

The most important and significant aspect of the Rio Summit was Agenda 21, a vast work program for the twenty-first century, representing the consensus reached by several states present at the summit. This historic document runs into 700 pages and embraces practically all areas of sustainable development. "It is a blueprint for a global partnership aimed at reconciling the twin requirements of a high-quality environment and a healthy economy for all people of the world."[5] Agenda 21 outlines global strategies for cleaning up the environment and encouraging environmentally sound development. The statement of principles on forests, aimed at preserving the world's rapidly vanishing tropical rainforests, is a nonbinding statement recommending that nations monitor and assess the impact of development on their forest resources and take steps to limit the damage done to them.[6] Thus, Agenda 21 and other Rio documents form a series of stepping stones toward a more socially, economically, and environmentally sustainable world.

INDIAN CONSTITUTION ON ENVIRONMENTAL JURISPRUDENCE

The Rio Declaration is considered a milestone in the development of international environmental law. Though it has always been characterized as a "soft" law, its impact both at international and domestic levels has been profound. In India, the post–Bhopal Gas Disaster (1984) era was a creative period for environmental jurisprudence. During this period, in the landmark Doon Valley case,[7] the Supreme Court dealt with the impact of mining in the Doon Valley region and through its orders impliedly generated a new fundamental right—"right of the people to live in healthy environment with minimal disturbance of ecological balance."

In this case, there were series of orders and in one of its orders, the court recognized the influence of the Stockholm Conference by accepting that this "conference and the follow-up action thereafter is spreading the awareness."[8] In the Kanpur Tanneries case,[9] the Supreme Court extensively quoted the Stockholm Declaration and strengthened the then nascent fundamental right to environment in India. In this case, the court gave preference to environment over employment and revenue generation. During this period, the Rio Declaration was also cited in the Law Society of India case.[10]

The Indian Constitution, besides recognizing civil and political rights, also guarantees the right to life with dignity. The Indian Constitution provides for environmental preservation and protection in its directive principles under Article 48A. The precautionary principle is one of the mechanisms and procedures by which possible danger to environment can be mitigated. Right from the independence of India, the application of the precautionary principle was not possible, because India was not open to understand the meaning and value of this principle. India started respecting this principle only after participating in the Rio Summit in 1992.

The right to life under Article 21 has been interpreted to mean a life of dignity to be lived in a proper environment free from the danger of diseases and infection. Clean surroundings lead to a healthy mind and healthy body. The right includes the right to enjoyment of pollution-free water and air in sufficient quantity for full enjoyment of life. If anything endangers or impairs that quality of life in derogation of laws, a citizen has the right to have recourse to Article 32 for removing the pollution of water or air which may be detrimental to their quality of life.

The first time an issue related to the environment was heard, the court held that it is always to be remembered that natural resources are permanent assets for mankind and not intended to be exhausted in one generation. In the Taj Trapezium Case (*M. C. Mehta v. Union of India*), while taking note of the disastrous effects on Taj Mahal due to emissions from Mathura Oil Refinery, the Supreme Court applied the principle of sustainable development and apart from passing several directions, it stepped in to execute and also supervise the consequent actions.

The polluter pays principle states that one who carries on a hazardous activity is liable to make good the loss or damage caused to another by such activity. Once a hazardous or inherently dangerous activity has been carried out, the person carrying out the activity is liable to make good the loss caused to any other person by the activity irrespective of the fact whether or not reasonable care was taken while carrying out the activity. In other words, the polluter pays principle means paying the cost of pollution.

The writ procedure is preferred over a conventional suit because it is speedy, relatively inexpensive, and offers direct access to the highest courts of the land. Nevertheless, class-action suits have their own advantages. The powers of the Supreme Court to issue directions under Article 32 and those of the high courts under Article 226 have attained greater significance in environmental litigation. Courts have made use of these powers to remedy past mala fides and to check immediate and future assaults on the environment.

The formulation of certain principles to develop a better regime for protecting the environment is a remarkable achievement. In the Bhopal Gas Tragedy case,[11] the Supreme Court formulated the doctrine of absolute liability for harm caused by hazardous and inherently dangerous industries by interpreting the scope of the power under Article 32 to issue directions or orders, whichever may be appropriate, in appropriate proceedings. According to the court, this power could be utilized for forging new remedies and fashioning new strategies.[12]

Almost twenty years after the Stockholm Conference, at the Earth Summit held in Rio de Janeiro in 1992, the attention of the international community was drawn to the bad shape our planet was in.[13] Principle 15[14] of the Rio Declaration 1992 clearly states that the participating nations must incorporate the precautionary principle in the national laws to control the environmental degradation, and this adoption should be done as per the capabilities of the respective nations. Moreover, the states should not wait for scientific certainty to protect the environment from irreversible damage. Objective 1[15] of the Cartagena Protocol on Biosafety to the Convention on Biological Diversity, adopted in the year 2000, clearly mentions that the precautionary approach should be adopted by the participating nations, as per the mandate of Principle 15 of the Rio Declaration, for the safe handling and transportation of living modified organisms, which are obtained by the application of modern biotechnology. In 2006, the Ministry of Environment and Forests, Government of India pronounced the National Environment Policy, in which the precautionary principle was adopted as a guideline for the preservation of environmental resources.

The Supreme Court in the Vellore citizens case[16] finally analyzed the precautionary principle and stated that this principle is part of the law of the land. In this case, the Supreme Court analyzed the concept of the precautionary principle and clarified that this principle in domestic law would first mean the adoption of environmental measures—that is, the state government or the statutory agencies will foresee the environmental degradation and will prevent such degradation by attacking the cause. Second, the government or agencies shall not wait for scientific evidence to show that there will be irreparable damage to the environment, and without waiting for such scientific evidence, they shall take appropriate measures to protect the environment. Third, the burden of proof shall not be with the complainant but with the respondent to prove that its action is environment friendly.

Therefore, as it was held in the Vellore Tanneries Pollution case[17] that the society has to prosper but not at the cost of the environment, and in a similar vein, the environment shall have to be protected but not at the cost of development of the society. The need of the hour is to strike a balance between the two—development on one side and a pollution-free environment on the other. Thus, sustainable development is the only answer, and administrative actions ought to proceed in accordance therewith and not against it.

Thus, Indian Jurisprudence on environmental damage is remarkable for both its procedural and substantive aspects. Apart from a few exceptions, the Indian courts have acted effectively more to abate environmental damage than to prevent future damage or remediate the consequences of past damage.[18]

CORPORATE SOCIAL RESPONSIBILITY AND SUSTAINABILITY

Corporate social and environmental reporting has received importance and attention in recent years as a part of the sustainable development process across the world. In India, standalone reporting practices exist, but with limited content and information. Professional companies are more inclined toward reporting their efforts rather than focusing on creating impact on the society. Family businesses' corporate social responsibility depends on the family's core emotional values and therefore does not focus on the reporting standards and disclosure with proper quantitative measures to look at the impact. There is an urgent need to develop a transparent reporting standard in India as part of a company's accountability toward all its stakeholders. The theme of corporate social responsibility is rather nascent in the Indian context as in the most developing economies.

WHY IS THERE A NEED TO CONSIDER THE RESPONSIBILITY OF CORPORATES?

A brief consideration of the present economic, population, and ecological realities suggests the importance of integrating these fields. Consider three relevant facts. First, a significant percentage of the world's population lives at or below a minimal level of subsistence. One quarter of the world's population lives in industrialized countries, and they consume 80 percent of the world's goods. To meet just the simple needs and minimum demands of the other 75 percent of the world's population, significant economic activity is necessary over the next few decades. One estimate holds that a fivefold increase in energy use and a five- to tenfold increase in economic activity would be required over the next fifty years to bring the standards of living for the present population of developing countries in line with those of people in the industrialized world.[19]

Second, even conservative estimates suggest that during these fifty years, the world population will double, bringing the total world population to over eleven billion.[20] Thus, economic activity needs to increase minimally by ten- to twentyfold to bring the standard of living of the actual world population in fifty years in line with that enjoyed by people in the industrialized present.[21]

Finally, we must recognize that the only source for this economic activity, ultimately, is the natural resources of the planet. The three standard factors of production—natural resources, capital, and labor—all derive from the productive capacity of the Earth. In simple terms, raw materials, energy, and food are the essential elements of all economic activity. Yet, the productive capacity of the Earth is already under significant stress. For example, one estimate suggests that if the world's population in forty years consumed nonrenewable mineral and petroleum resources at the current US rates, these resources would last fewer than ten years.[22]

These three factors—deep worldwide poverty, increasing population growth, and limited resources—raise a serious economic and moral dilemma. Significant economic activity will be necessary to meet the basic needs of an increasing human population, yet economic growth itself is responsible for much of the environmental degradation which already jeopardizes the possibility of meeting even present needs. It would seem that continued economic growth alone will not resolve this dilemma.

Classical and Neoclassical Models

Since economic growth is an assumed good within the economic system, standard views of corporate social responsibility implicitly presuppose the moral legitimacy of economic growth. For example, the classical model of corporate social responsibility argues that economic efficiency and obedience to the law is sufficient for satisfying moral responsibility. Neoclassical models argue that once minimal moral constraints are met, economic efficiency should remain the primary measure of the social responsibility of a business. In contrast, if any consensus has emerged among environmental philosophers, it is that unrestrained markets and economic growth are ecologically and ethically deficient. Economic sustainability, in which a qualitative understanding of "development" replaces the more quantitative conception of "growth," provides a more acceptable economic vision according to many environmental philosophers.

Corporate Environmental Responsibility and Competitive Advantage

Corporate Environmental Ethics: The measurement of corporate environmental ethics includes four items:

1. the company has clear and concrete environmental policies;
2. the company's budget planning includes the concerns of environmental investment or procurement;
3. the company has integrated its environmental plan, vision, or mission to its marketing events; and
4. the company has integrated its environmental plan, vision, or mission to company's culture (Henriques and Sadorsky 1999).

Green Product Innovation: The measurement of green product innovation includes three items:

1. the company chooses those materials for a product that produce the least amount of pollution for conducting product development or design;
2. the company uses the fewest amount of materials to comprise a product for conducting product development or design; and
3. the company would circumspectly deliberate whether a product is easy to recycle, reuse, and decompose for conducting product development or design (Utterback and Abernathy 1975).

Green Process Innovation: The measurement of green process innovation includes three items:

1. the manufacturing process of the company effectively reduces the emission of hazardous substances or waste;
2. the manufacturing process of the company reduces the consumption of water, electricity, coal, or oil; and
3. the manufacturing process of the company reduces the use of raw materials (Utterback and Abernathy 1975).

Competitive Advantage: The measurement of competitive advantage includes five items:

1. the quality of the products or services that the company offers is better than that of the competitors' products or services;
2. the company is more capable of R&D than the competitors;

3. the company has better managerial capability than the competitors;
4. the company's profitability is higher than that of the competitors; and
5. the corporate image of the company is better than that of the competitors.

THE COALITION FOR ENVIRONMENTALLY RESPONSIBLE ECONOMIES PRINCIPLES

The CERES Principles are a model corporate code of environmental conduct created by the Coalition for Environmentally Responsible Economies (CERES), a coalition of investors, public pension trustees, foundations, labor unions, and environmental, religious, and public interest groups.

By endorsing the CERES Principles, companies not only formalize their dedication to environmental awareness and accountability but also actively commit to an ongoing process of continuous improvement, dialogue, and comprehensive, systematic public reporting. The individual CERES Principles are explained below.

Protection of the Biosphere

We will reduce and make continual progress toward eliminating the release of any substance that may cause environmental damage to the air, water, or the Earth, or its inhabitants. We will safeguard all habitats affected by our operations and will protect open spaces and wilderness, while preserving biodiversity.

Sustainable Use of Natural Resources

We will make sustainable use of renewable natural resources, such as water, soils, and forests. We will conserve nonrenewable natural resources through efficient use and careful planning.

Reduction and Disposal of Wastes

We will reduce and where possible eliminate waste through source reduction and recycling. All waste will be handled and disposed of through safe and responsible methods.

Energy Conservation

We will conserve energy and improve the energy efficiency of our internal operations and of the goods and services we sell. We will make every effort to use environmentally safe and sustainable energy sources.

Risk Reduction

We will strive to minimize the environmental, health, and safety risks to our employees and the communities in which we operate through safe technologies, facilities, and operating procedures, and by being prepared for emergencies.

Safe Products and Services

We will reduce and where possible eliminate the use, manufacture, or sale of products and services that cause environmental damage or health or safety hazards. We will inform our customers of the environmental impacts of our products or services and try to correct unsafe use.

Environmental Restoration

We will promptly and responsibly correct conditions we have caused that endanger health, safety, or the environment. To the extent feasible, we will redress injuries we have caused to persons or damage we have caused to the environment and will restore the environment.

Informing the Public

We will inform in a timely manner everyone who may be affected by conditions caused by our company that might endanger health, safety, or the environment. We will regularly seek advice and counsel through dialogue with people in communities near our facilities. We will not take any action against employees for reporting dangerous incidents or conditions to management or to appropriate authorities.

Management Commitment

We will implement these principles and sustain a process that ensures that the board of directors and the chief executive officer are fully informed about pertinent environmental issues and are fully responsible for the environmental policy. In selecting our board of directors, we will consider demonstrated environmental commitment as a factor.

Audits and Reports

We will conduct an annual self-evaluation of our progress in implementing these principles. We will support the timely creation of generally accepted environmental audit procedures. We will annually complete the CERES report, which will be made available to the public.[23]

In May 1992, several publicly held corporations joined previous privately held signatories after the principles were amended to reflect major concerns corporations expressed in discussions with CERES. The CERES Principles provide a viable alternative to treaties, legal codes, and industry principles. Implementing the principles is not without cost, yet the long-term viability of any corporation must be measured ecologically as well as economically. The principles provide a framework for that measurement.

Since the promulgation of the principles three years ago, the CERES proponents and corporate representatives have engaged in lively dialogue. Flexibility on both sides has yielded a productive, nonadversarial relationship conducive to cooperation on the most difficult environmental problems. Whether the principles will become a widely recognized standard for public environmental accountability remains to be seen. In the meantime, the principles have already challenged many corporations to accept greater environmental responsibility and accountability.[24]

VALDEZ PRINCIPLES

On September 7, 1989, CERES proposed a new approach to corporate environmental responsibility in the form of a voluntary code of conduct called the Valdez Principles.[25] The Valdez Principles are progress-oriented. They call on corporations to protect the environment aggressively, not merely to comply with the minimum environmental standards set by federal, state, and local governments. The audit and disclosure provisions of the Valdez Principles are particularly ambitious because, in addition to asking corporations to go beyond what is currently required by law, they potentially expose signatory corporations to increased litigation, increased costs, and disclosure liability beyond that required by federal and state laws.[26]

The Valdez Principles support a wide range of environmental issues. Protection of the biosphere is one of its objectives, and it encourages industries to minimize or eliminate the emission of pollutants. The principles are also devoted to protecting biodiversity and insuring the sustainable development of land, water, forests, and other natural resources. The principles advocate the use of recycling whenever possible, support safe disposal methods, and encourage the use of safe and sustainable energy sources.

Energy efficiency is also a goal, as well as the marketing of products that have minimal environmental impact. The principles also call for corporations to have at least one board member qualified to represent environmental interests and a senior executive responsible for environmental affairs.

Other goals include damage compensation, disclosure of accidents and hazards, and the creation of independent environmental audit procedures.

Many major corporations have indicated an interest in these principles, but few have signed them. Some executives have observed that many aspects of the Valdez Principles are already required by government regulations and internal policies.[27]

Perhaps then the most significant feature of the Valdez Principles is not what they have accomplished but the circumstances of their origin. A major disaster often engenders a social and political climate that is, at least temporarily, receptive to reform. In this case, it was a rare coalition between financial investors and environmental groups. Many have argued that the principles had unrealistic goals, but some see in their development hope for the future.[28] Meanwhile, the atmosphere for the acceptance and success of the Valdez Principles continues to ripen.

CONCLUSIONS

Dynamic economic equilibrium involves moving away from the concept of growth (quantitative improvement) toward development (qualitative improvement), but not simple development, rather environmentally sustainable development that does not preclude the ability of the environment to provide raw materials and energy and absorb wastes and residues. Moreover, such development entails the consideration of human ecology, so that it is socially sustainable. Implementing ecological economics reinforces a humanistic character. This will boost the formation of a new development concept of sustainable development, environmentally and socially sustainable, represented by human development that requires investment in people, through increased educational opportunities, better health insurance systems, and emergence of new jobs—that is, human development concerning both human capacity development and productive use in ecological conditions. Human development involves the development of people, by people, which includes participatory approaches.[29]

NOTES

1. M. C. Mehta, Growth of Environmental Jurisprudence in India, p. 71, 1999.
2. Marchello, Perrini, Serafini, & Diritto dell'Ambiente, 2002, p. 15; Kiss & Beurier, 2010.
3. Report of the World Commission on Environment and Development: Our Common Future, http://www.un-documents.net/our-common-future.pdf.
4. https://www.britannica.com/event/United-Nations-Conference-on-Environment-and-Development.

5. Michael Keating, *The Earth Summit Agenda for Change*.

6. http://www.sustainable-environment.org.uk/Action/Agenda_21.php.

7. RLEK Dehradun, v. State of UP. AIR 1985 SC 652. Three judges bench order of March 12, 1985.

8. AIR 1987 SC 359, 363 (Para 19) order of Dec. 18, 1986.

9. M. C. Mehta, v. Union of India AIR 1988 SC 1037. See Para 4 (pp. 1038–1040) for detailed discussion of Stockholm Declarations by Justice Venkataramiah.

10. Law Society of India v. Fertilizer & Chemical Travancore Ltd. AIR 1994 Ker. 308.

11. 1990 AIR 273, 1989 SCC (2) 540.

12. http://www.legalserviceindia.com/articles/jjj.htm.

13. United Nations Documents, 1992 Declaration.

14. Principle 15: In order to protect the environment, the precautionary approach shall be widely applied by states according to their capabilities. Where there are threats of serious or irreversible damage, lack of full scientific certainty shall not be used as a reason for postponing cost-effective measures to prevent environmental degradation.

15. Objective 1: In accordance with the precautionary approach contained in Principle 15 of the Rio Declaration on Environment and Development, the objective of this protocol is to contribute to ensuring an adequate level of protection in the field of the safe transfer, handling, and use of living modified organisms resulting from modern biotechnology that may have adverse effects on the conservation and sustainable use of biological diversity, taking also into account risks to human health, and specifically focusing on transboundary movements.

16. Vellore Citizens Welfare Forum v. Union of India, AIR1996 SC 2715.

17. AIR 1996 SC 2715: (1996) 5 SCC 647.

18. Published in Review of European Community and International Environmental Law Vol. 5, No. 4 (1996), p. 395 by Michael R. Anderson & Anees Ahmed, 2004, Universal Law Publishing Co. Pvt Ltd.

19. 1 Jim MacNeill, "Strategies for Sustainable Development", in Managing Planet Earth (Scientific American, 1990), pp. 109–111.

20. Present estimates suggest that the rate of population increase is one billion people every 10 years. The doubling to 11 billion in fifty years is "conservative" in the sense that it assumes, contrary to trends, that the rate of increase will remain constant.

21. Herman Daly points out that there are two important reasons why doubling the population would require significantly more than a doubling of economic activity to meet constant demand. First, allowance must be made for the tremendous capital accumulation that would be necessary to transform all these resources into final products. Second, the mineral and energy resources needed for such growth would need to come from increasingly less accessible and low-grade deposits; we have already taken the readily accessible and cheap iron, coal, oil, aluminum, uranium, timber, and so on. See Herman Daly, "Sustainable Growth: An Impossibility Theorem", reprinted in Valuing the Earth, edited by Herman Daly and Kenneth Townsend (Boston: MIT Press, 1993), pp. 267–273.

22. Robert Frosch and Nicholas Gallopoulos, "Strategies for Manufacturing", Managing Planet Earth, p. 98.

23. The Coalition for Environmentally Responsible Economies (CERES) Principles, https://www.gdrc.org/sustbiz/ceres-principles.html.

24. These publicly held corporations include Ben & Jerry's Homemade and Ringer Corporation. CERES, supra note 12, at 3–4.

25. Coalition for Environmentally Responsible Economies [hereinafter CERES], Valdez Principles (Sept. 7, 1989) (hereinafter Valdez Principles).

26. Feder, Who Will Subscribe to the Valdez Principles?, N.Y. Times, Sept. 10, 1989, § 3, at 6, col. 1.

27. Valerie Ann Zondorak, A New Face in Corporate Environmental Responsibility: The Valdez Principles, B. C. Envtl. Aff. L. Rev. Vol. 18 (1991), p. 457.

28. "Valdez Principles," Environmental Encyclopaedia., Retrieved January 11, 2019 from Encyclopedia.com: https://www.encyclopedia.com/environment/encyclopedias-almanacs-transcripts-and-maps/valdez-principles.

29. Environmental Protection—An Integral Part of Sustainable Development, Journal of Knowledge Management, Economics and Information Technology.

REFERENCES

Henriques, I. and Sadorsky, P. The Relationship between the Environmental Commitment and Managerial Perceptions of Stakeholder Importance, The Academy of Management Journal, 42(1), (February 1999).

James, M. Utterback and William, J. Abernathy. A Dynamic Model of Process and Product Innovation, OMEGA, Vol. 3, No.6 (December 1975).

Chapter 8

Global Warming and Greenhouse Effect

Priti Chahal

INTRODUCTION

Globalization has become one of the most fashionable terms in contemporary political and academic debates. It covers a wide range of distinct political, economic, environmental, and cultural trends. Along with globalization, green thought has become very popular in recent times. Man has been intervening in nature for a long time, but the rapid growth of industrialization during the twentieth century has accelerated this process of intervention to worrying levels. There is no doubt that industrialization increased production by leaps and bounds and that it has been helpful in wiping out poverty, ignorance, disease, and illiteracy, and in bringing prosperity for certain societies. But the fundamental question being raised during the past three decades is, what is the cost of this development? Industrialization has brought pollution, which is undermining the basic biological systems upon which the life of the plants rests. The effects of development on air, water, land, and climate have been quite damaging. Factors such as pollution of air, airborne lead, acid rain, emission of carbon dioxide, ozone depletion, soil erosion, deforestation, silting of rivers and reservoirs, problems regarding disposal of solid waste, and toxic wastage are affecting the health of people adversely. The theories of development of industrial societies did not take into account the benefits of clear water, stable atmosphere, or predictable climate. As one author remarked, it did not occur to the economists that if our activities interfere too radically with the working of nature, then nature might no longer be capable of providing the benefits we have been taking for granted and upon which our survival depends.

Environment is a system, which includes all living things, and air, water, and soil, which is their habitat. Human beings are a part of this immensely complex and interrelated natural world. What we sow in terms of industrial pollution, we will reap from the instability of the ecosphere.

ENVIRONMENT AS AN INTERNATIONAL MOVEMENT

The key theme of the environment movement is the insistence that the major problem we face is neither capitalism nor communism but industrialism. It is critical of the belief that human needs can only be met through the permanent expansion of the process of production and consumption regardless of the damage done to the planet and to the rights of the future generations. Environmentalism as a political ideology is concerned with the relationship between human beings and their environment and among human beings themselves. It finds the concept of development through industrialization as wrong on a number of grounds.

First, according to Fritz Schumacher, the modern industrial system with all its intellectual sophistication consumes the very basis on which it has been erected. By consuming recklessly the nonrenewable sources of energy, the industrial societies are digging their own collective grave.

Second, the industrially developed societies are dragging the rest of the world with them into a grave for two reasons:

1. The rate of production and consumption in such societies is higher than that in the developing countries. So the per capita rate of resource use and pollution created is proportionately more.
2. Such high rate of production and consumption is the aspiration of all developing countries. Such aspirations can only be fulfilled across the planet with incurring untold and irreversible damage to the ecosystem.

Third, the tendency of industrial development to expand production and consumption is incompatible with the finite nature of the planet. Soon the limits of expansion will be reached. Either the resources will run out, or the planet's capacity to absorb toxic waste will exhaust. Along with this, the environment is spoiled and the quality of life worsens. Sustainability and industrialism are mutually exclusive.

Fourth, industrial development is not an answer to environmental problems. It can provide temporary success but cannot provide lasting solutions.

The seriousness of environmental degradation was felt during the 1960s and 1970s. A number of writings such as Rachel Carson's *Silent Springs* (1962), Paul Ehrlich's *The Population Bomb*, and Garett Hardin's *Tragedy of the Commons* raised the specter of not only environmental collapse but also its relation to overpopulation.

The Stockholm Conference (1972) was the first conference on environment at the global level which placed environment on the political agenda. It held that solving environmental problems was a political question which could no longer be left to scientists, experts, or private individuals, and that it was imperative for all nations to act together in order to preserve the environment for the present and future generations.

Before the Stockholm Conference, there was no real politics of environment. Even political theory never concerned itself with the political nature of ecological issues. Nature was considered to be a bundle of abundant natural economic resources, available to human beings to be exploited, battled against, conquered, or molded according to their needs and requirements.

GLOBALIZATION AND THE ENVIRONMENT

Environmentalism is an issue on which globalization has had the greatest impact. The original global issue is nature itself. Long before humans invented environmentalism and long before humans, the planet was chugging along as a well-balanced ecosystem. Fresh oxygen was pumped into the atmosphere by huge rainforests, the big fished culled the little fish, and natural fires managed prairies. Environment and globalization have compressed the world, and people are becoming aware that there is only one planet.

The effects are global and the problems can only be tackled through cooperation at the global scale. Again some problems relate to the exploitation of global common resources such as oceans, deep-sea bed, atmosphere, and outer space. Many scholars argue that the world's genetic resources are a common heritage and should be preserved in the common interest of the humanity.

Then there are many problems that are transnational which cross the state boundaries, such as the emission of gases. For example, the emission of sulfur dioxide by one country can be taken to another country through winds and cause acid rain there. State or nonstate actors from outside the region may contribute to the problems or to efforts to tackle them. Lastly, overexploitation of resources or environmental degradation, which may be local, can have global problems such as unsustainable agricultural practices, soil degradation, desertification, deforestation, and river pollution. These problems are linked to broader political and socioeconomic processes which are themselves part of a global political economy.

Economic development is directly or indirectly linked to industrial issues. An increase in production leads to the generation of difference types of industrial wastes. Industrial activities use a range of chemicals in the production of cosmetics, drugs, food, dyes, dairy products, paper, battery, and electronic items to keep modern life humming. These chemicals, after fulfilling their roles in the production process, end up accumulating in the environment and degrade the environmental quality. To minimize the impact of industrial pollution, the mass media and government should work on spreading awareness regarding the issues of industrial pollution and its adverse health impact. Changes in lifestyle, environmental education, self-awareness, and realization are also necessary as most of the people are unaware of the hazards of industrial pollution. We should reject products which use ingredients such as solvents, acids and heavy metals, plastic cup, bottles, and straw. If no one purchases such products, then industries will no longer manufacture these products that degrade the environment. Last but not least, the central and state governments must work together to identify and implement long-term solutions.

A task group set up by the World Health Organization has warned that climate change may have a serious impact on human health. Climate change will increase existing health problems and may also bring new and unexpected ones. Strategies aimed at reducing the potential health impacts of anticipated climate changes should include the monitoring of infectious diseases and disease vectors to detect early changes in the incidence of diseases and the geographical distribution of vectors; environmental management measures to reduce risk; disaster preparedness for floods or droughts; and their health-related consequences. It will be necessary to educate and create early warning systems for epidemic preparedness. Improved water and air pollution control will become increasingly essential for human health. Public education will have to be directed at changes in personal behavior. The training of researchers and health professionals is essential toward the world becoming more responsible for the expected outcome of global climate change (GCC).

GLOBAL WARMING

Gases including carbon dioxide, nitrous oxide, methane, and water vapor trap heat from the Sun within the atmosphere. Acting like the panes of glass in a greenhouse, they ensure that temperatures close to the Earth's surface are much higher than they would otherwise be. In this way, the greenhouse effect makes life, as we know it, possible. However, this system has recently come under heavy pressure. Since the Industrial Revolution, humankind has been extracting and burning fossil fuels at increasing rates, releasing significant amounts of greenhouse gases into the atmosphere. As concentrations of greenhouse gases have increased, so has the strength of the greenhouse effect. The United Nations Intergovernmental Panel on Climate Change (IPCC), in its third and most recent assessment, published in 2018, suggests that there is new and stronger evidence that most of the warming observed over the past fifty years is attributable to human activities. The human activities that are responsible for this effect on the environment are the historical use of fossil fuels in industrial processes (in Europe and the United States) and deforestation. Moreover, the use of chlorofluorocarbons (CFCs) in various industrial and commercial machineries such as air conditioners and refrigerators was initially favored because their virtue is that they are very stable and react with almost nothing, until they drift into the stratosphere, where direct ultraviolet (UV) radiation breaks them up, releasing agents that in turn rupture ozone molecules. This leads to depletion of the ozone layer, while increasing the volume of other gases, thereby disturbing the balance of gases and leading to increased warming of the Earth. The IPCC report also states that average global temperatures are projected to increase by 1.4–5.8 degrees Celsius over the next 100 years because of the enhanced greenhouse effect. Owing to this warming, glaciers and polar icecaps are expected to melt, causing sea levels to rise by anything between 9 and 88 centimeters in the twenty-first century. The IPCC also expects significant changes in patterns of rainfall—including monsoons—and more extreme weather events.

Agricultural systems contribute to methane emissions through several mechanisms:

1. The cultivation of soils resulting in the loss of soil organic matter;
2. The cleaning of forests to create new cropland;
3. The direct use of fossil fuels in farm operations; and
4. The indirect use of embodied energy in inputs that are energy-intensive to manufacture.

At the end of the day though, it needs to be remembered that the effect of global warming visible today is the result of accumulation of greenhouse gases over the period of time that the industrialized world has contributed to it, and so, it needs to take responsibility for it.

Carbon dioxide is not rinsed out of the air like soot; rather, it is very slowly absorbed by the oceans and by living things, at rates that cannot be significantly accelerated. Its impacts, great or small, cannot be reversed quickly. So, the combustion history of the twentieth century has already partly determined conditions in the next several centuries to come.

Industrialized countries ought to invest in green technologies using alternate forms of energy, which they have done, but because they are not sure of the returns from those and the present dispensation provides an assured rate of profit, they have not shown much enterprise on this account. It does, additionally, provide a warning to the developing countries that they too need to modify or research into alternate technologies that do not use fossil fuels, so that they do not worsen the problem in the future. The ownership of liability on these emissions is the source of the controversy over the Kyoto Protocol.

CAUSES OF GLOBAL WARMING: THE GREENHOUSE EFFECT

The greenhouse effect is the process by which radiation from a planet's atmosphere warms the planet's surface to a temperature above what it would be without its atmosphere. If a planet's atmosphere contains radioactively active gases (i.e., greenhouse gases) they will radiate energy in all directions. Burning of coal, oil, and natural gas releases carbon dioxide which is collected in the atmosphere like a thickening blanket, trapping the Sun's heat and causing the planet to warm. Burning of these fossil fuels, according to scientists, is changing the Earth into a hothouse, changing climate worldwide. Combined with the destruction of huge areas of rainforests, the amount of carbon dioxide and other heat-trapping gases are leading an increase in the Earth's average temperature. The increased amount of carbon dioxide and other greenhouse gases is primarily caused by human activities such as the burning of fossil fuels, land clearing for agriculture, and so on, leading to an increase in the greenhouse effect.

What Is Greenhouse Effect?

Greenhouse is the name given to a glasshouse constructed to keep delicate and rare plants that require warmth and protection from weather. The house is constructed using glass panels. The glass panels allow sunrays and heat to pass through the glasshouse. The heat that enters the glasshouse cannot escape because the glass panels send the heat back inside the glasshouse. This makes the greenhouse warmer than the outside environment. This is called the greenhouse effect.

An example of the effect can be observed in the case of a car that when parked in the Sun with all doors and windows closed gets heated up.

Our Earth's atmosphere also acts as a glasshouse. There is a layer of different gases around the Earth. Some of these gases such as carbon dioxide, ozone, methane, nitrogen oxide, CFCs, and water vapor have the property of trapping the heat energy of the Sun. These gases are therefore called greenhouse gases. They do not allow the heat to escape back into space. This keeps the atmosphere warm. The heating of the Earth's atmosphere because of the trapping of heat energy reflected from the Earth's surface by greenhouse gases in the atmosphere is called the greenhouse effect.

Human activities such as burning of fossil fuels in automobiles and industries, and cutting down of forests (deforestation) increase the level of carbon dioxide and many other harmful gases in the atmosphere. This has resulted in increased greenhouse effect.

The greenhouse effect leads to the temperature rising because of the Sun's heat and light trapped in the Earth's atmosphere. This is similar to the case of heat getting trapped in a car standing in the Sun. On a very hot day, the car gets hotter when it is out in the parking. This is because the heat and light from the Sun can get into the car, by going through the windows, but it cannot get out. This is what the greenhouse effect does to the Earth. The heat and light can get through the atmosphere, but it cannot get out. As a result, the temperature rises.

The problem is that the level of these gases has increased significantly since pre-industrial times or around 1750. This can be attributed largely to human activities, mostly fossil fuel use and land use change. Further, it is exacerbated by the removal of traditional sinks such as forests, fossil fuels, and ocean plankton that kept carbon fixed and locked up. Human activity has been increasing the concentration of greenhouse gases in the atmosphere, particularly carbon dioxide from the combustion of coal, oil, and gas, plus a few other gases.

As a result, the global surface temperature has increased by about 0.6 ± 0.2 degrees Celsius since the late twentieth century and by about 0.2–0.3 degrees Celsius over the past thirty years.

Over the past century, the human species has turned the Earth into a huge unplanned experiment. By releasing unprecedented amounts of greenhouse gases such as carbon dioxide, methane, CFCs, nitrous oxide, and other gases that deplete the ozone layer into the atmosphere, we have in effect turned up the global thermostat. Greenhouse gases act as a glasshouse covering a sink from all sides and allowing light energy to pass through but then trapping the reemitted heat.

Carbon dioxide accounts for half of the global warming. Nitrous oxide is the by-product of the burning fossil fuels. Burning of natural gas releases 70 percent as much carbon dioxide per unit of energy as the burning of oil and coal does. Forests and oceans are natural sinks for carbon dioxide but are unable to absorb the quantities currently being emitted. Deforestation releases large quantities of carbon dioxide as well as methane, carbon monoxide, ozone, and nitrous oxide. Swamps, cattle yards, rice paddies, landfills, termites, and fuels produce methane, which is about 13 percent of the greenhouse gases. CFCs used in refrigerators and air conditioners account for 17 percent of the greenhouse effect.

With human advances and technology, new types of greenhouse gases have been introduced into the atmosphere. For this reason, the greenhouse effect in our world today is accelerating at an abnormal rate. Scientists claim that if greenhouse gases continue to rise as they have in the past several decades, then during the twenty-first century the temperature will also rise by several degrees. The main concern of this Earth warming is the effects on the human life and the ecosystem.

GLOBAL WARMING AND ITS EFFECTS

The potential dangers of global warming are being increasingly studied by a wide global consortium of scientists, who are increasingly concerned about its potential long-term effects on our natural environment and on the planet.

The predicted effects of global warming are many and various, both for the environment and for human life. These effects include sea level rise, impact on agriculture, reduction in the ozone layer, increased intensity and frequency of extreme weather events, and the spread of diseases. However, the extent and likelihood of these consequences is a matter of controversy.

Global warming will affect the climate everywhere in the world. With temperature changing, it will directly affect what species—both plants and animals—can live and prosper. States all over the world have programs and groups that try to encourage ways that will reduce greenhouse gas emission in their territory. Passing regulations to reduce automobile carbon dioxide emissions and offering incentives and covenants for manufacturers and other large contributing organizations are some of the ways through which states are trying to reduce greenhouse gases from our atmosphere. The states and the people are beginning to realize the dangerous possibilities that will affect their lives in the near future and they are willing to do something about it.

Pollution and Acid Rain

When fossil fuels such as coal, oil, and natural gas are burned, chemicals such as sulfur dioxide and nitrogen oxides are produced. These chemicals react with water and other chemicals in the air to form sulfuric acid, nitric acid, and other harmful pollutants such as sulfates and nitrates.

These acid pollutants spread upward into the atmosphere and are carried by air currents, to finally return to the ground in the form of acid rain, fog, or snow. The corrosive nature of acid rain causes many forms of environmental damage. Acid pollutants also occur as dry particles and gases, which when washed from the ground by rain add to the acids in the rain to form an even more corrosive solution. This is called acid deposition.

The best way to stop the formation of acid rain is to reduce the emissions of sulfur dioxide and nitrogen oxides into the atmosphere. This can be achieved by using less energy from fossil fuels in power plants, vehicles, and industries. Switching to cleaner-burning fuels is also a way out, for example, using natural gas which is cleaner than coal or using coal with lower sulfur content. Developing more efficient vehicles will reduce pollutants from being released into the air.

Ozone Layer Depletion

Ozone is formed by the action of sunlight on oxygen. It forms a layer 20–50 kilometers above the surface of the Earth. This action takes place naturally in the atmosphere, but is very slow. Ozone is a highly poisonous gas with a strong odor. It is a form of oxygen that has three atoms in each molecule. It is considered a pollutant at the ground level and constitutes a health hazard by causing respiratory ailments such as asthma and bronchitis. It also causes harm to vegetation and leads to a deterioration of certain materials such as plastic and rubber. Ozone in the upper atmosphere, however, is vital for all forms of life as it protects the Earth from harmful UV radiations of the Sun. The ozone layer in the upper atmosphere absorbs the UV radiation, preventing it from reaching the Earth's surface.

The destruction of the ozone layer causes increased incidence of skin cancer and cataracts. It also causes damage to certain crops and plankton, thus affecting natural food chains and food webs. This decrease in vegetation leads to an increase in carbon dioxide.

With the signing of the Montreal Protocol in 1987—a treaty for the protection of the ozone layer—the use of CFCs was to be banned by the year 2000, after which the ozone layer was expected to slowly recover over a period of about fifty years. Although the use of CFCs has been reduced and is now banned in most countries, other chemicals and industrial compounds such as bromine, halocarbons, and nitrous oxides from fertilizers continue to attack the ozone layer.

Nuclear Accidents and Nuclear Holocaust

Nuclear energy was researched and developed as an alternate source of clean cheap energy compared to fossil fuels. Although this did happen, along with the benefits of nuclear energy came its downfalls. In the short history of nuclear energy, there have been a number of accidents that have surpassed any natural calamities or other energy source extractions in their impact. A single nuclear accident causes loss of life, long-term illnesses, and destruction of property on a large scale and for a long period of time. Radioactivity and its fallout lead to cancer, genetic disorders, and death in the affected area for decades after the accident, thus affecting all forms of life for several generations. The use of nuclear energy in war has had devastating effects on humans and on the Earth. In the only use of nuclear power in war, the United States dropped two atomic bombs over the Japanese towns of Hiroshima and Nagasaki in 1945. These two atomic bombs killed thousands of people, left many more thousands injured, and destroyed everything for miles around. The effects of the radiation from these nuclear bombs can still be seen today in the form of cancer and genetic mutations in the affected children and survivors of the incident.

Spread of Diseases

It is expected that global warming will favor the breeding and spread of mosquitoes in temperate areas. These are notorious vectors for the spread of a large number of diseases including malaria, elephantiasis, yellow fever, chikungunya, and dengue. Chikungunya fever is an emerging disease in India and is characterized by fever, rash, and severe joint pain.

Impact on Wildlife

About 20–30 percent of plant and animal species could be at risk of extinction during this century if temperatures continue to rise. Reduction of tropical forests, savannas, biodiversity, Great Barrier Reef, and species extinction is expected in several parts of the world. With the rise of global mean temperature during the twenty-first century, vegetation in the temperate regions may extend toward poles.

Impact on Weather, Climate, and Food Production

Major weather changes such as alterations in precipitation patterns, and increases in forest fires, hurricanes, cyclones, tornadoes, and heat wave intensities are expected as a result of global warming. As per the IPCC report, food and agricultural production in some areas is expected to decrease, though some mid- to high-altitude regions could see an increase. Poor countries are expected to be more vulnerable to climate change owing to the lack of technology and economic resources.

Biodiversity

A changing climate and global warming are considered to be major potential threats to biodiversity. Increasing global temperatures will affect weather, precipitation patterns, species distribution, and plant productivity on the

Earth. Marine biodiversity will be adversely affected as a result of an increase in atmospheric carbon dioxide because the oceans act as sinks for carbon dioxide. Biodiversity provides a variety of direct and indirect services, without which we cannot survive for a moment. It is the source of food, fodder, fiber, jute, spices, rubber, timber, leather, medicine, dyes, oil, and so on. Biodiversity maintains ecological balance by nutrient recycling; soil formation; air and water purification; and carbon, oxygen, nitrogen, and water cycles. It regulates the climate and precipitation, and lessens the impact of climate change and global warming. It has cultural and aesthetic values, for example, bird watching, ecotourism, and gardening recreation.

Biodiversity is under serious threat as result of unsustainable economic activities. The main threats to biodiversity are rapid population growth, urbanization, unsustainable resource consumption, overexploitation of natural resources, and environmental pollution.

Impact on Glaciers and Sea Level

Global warming has led to negative glacier mass balance, causing glacier retreat around the world. It is estimated that a net decline has occurred in 142 of the 144 mountain glaciers from 1900 to 1980. Since 1980, the global glacier retreat has increased significantly. Increasing temperatures are expected to cause continued retreat in the majority of alpine glaciers around the world. Increased melting would cause greater flow for several decades after which some areas of the most populated regions on the Earth are likely to run out of water. Also, there is likely to be a rise in sea level from glacier melting. A rise of 20 centimeters is expected by 2030, with many cities including Mumbai facing the risk of drowning.

Financial Effects

The United Nations Environmental Programme (UNEP) announced that severe weather events around the world made 2005 the most costly year on record, although there is no way to prove whether the occurrence of hurricanes was affected by global warming. Preliminary estimates presented by the German Insurance Foundation put the economic losses at more than $200 billion with insured losses rising at more than $70 billion. Financial institutions including the world's two largest insurance companies have estimated that the increased frequency of several climate events coupled with social trends could cost almost $150 billion each year in the next decades. These costs, through increased costs related to insurance and disaster relief, would burden taxpayers and industry alike.

REMEDIES FOR GLOBAL WARMING

Now the big question is—what can be done? The answer is—reduce the rate at which we add carbon dioxide to the atmosphere by burning less coal, oil, and natural gas. In this context, five categories of actions have been proposed to reduce the level of harmful gases:

- Reduction in energy use (conservation)
- Shift from carbon-based fossil fuels to alternative energy sources
- Creation of carbon capture and storage sinks
- Carbon sequestration (i.e., capturing carbon dioxide before it is released and burying it within geologic formations from which it is highly unlikely to escape)
- Planetary engineering to cool the Earth

Apart from these, a number of strategies have been recommended to reduce global warming. Some of them are the development of new technologies, wind power, nuclear power, solar power, renewable energy, biodiesel, electric or hybrid automobiles, fuel cells, energy conservation, carbon taxes, enhancing natural carbon dioxide sinks, and carbon capture and storage. Some environmentalist groups encourage individual action against global warming, often aimed at the consumers.

Efforts to reduce global warming go hand in hand with enhancing oil security. Low- and zero-carbon energy sources, including many biofuels, are renewable and can be produced domestically, reducing dependence on petroleum. Brazil, for example, derives one-third of its transport fuel from ethanol produced from sugarcane. A task force has recommended that the United States should give subsidy to produce biofuels instead of food crops.

Mankind must turn to renewable forms of energy not because of dwindling oil supply but because of the mounting and unimpeachable evidence that we have a profound carbon problem on our hands. Even if we discover billions of new barrels of oil in the ground, we cannot keep burning them—and pumping vast amounts of carbon dioxide and other greenhouse gases into the atmosphere—without potentially catastrophic consequences.

According to the findings of the UN IPCC, in order to stabilize greenhouse gases in the atmosphere, global emissions must be reduced to at least 60 percent below the 1990 levels. That will need a radical change in the way the world uses energy, and to accomplish that, many people feel, will require nothing less than a new industrial revolution, an overwhelming retreat from society's mass reliance on the carbon fuels—oil, gas, and coal—that have powered the global economy for more than a hundred years.

EFFORTS AT UN LEVEL

Since the end of 1980s, there has been a serious international concern that anthropogenic emissions of greenhouse gases such as carbon dioxide, methane, nitrous oxide, and CFCs could be affecting the Earth's overall energy balance and causing rapid global warming and climate change. In 1988, the IPCC was formed under the auspices of UNEP and World Metrological Organization to examine the risks of such climate change. An international conference on climate change in 1992 in Rio de Janeiro adopted a Framework Convention on Climate Change (FCCC), which was signed by 153 countries and came into force within 19 months on March 21, 1994. The framework convention established the principles, aims, institutions, and procedures that should subsequently be developed. The objective of the FCCC was to achieve stabilization of greenhouse gas concentrations in the atmosphere at a level that would prevent dangerous anthropogenic interference with the climate system. Such a level should be achieved within a timeframe sufficient to allow ecosystems to adapt naturally to climate change, to ensure that food production is not threatened, and to enable economic development to proceed in a sustainable manner. Recognizing that the developed countries should take the lead, these states should, as a first step, individually or jointly return to their 1990 levels of greenhouse gas emissions. But this was not legally binding. The importance of the framework was that the parties must provide such information as their national greenhouse gas emissions, their emission projections, and their policies to limit the emission of gases. This would be reviewed internationally so as to provide stimulation for further negotiations.

The next important step in this direction was international agreement on climate change, popularly known as the Kyoto Protocol. It is an amendment to the UNFCCC. Countries that ratified this protocol agreed to reduce their emissions of carbon dioxide and five other greenhouse gases, or engage in emissions trading if they maintain or increase any of these gases.

IMPACT OF CLIMATE CHANGE IN INDIA

The possible adverse impacts of climate change and global warming in India include adverse impacts on public health, water availability, forest, coastal areas, agriculture, and food production. A sea level rise of 15–38 centimeters is projected along India's coasts by the mid-twenty-first century and 46–59 centimeters by 2100 (NAPCC, MoEF&CC). It has also been projected by the Indian Agricultural Research Institute (IARI) that every 1 degree Celsius rise in temperature would reduce wheat production by 4–5 million tons and loss of food production by 10–40 percent by 2100. Based on the regional climate model, it has been projected that 77 percent of the forests in the country are likely to experience a change in their type and products. Extreme events such as cyclones, floods, and droughts will be very common in the country.

INDIAN'S EFFORTS TO FIGHT AGAINST THE ADVERSE IMPACTS OF CLIMATE CHANGE

A number of steps have been taken in India to minimize the adverse impacts of climate change and global warming. India has increased its spending on adaptation programs to 2.6 percent of GDP and has started the afforestation program under the Compensatory Afforestation Fund Management and Planning Authority (CAMPA). The country has also promised to create an additional carbon sink of 2.5–3 billion tons of carbon dioxide through forests and tree cover by 2030 (MoEF&CC, 2016). Under the National Water Policy (2002), it has been made mandatory to construct rooftop and other types of rainwater harvesting systems. According to the Coastal Regulation Zone (CRZ) notification, restrictions have been enforced in the area of seashores to protect the ecologically sensitive biodiversity. No development zone of 50 meters around the coastal areas has also been proposed to protect the biodiversity.

A star-based leveling program for electrical appliances has been introduced by the Bureau of Energy Efficiency for air conditioners, refrigerators, and tube lights to save energy and make the consumer aware. These levels provide information about the amount of energy consumption by an electrical appliance. Improved fuel standards such as Bharat Stage and compressed natural gas (CNG) driven vehicles have been introduced in Delhi and other cities. India released its ambitious National Action Plan on Climate Change (NAPCC) to mitigate and adapt to global warming and climate change on June 30, 2008. It includes National Solar Mission, the National Mission for a Green India, and so on. The main purpose of all these missions and programs is to minimize the adverse impact of climate change and global warming.

INTERNATIONAL NEGOTIATIONS AND INDIA

Since the 1990s onward, the focus of the entire world was shifted to protect the ecological systems of the planet. As an emerging leader of the developing countries, India was expected to lead the show. Before the 1990s, the debate between the North and South was related to material advancement. However, in the 1990s the nature of the debate changed. The focus shifted to the degree of carbon emissions. Developing countries are now blaming the developed countries for the degradation of the world's ecosystems. India as a leader of the South (developing countries) has taken a tough stand in this regard. It has consistently maintained that developing countries including India should not be forced to reduce carbon emissions. The basic argument that was given was that till recently the developed countries (most prominently the United States) have been responsible for the world's total pollution. If at all any target is going to be fixed, the developed nations must lead the way. Starting from Kyoto Protocol to the recent negotiations held in Bali, what is evident is that India has been able to form a cartel of developing countries to put pressure on the United States and other developed nations to accept their terms and conditions. This is a significant development as far as international politics is concerned. India has demonstrated its ability to lead the developing nations.

IMPORTANT STRATEGIES TO DEAL WITH CLIMATE CHANGE AND GLOBAL WARMING

Some of the important strategies that could reduce the increasing concentration of greenhouse gases and the adverse impact of global warming include

i. Minimizing the use of nitrogenous fertilizers for reducing nitrogen oxide emissions
ii. Developing substitutes for ozone-depleting substances
iii. Limiting the use of fossil fuels by using renewable energy resources
iv. Replacing incandescent light bulbs with compact fluorescent light (CFL) and light emitting diode (LED) bulbs
v. Promoting the use of CNG-driven vehicles, metros, and battery-operated vehicles (the transport sector accounts for more than 30 percent of carbon dioxide emissions)

Scientists have established a clear link between the increase in global mean temperature, climate change, global warming, and their adverse impact on every component of the environment. Most of the climate scientists agree that global warming is real and human interference with nature is the main cause of climate change and global warming. Among the prominent greenhouse gases, carbon dioxide is the main contributor for an increase in the global mean temperature and the associated adverse impacts on health, agriculture, food production, sea level, forests, weather, and glaciers.

To minimize the adverse impacts of global warming and climate change, several international and national efforts have been made in the form of conventions and treaties. India has also played an important role in reducing greenhouse gas emissions by increasing forest cover, harnessing solar and hydro energy, and implanting international and national environmental programs within a pro-poor policy framework.

CONCLUSIONS

The human species, which once had a role in environment conservation, has, over the years, effectively destroyed the environment. This was made possible by the development of a socioeconomic and technological system that over the past 200–300 years allowed society to initiate major changes in its relationship with the other elements in the environmental system. Indeed, in many ways human beings no longer see themselves as part of the environment. Such detachment has undoubtedly contributed to the problems that have arisen in the environment. There is a perception among the environmentalists that the situation will be improved only when humans once again begin to consider themselves as an integral part of the natural environment.

Much of the difficulty associated with the attempts to solve environmental problems arises from the socioeconomic and political consequences of the required changes, which are perceived by some to be even more detrimental to society than the continued existence of the problem. Given the complexity of the environmental problems being considered, there is no one approach that satisfies all needs. Solutions will have to be flexible enough to deal with issues that have arisen as a result of deliberate human interference in the environment as well as those that arose inadvertently, perhaps as a byproduct of some activity designed to improve the quality of life. Environmental degradation is a global problem. Hence, it needs cooperation on a global scale.

The United Nations Commission on Sustainable Development has assumed the task of promoting the concept and its implementation. In one of its reports, it concluded that some progress had been made in reducing poverty, curbing pollution, and slowing the rate of environmental degradation, but overall the global environmental has continued to deteriorate and many nations have not lived up to the commitments they had made at the Earth Summit. In short, although the policies and principles of sustainable development are now well established, there is a considerable lag in putting them into practice.

Whatever may be the outcomes of the process of sustainable development, it is very clear that the society cannot sit idly and wait for results. People are an integral part of the environment and responsible for the environmental deterioration that has occurred. Hence, they must also participate in the search for alternatives and solutions. Sustainable development offers the greatest promise, but it is also the approach that demands the greatest individual sacrifice. Success or failure in slowing and then reversing environmental deterioration will depend on society's willingness to face these challenges and accept the sacrifices, or ignore them and suffer the consequences.

BIBLIOGRAPHY

Agarwal, A., Narain, S. and Sharma, A. (eds), Green Politics. New Delhi, 1999.

Baylis, John and Smith, Steve, The Globalization of World Politics. New Delhi: Oxford University Press, 2005.

Bhatt, S., Biodiversity: A Manual for College Teachers. Ahmedabad: Centre for Environment Education, 1997.

Boehmer-Christiansen, S., 'Global climate Protection Policy: The Limits of Garner Robert', Environmental Politics Change, Vol. 4 No. 2, 1994.

Gadgil, M., 'Let the People Speak', Hindu Survey, 1998.

Hajer, Maarten A., The Politics of Environmental Discourse Ecological Modernization and the Policy Process. London: Oxford University Press, 1995.

Harris, Frances, Global Environmental Issues. John Willey & Sons, 1994.

Hurst, P., Rainforest Politics: Ecological Destruction of South-East Asia. London: Zed Books, 1990.

Kirkby, John, Phil O'Keefe and Lloyd Timberlake (eds), 'Biodiversity' (Chapter 1), 'Climate Change and Energy' (Chapter 2) and 'Global Warming' (chapter 10). The Earthscan Reader in Sustainable Development. London: Earthscan Publishing Ltd., 1995.

Kothari, A., Understanding Biodiversity: Life Sustainability and Equity, 1997.

Lamber, Mark and Vogler, John (eds), The Environment and International Relations. London: Routledge, 1995.

McCormick, John, The Global Environmental Movement. London: John Willey & Sons, 1995.

McNeill, J. R., Something New Under the Sun: An Environmental History of the Twentieth-Century World. New York: Norton, 2001.

Meyer, M. and Abich, K., 'Winners and Losers in Climate Change' in W. Sachs (ed.) Global Ecology: A new of Political Conflict. London and New Jersey: Zed Books, 1993.

Mukherji, Shormila, Fragile Environment. New Delhi: Manak Publications, 2004.

Nicholson, Michael, International Relations, A Concise Introduction. New York: New York University Press, 2002.

Pretty, J. and Ball, A., Agricultural Influences on Carbon Emissions and Sequestration: A Review of Evidence and the Emerging Trading Options. Centre for Environment and Society. Occasional Paper 2001–03, University of Essex, 2001.

Ramanthan, U., Review of Clouds of Injustice: Bhopal Disaster 20 Years On. London: Amnesty International, 2004.

Rasmussen, P.E., Goulding, K.W.T., Brown, J.R., Grace, P.R., Janzen, H.H. and Korschens, M., Long-Term Agro Ecosystem Experiments: Assessing Agricultural Sustainability and Global Change'. Science, 1998.

Reicosky, D.G., Kemper, W.D., Langdale, G.W., Douglas, C.L. and Rasmussen, P.E., 'Soil Organic Matter Changes Resulting from Tillage and Biomass Production'. Journal of Soil and Water Conservation, 1995.

Robertson G.P, Paul, E.A. and Harwood, R.R., 'Greenhouse Gases Intensive Agriculture: Contributions of Individual Gases to Radioactive Warming of the Atmosphere'. Science, 2000.

Seminar, Elusive Justice: A symposium on the Bhopal Disaster after Twenty Years'. December, 2004.

Shiva, V. (eds), Biodiversity: Social and Ecological Perspectives. London: Zed Books, 1991.

Shiva, V., 'Global Warming Caused by Rich Countries'. Third World Resurgence, No. 1, September, 1990.

Smith, D., The Penguin State of the World Atlas, 2003.

Smith, Z.A., The Environmental Paradox. London: Prentice Hall, 2000.

Speth, James Gustave, Global Environmental Challenges: Transitions to a Sustainable World. New Delhi: Orient Longman, 2004.

USDA, Growing Carbon: A New Crop that Helps Agricultural Producers and the Climate Too. Natural Resources Conservation Service. Washington DC, 2000.

Weiszacker, Christine Won, 'Competing Notions of Biodiversity' in W. Sachs (ed.) Global Ecology: A New Arena of Political Conflict. London, New Jersey: Zed Books, 1993.

Chapter 9

Law Governing Environmental Impact Assessments at the International Level

Amrit Kaur Pannu

INTRODUCTION

"Transboundary environmental governance" is used to describe a range of regulatory processes in order to assess, mitigate, and compensate for the impact of human activities on the environment. The main processes used are prior environmental impact assessments (EIAs) or strategic environmental assessments (SEAs). The term "transboundary" does not only apply to situations where the impact occurs within the jurisdiction of another state, it includes effects beyond any state's jurisdiction as well. Such governance pertains to activities carried out by state actors, nonstate entities such as global and regional organizations, marine industries such as shipping and fisheries, offshore mining industries, marine scientific researchers, and so on. The duty of a state to conduct an EIA has gradually gained the status of a fundamental principle in international law based on the recent shift from measures of control to a more preventive approach.[1] An EIA has been defined as

> a systematic process of determining and managing (identifying, describing, measuring, predicting, interpreting, integrating, communicating, involving, and controlling) the potential (or real) impacts (direct and indirect, individual and cumulative, likelihood of occurrence) of proposed (or existing) human actions (projects, plans, programs, legislation, activities) and their alternatives on the Environment (physical, chemical, biological, ecological, human health, cultural, social, economic, built, and interrelations).[2]

At the domestic level, an EIA would help to arrive at a fully informed decision while accounting for potential effects on the environment by the proposed activity. It would provide an opportunity to voice the concerns of those affected and to help them understand the activities being undertaken.[3] The process calls for exchange of information, notification, and mutual consolation in case of transboundary harm, and the assessment would also provide the affected state with an opportunity to consult with the originating state by considering the results from the assessment report.[4] The originating state has the option to exercise command and control measures with regard to the proposed activity such that it can completely deny authorization of it and could make the authorization conditional as long as the design was modified to mitigate damage or a less harmful alternative could be adopted.[5]

NO-HARM PRINCIPLE AND TRANSBOUNDARY ENVIRONMENTAL ASSESSMENT

The no-harm principle does not apply to completely avoid any harm; a certain threshold must be met—in order to be prohibited, the activity engaged should have a "significant adverse impact."[6] The state should not be responsible for all the damage that has occurred but only that which it failed to prevent.[7] As a general principle, state authorities should not authorize operations that negatively impact the interests of other states.[8] The International Court of Justice (ICJ) in the Nuclear Weapons Advisory Opinion reiterated the same principle with reference to high seas and deep seabed.[9] The principle imposes a standard of due diligence to be observed by states when authorizing private entities to operate projects; it is a way of creating an institutional process that should be followed diligently.[10]

This chapter explores the concept of EIAs and their relevance in controlling the harm arising out of land-based sources of marine pollution. A description of the no-harm principle and of transboundary environmental assessment has been used to provide context. The next section addresses transboundary harm caused by land-based sources of marine pollution and further discusses international and regional instruments that states have adopted as an effort to increase their accountability and to encourage them to undertake EIAs. Further, the subsequent section states examples of two cases where the court has pressed upon the importance of such assessments. Finally, the conclusion acknowledges the existence of multiple bilateral and multilateral instruments; however, it also points out the difference between developing and developed countries and the fact that the level of development is an important factor toward implementing laws protecting the environment.

TRANSBOUNDARY HARM ARISING OUT OF LAND-BASED SOURCES OF POLLUTION

The maximum impact suffered by the marine environment is through land-based sources of pollution, including industrial, agricultural, and urban waste discharges which are either directly released or via outflows or pipelines. The waste can also be transported through internal water bodies such as rivers that ultimately flow into the sea. When excessive nutrients are introduced into the environment through the named sources, it increases the plant life that elevates the amount of oxygen-consuming bacteria, causing eutrophication.[11] The pollution resulting from the activities undertaken by one state can affect the natural environment of another state owing to the transboundary movement of polluting agents.[12]

The United Nations Convention for the Law of the Sea (UNCLOS) does not define land-based sources of pollution. However, it does include provisions on land-based activities, which are capable of resulting in "substantial pollution of or significant and harmful changes to the marine environment," to undergo an EIA prior to their approval.[13] The precautionary principle is reflected within the terminology of Article 194[14] of UNCLOS as well as other instruments that include the exercise of due diligence as part of the responsibilities of states. It ensures that any harm must be prevented. The *Corfu Channel*[15] judgement very clearly indicates that the responsibility of a state can only be invoked in case of foreseeable risks. An EIA must be conducted prior to sanctioning projects that are likely to have an adverse impact on the environment. It could be the environment of the state in whose jurisdiction the polluting activity is being carried out, or the jurisdiction of other states for which action may be brought.[16] Article 204 of UNCLOS provides for monitoring the risks or effects of pollution. It states the need to "observe, measure, evaluate and analyze, by recognized scientific methods, the risks or effects of pollution of the marine environment." Any activities that are authorized by the state shall be under surveillance to determine the likelihood of pollution of the environment caused by them.[17] When the probability of resulting harm is established, the responsibility to prevent, reduce, and control lies with the state. It helps with the identification of specific areas that are at a higher risk and require attention.[18] The no-harm principle applies in curtailing pollution from land-based sources. It is customary international law as well as the subject matter of general principles of international law that requires states to refrain from causing serious harm to the environment of other states. The arbitral award delivered in the *Trail Smelter* case held Canada responsible for the damage that was caused by fumes emanating from a privately owned smelter located within the state. The case also brings to light the contents of Principle 21 of the Stockholm Declaration on Human Environment, 1972, which provides that states should act pursuant to their own environmental policies when exploiting natural resources within their jurisdiction; however, they must exercise caution and ensure that such acts do not cause damage beyond their own territorial jurisdiction. The said principle does not only apply to damage being caused to other states, it also encompasses common spaces and the marine environment in general. Article 194 of UNCLOS reflects that the scope of the principle is within the law of the sea with regard to all forms of pollution including that which results from land-based sources. The judgement of the ICJ in the *Corfu Channel* case refers to the duty imposed on states to contravene any such activities taking place within their jurisdiction that may result in a violation of rights of other states. The draft articles of the ILC also take into consideration the responsibility of states to prevent, reduce, and control pollution, especially in context to "watercourse states." Article 7 imposes the obligation to exercise due diligence in a manner that no harm comes to the watercourse states during the utilization of an international watercourse.[19] Internationally, the non-binding Montreal Guidelines for the Protection of Marine Environment against Pollution from Land-based Sources, 1985 incorporate in paragraph 10 the requirement for states to adopt a "comprehensive environmental management approach to the prevention, reduction and control of pollution from land-based sources."[20]

INTERNATIONAL INSTRUMENTS OF TRANSBOUNDARY GOVERNANCE

There is a broad range of multilateral and bilateral instruments that specifically relate to EIAs. The Environmental Protocol to the Antarctic Treaty provides for the carrying out of EIAs within the territories of the states party to the Antarctic Treaty as well as for "areas beyond national jurisdiction" (ABNJ). Principle 17 of the Rio Declaration states, "EIA, as a national instrument, shall be undertaken for proposed activities that are likely to have a significant adverse impact on the environment and are subject to a decision of a competent national authority."

It can be inferred from the language used here that EIAs are a requirement in international law. When activities resulting in environmental harm are undertaken by a state and the effects could be borne by other states, it violates the international obligation to "respect the environment of other States or of areas beyond national control." The missing aspect of the definition is that it does not impose any specific standards in relation to conducting EIAs.[21] Agenda 21, a plan of action undertaken for the Rio Declaration, pressed the need to undertake EIAs for all states with a view to protect the environment.[22] There are various instruments based solely on regulating the conduct of EIAs, as well as those relating to the environment containing provisions that impose a requirement to conduct EIAs; binding instruments require an assessment to be conducted in circumstances specified by them.

The United Nations Environment Programme (UNEP) guidelines regard "nature and location of the proposed activity" as criteria when assessing environmental impacts.[23] The World Bank assesses the following factors—"type, location, sensitivity, and scale of the project, nature and magnitude of the potential impact"—to determine which of the three categories a project belongs to. Category A includes projects that will have "significant adverse environmental impacts" and an assessment is mandatory; Category B includes projects with "some adverse impacts but a lesser degree of significance" and an initial assessment is to be conducted to determine whether there is need for a full EIA; and Category C projects do not require to be assessed as they have no significant impacts.[24] The approach of the Asian Development Bank is very similar to the World Bank's. The Antarctic Protocol has a two-step approach that begins with an initial assessment followed by a "comprehensive environment evaluation" for projects that are likely to have more than just a minor environmental impact.[25] UNEP Goals and Principles of EIA, 1987 are among the initial documents containing procedures to meet the objectives of EIAs.[26] Principle 1 includes the description of the activity proposed to be undertaken—a description of the environment, including details which will help to identify the effects of the activity on it, practical alternatives, all kinds of impact on the environment whether direct, indirect, cumulative, short term, or long term; any gaps in knowledge or uncertainties; and lastly whether the activity will result in transboundary harm or harm to the environment of another state. It is crucial to include areas beyond national jurisdiction and transboundary harm within the contents of EIAs to understand the overall implications of the activity. Principle 11 takes areas beyond national jurisdiction a little further by encouraging the adoption of bilateral, multilateral, and regional instruments of consultation. The principles also include mechanisms which will assist in determining the effects of a project. They promote listing of activities which will most likely produce or not produce significant effects, separately listing areas of special importance as well as listing categories of available resources. They also promote an initial evolution prior to the assessment when determining its necessity. As for public participation, Principle 7 imposes the obligation to consult with stakeholders.[27]

Convention on Biological Diversity 1992[28]

The Convention on Biological Diversity (CBD) is a binding instrument that requires an identification of adverse activities and monitoring of projects, and determining whether the anticipated effects occur or not. The convention's provisions apply to areas beyond national jurisdiction. The EIA obligations discussed within the convention also comprise the subject matter of the

CBD voluntary guidelines; they raise questions related to the impact upon biodiversity:

> Would the intended activity affect the biophysical environment directly or indirectly in such a manner or cause such biological changes that it will increase the risks of extinction of genotypes, cultivars, varieties, populations of species, or the chance of loss of habitats or ecosystems?
>
> Would the intended activity surpass the maximum sustainable yield, the carrying capacity of a habitat/ecosystem or the maximum allowable disturbance level of a resource, population or ecosystem, taking into account the full spectrum of values of that resource, population or ecosystem? Would the intended activity result in changes to, and/or rights over, biological resources?[29]

The United Nations Convention for the Law of the Sea (UNCLOS

Article 206 states the need to assess potential effects arising out of planned activities undertaken by states if they are likely to result in substantial harm, pollution, or changes to the marine environment. It further imposes the requirement to communicate the reports of these assessments to other states. This is generally accepted as an obligation to conduct an EIA despite the term not being expressly used.[30] However, the convention specifies that a need to conduct an assessment only arises when there is scope for "substantial pollution" or "significant harm," and so far there is no scale upon which the degree of harm can be measured and sates need to exercise discretion in the matter.

Articles 204, 205, and 206 of UNCLOS present the provisions related to EIAs for land-based sources of marine pollution, including dumping at sea.

It can be said that the language used in Article 206 is vague in the sense that there are many unspecified factors; for example, the clause relating to which state is responsible is to be invoked for assessing the impacts arising out of a project falling within the jurisdiction of multiple states. No specific criterion has been outlined to be fulfilled by the assessing state. The provision also fails to state the international standards that would apply during the assessment if it were to be carried out by one or several states jointly. The outcome of such leniency could only mean that information may not be available to the states affected well in time to take action owing to the absence of specific provisions regarding notification and consultation.[31] Instead of stating procedural requirements, the article permits states to determine the same as per their own understanding and national policies. The issue arising out of self-determination was that developing states, particularly during the time of the adoption of UNCLOS, could not have been expected to have standards similar to those of developed nations.[32]

Espoo Convention

The United Nations Economic Commission for Europe negotiated the Convention on Environmental Impact Assessment in a Transboundary Context (Espoo Convention).[33] The spread of EIA in national policymaking was what led to the emergence of transboundary-EIA-based instruments. It must be noted that while drafting transboundary procedures, all states have different national policies, and so their procedures will certainly differ from one another. It would be quite ideal to have a similar procedure among states with similar domestic policies, such as the case is with the EU.[34] It is the only formally binding treaty along with the Protocol to the Antarctic Treaty on Environmental Procedure, 1966 that contains comprehensive requirements with respect to EIAs. The prime objective of the two treaties is to ensure reciprocity between states with regard to the contents of assessments undertaken by them and to abide by the requirements of notification and mutual consultation.[35] The convention includes three annexes that contain lists. Annex I lists those activities that are likely to have "significant adverse environmental impacts." Annex III contains the general criteria for nonlisted activities in order to determine if they may have a significant impact. If that is in fact true for a particular project, it is to be treated as it were already mentioned in Annex I. The interstate process is relevant for transboundary harm. But as the case was before, the decision maker is always the state in whose jurisdiction the activities are taking place. The European Bank for Reconstruction and Development (EBRD) has adopted an approach similar to that of the Espoo Convention. However, the determination is to be made by their staff under the bank's environmental procedure.[36] What sets the convention apart from the provisions of UNEP EIA Goals and Principles is that only transboundary environmental impact is considered by it. Hence it does not cover domestic pollution and harmful impact on the marine environment beyond the jurisdiction of any states.[37]

Regional Instruments

At the regional level, there exists an identical mix of instruments binding and nonbinding. Some instruments on EIAs that are modeled similarly to the Espoo Convention are the Kuwait Convention 1978, Draft Protocol and Guidelines on EIA in a Transboundary Context for the Caspian Sea, and the agreement among South-Eastern European states to implement the Convention on Environmental Impact Assessment in a Transboundary Context (Bucharest, 2008), among others. The first multilateral environmental agreement or regional convention to contain an obligation to conduct an assessment was the 1978 Kuwait Convention for Cooperation on the Protection of the Marine Environment from Pollution.[38] Article XI states,

"Each Contracting State shall endeavor to include an assessment of the potential environmental effects in any planning activity entailing projects within its territory, particularly in coastal areas which may cause significant risks of pollution in the Sea Area."[39]

Kiev Protocol[40]

The 2003 Protocol on Strategic Impact Assessments to the Espoo Convention is about SEAs in a domestic sphere. It imposes the requirement of an SEA to be undertaken for certain programs specified within its contents. These have been determined on the basis of their effects on the environment and health, reason being, such aspects must be covered in the process of policymaking. Article 2(6) of the protocol includes the evaluation of both environmental as well as health effects; it further emphasizes the importance of public participation.[41] The various sectors that must conduct SEAs are agriculture, forestry, fisheries, energy and industry, mining, transport, regional development, waste management, telecommunications, tourism, town and country planning, and land use. Annex II of the Espoo Convention contains a list of projects that require an EIA under national legislation, but the protocol is not limited to the contents of the annexes. It applies wherever necessary steps need to be taken within the state. The methodology used could vary between a case-by-case examination or specific listing based on the effects of their activities on the environment and health.[42]

Madrid Protocol and Arctic EIA Guidelines[43]

The Protocol on Environmental Protection to the Antarctic Treaty applies a complex and multidimensional screening mechanism for activities requiring EIA. It functions in context to areas beyond national jurisdiction as well. Its provisions apply to government-initiated as well as private sector activities within the Antarctic treaty area. The process is divided into three levels, starting with a preliminary assessment carried out at the national level for all activities proposed to be undertaken. If the report suggests a minor or transitory impact, then the next level of initial environmental evaluation is carried out. Lastly, if the report of the second assessment suggests more than a minor or transitory impact, the final level of a comprehensive EIA must be undertaken.[44]

The Guidelines for Environmental Impact Assessment in the Artic are not formally binding on the states. They include both renewable and nonrenewable sources of natural resources exploited for use by public sector activities, military activities, and infrastructural development. The mechanism implemented for examining is a case-by-case basis or applying mandatory assessments of listed harmful activities. They have employed the "sensitivity criteria" that takes into consideration the time period of the project, status of marine species in the area, habitats and ecosystems located within the area, the level of emissions of a project, and so on.[45]

1985 Council Directive

With the enforcement of the European Council Directive of 1985, EIAs were incorporated into the environmental protection plans of the EU.[46] The requirements under the directive were that prior to giving consent for projects of a public and private nature, if they were to have a significant impact on the environment, the developer together with the authority in charge of granting approval for the said project must put together an assessment. The directive, however, does not apply to national defense projects.[47]

CASES

Highlighting the Significance of EIAs in International Law

Singapore Land Reclamation Case[48]

The case took place between the states of Singapore and Malaysia. The main issue contended by Malaysia was the "threat of serious harm to the marine environment" arising out of a land reclamation project undertaken by Singapore in the Johor Straits. It was further contended that Singapore was in breach of the obligation to undertake an EIA as well as notify and consult Malaysia with respect to the assessment report. While awaiting the constitution of an arbitral tribunal, provisional measures were sought from the International Tribunal for the Law of the Sea (ITLOS). The tribunal required the project to be assessed by experts and for means of mitigating any damage to be devised, based on Singapore's agreement to exchange information and consult with Malaysia. The report of the study conducted by a group of experts, although not referred to as an EIA, fulfilled the requirements. It established that the possibility of harmful impact on the environment was not subject to exclusion, and mitigation measures were devised as part of the report.[49]

MOX Plant Case[50]

The dispute arose between the UK and Ireland, concerning a nuclear fuel reprocessing plant set up by the UK. The EIA issue was based on the requirement of Article 206 of UNCLOS, an obligation the UK had not adequately fulfilled. Concerns were raised about discharges of radioactive isotopes being released into the Irish Sea, thereby affecting their marine environment.

Ireland contended that the UK was in breach of an obligation having inadequately assessed the impact of the MOX plant. The assessment failed to include important aspects such as individual sources of discharge into the Irish Sea, the cumulative impact of such discharges, and accidental releases arising out of transportation of nuclear material. No alternative measures were even considered in the report. The very essence of the argument put forward by Ireland was that "the content of the duty to assess should be determined with reference to common standards of EIA accepted by States in other international instruments." They highlighted the requirements set within the Espoo Convention, the EC EIA Directive, and the UNEP EIA Principles stating they were binding on the UK, further arguing the need to compile an updated assessment report owing to the lapse of time since the original assessment. The UK's position was that first, Article 206 applies only once the construction of the plant has been approved, and second, the requirement to conduct an assessment was only necessary where there was an indication of "substantial pollution" or "significant and harmful change to the marine environment," in determining which states were permitted to exercise discretion and the UK had complied with the said requirements whereas Ireland had failed to prove otherwise.[51]

The case puts forward the question of necessity of an EIA where large-scale industrial activities carrying a risk toward the environment take place. Ireland presented an argument drawing from various sources on international law that the EIA undertaken had proved to be inadequate. However, the law does not answer the question regarding the adequacy of an EIA.[52]

Both the cases mentioned above are concerned with the application of UNCLOS with significance being placed on cooperation among states and notification followed by mutual consultation. They discuss the importance of EIAs, the prevention of pollution of the marine environment, and wherever applicable, liability for harmful impact on the seas. Despite not providing any outcome about conducting an EIA, the cases highlight examples of state practices where harmful activities affecting the environment are recognized and measures to mitigate the damage are taken through consultation with the affected state.[53]

CONCLUSIONS

The oceans of the world are all connected to one another, and a single state cannot be given the responsibility to make sure that the marine environment remains unaffected by human activities and the pollution caused by them. The protection of the environment is a common concern of mankind.[54] There are numerous international instruments that establish EIA requirements on states;

they have become a requirement of general international law. The different criteria involved in undertaking the assessments are also readily available to states willing to carry out an assessment. It is even contended that EIAs be a subject of customary law, and states must carry out this responsibility in the spirit of international law and to comply with the rules to control and manage transboundary harm, especially where multiple states are involved. The main problem arises out of the unwillingness of states to comply with the said rules and also the difference in the nature of EIA commitments in various treaties. There remains unspecified procedures if they even include one; the requirements mentioned are mostly vague and are not supported by substantive procedure. A great deal is left to the states to determine, and so the issue in the MOX Plant case[55] is proof of resulting disputes. Ireland contended that the assessment report provided by the UK was inadequate. Another issue lies in the fact that so far states have not contested the existence of the duty to conduct an EIA. Ireland had advanced the argument that an appropriate EIA had not been conducted, but the necessity to undertake the assessment was not put forward. The cases stand as important pieces of evidence suggesting the necessity to determine the amount of damage the proposed activities would lead to.[56] The objectives behind commitments in one treaty may differ largely from those that support the inclusion of similar provisions in a different treaty. Domestic EIA systems can never be expected to reach a common level because of the difference in levels of development of states.[57] In many developing countries, EIA regimes only exist because of enormous pressure from international institutions. It mostly happens that development banks encourage activities that carry EIA requirements as part of the procedure. But so often they are broadly incorporated into the domestic legislation, and no detailed requirements or procedures are set up. The main limitation is also lack of capacity of these states to carry out assessments on all projects. They do not have access to scientific information or expert opinions. Even the technological development adds to this factor. Sometimes financial resources are insufficient for them to comply properly. It is also very difficult to ensure public participation in an orderly fashion with the populations likely to be affected in developing countries. The process simply becomes a political issue rather than an environmental one. The only suggestion to counter these hindrances is to keep in mind differing political, social, and economic backgrounds in these states.[58]

NOTES

1. Kevin R. Gray, "International Environmental Impact Assessment: Potential for a Multilateral Environmental Agreement" 11 (1) Colorado Journal of International Environmental Law and Policy, 2000 pg. 83, 88.

2. David P. Lawrence, Environmental Impact Assessment: Practical Solutions to Recurrent Problems (Wiley-Interscience 2003) pg. 7.

3. Maki Tanaka, "Lessons from the Protracted Mox Plant Dispute: A Proposed Protocol on Marine Environmental Impact Assessment to the United Nations Convention on the Law of the Sea", 25(2) Michigan Journal of International Law, 2004 pg. 356, 357.

4. Phoebe Okowa, "Procedural Obligations in International Environmental Agreements", 67(1) The British Year Book of International Law, 1997 pg. 279, 280, 302.

5. Gunther Handl, "State Liability for Accidental Transnational Environmental Damage by Private Persons", 74 American Journal of International Law, 1980 pg. 557.

6. Trail Smelter Arbitration (United States v Canada) (1941) 3 RIAA 1905; Rachel Lorna Johnstone, "Evaluating Espoo: What Protection does the Espoo Convention Offer the Arctic Marine Environment?", 5(1) The Yearbook of Polar Law Online, 2013 pg. 339.

7. Rachel Lorna Johnstone, "Evaluating Espoo: What Protection does the Espoo Convention Offer the Arctic Marine Environment?", 5(1) The Yearbook of Polar Law Online, 2013 pg. 339.

8. James Cameron (correspondence author), Juli Abouchar, "The Precautionary Principle: A Fundamental Principle of Law and Policy for the Protection of the Global Environment", 14 Boston College International and Comparative Law Review, 1991 pg. 22.

9. Legality of the Threat or Use of Nuclear Weapons (Advisory Opinion),ICJ Reports, 1996 pg. 254 para 29.

10. Pulp Mills on the River Uruguay (Argentina v Uruguay) (Merits) ICJ Reports, 2010 pg. 14 para 197.

11. V. H. Smith, G. D. Tilman, J. C. Nekola, "Eutrophication: Impacts of Excess Nutrient Inputs on Freshwater, Marine, and Terrestrial Ecosystems", 100(1) Environmental Pollution, 1999 pg. 182 table 3.

12. S. D. Murphy, "Prospective Liability Regimes for the Transboundary Movement of Hazardous Wastes", 88(1) American Journal of International Law, 1994 pg. 25.

13. United Nations Convention on Law of the Sea (adopted 10 December 1982, entered into force 16 November 1994) 1833 UNTS 3 (UNCLOS) Art. 206.

14. United Nations Convention on Law of the Sea (adopted 10 December 1982, entered into force 16 November 1994) 1833 UNTS 3 (UNCLOS) Art. 194.

15. Corfu Channel Case (United Kingdom v. Albania) (Assessment of Compensation) 15 XII 49 ICJ Reports 1949 pg. 244.

16. Alan Boyle, "Land-based Sources of Marine Pollution—Current Legal Regime", 16(1) Marine Policy, 1992 pg. 22.

17. United Nations Convention on Law of the Sea (adopted 10 December 1982, entered into force 16 November 1994) 1833 UNTS 3 (UNCLOS) Art. 204.

18. James Harrison, "Saving the Oceans through Law: The International Legal Framework for the Protection of the Marine Environment" (Oxford: Oxford University Press 2017) pg. 67

19. Stephen McCaffrey, "The International Law Commission Adopts Draft Articles on International Watercourses", 89(2) American Journal of International Law, 1995 pg. 399.

20. UNEP Governing Council, Montreal Guidelines for the Protection of the Marine Environment against Pollution from Land-based Sources, Decision 13/18, 1985.

21. Philippe Sands, Principles of International Environmental Law (Cambridge; New York: Cambridge University Press 2003) pg. 800.

22. Agenda 21: Programme of Action for Sustainable Development, (1992) GAOR Session 47th Session, U.N. Doc. A/CONF.151/4 para. 17.18, 17.18, 17.19, 17.20.

23. UNEP Governing Council, Goals and Principles of Environmental Impact Assessment, Decision 16/25 (17 June 1987) UN Doc. UNEP/GCIDEC/14/25.

24. World Bank, Environmental Assessment, in the World Bank Operational Manual: Operational Policies (1999) OP 4.01 no. 8.

25. Maki Tanaka, "Lessons from the Protracted Mox Plant Dispute: A Proposed Protocol on Marine Environmental Impact Assessment to the United Nations Convention on the Law of the Sea", (2004) 25(2) Michigan Journal of International Law pg. 403.

26. UNEP Governing Council, Goals and Principles of Environmental Impact Assessment, Decision 16/25 (17 June 1987) UN Doc. UNEP/GCIDEC/14/25.

27. Transboundary Book - Robin Warner, Simon Marsden, Transboundary Environmental Governance: Inland, Coastal and Marine Perspectives (Farnham, Surrey, England; Burlington, VT: Ashgate 2012) pg. 301, 302.

28. Convention on Biological Diversity (adopted on 5 June 1991, entered into force on 29 December 1993) 1760 UNTS 79 ("Biodiversity Convention").

29. Robin Warner, Simon Marsden, Transboundary Environmental Governance: Inland, Coastal and Marine Perspectives (Farnham, Surrey, England; Burlington, VT: Ashgate 2012) pg. 303.

30. James Harrison, "Saving the Oceans through Law: The International Legal Framework for the Protection of the Marine Environment" (Oxford: Oxford University Press; 2017) pg. 32.

31. Maki Tanaka, "Lessons from the Protracted Mox Plant Dispute: A Proposed Protocol on Marine Environmental Impact Assessment to the United Nations Convention on the Law of the Sea", 25(2) Michigan Journal of International Law, 2004 pg. 356.

32. Neil Craik, The International Law of Environmental Impact Assessment: Process, Substance and Integration (Cambridge: Cambridge University Press 2008) pg. 99.

33. Convention on environmental impact assessment in a transboundary context (adopted on 25 February 1991, entered into force on 10 September 1997) (1992) OJ C104 ("Espoo Convention").

34. Robin Warner, Simon Marsden, Transboundary Environmental Governance: Inland, Coastal and Marine Perspectives (Farnham, Surrey, England; Burlington, VT: Ashgate 2012) pg. 325, 326.

35. Neil Craik, The International Law of Environmental Impact Assessment: Process, Substance and Integration (Cambridge: Cambridge University Press 2008) pg. 101, 104.

36. Maki Tanaka, "Lessons from the Protracted Mox Plant Dispute: A Proposed Protocol on Marine Environmental Impact Assessment to the United Nations Convention on the Law of the Sea", (2004) 25(2) Michigan Journal of International Law pg. 403.

37. Neil Craik, The International Law of Environmental Impact Assessment: Process, Substance and Integration (Cambridge: Cambridge University Press 2008) pg. 102.

38. Kuwait Regional Convention for Co-operation on the Protection of Marine Environment from Pollution (adopted on 24 April 1978, entered into force on 30 June 1979).

39. Kuwait Regional Convention for Co-operation on the Protection of Marine Environment from Pollution (adopted on 24 April 1978, entered into force on 30 June 1979) Art. XI.

40. Protocol on Strategic Environmental Assessment to the Convention on Environmental Impact Assessment in a Transboundary Context (adopted on 21 May 2003, entered into force on 11 July 2010) 2685 UNTS 140 ("Kiev Protocol").

41. Protocol on Strategic Environmental Assessment to the Convention on Environmental Impact Assessment in a Transboundary Context (adopted on 21 May 2003, entered into force on 11 July 2010) 2685 UNTS 140 ("Kiev Protocol") Art. 2(6).

42. Robin Warner, Simon Marsden, Transboundary Environmental Governance: Inland, Coastal and Marine Perspectives (Farnham, Surrey, England; Burlington, VT: Ashgate 2012) pg. 309.

43. Protocol on Environmental Protection to the Antarctic Treaty (adopted on 4 October 1991, entered into force on 14 January 1998) 30 ILM 1455 ("Madrid Protocol").

44. David Lyons, "Environmental Impact Assessment in Antarctica under the Protocol on Environmental Protection", 29(169) Polar Record, 1993 pg. 113.

45. Robin Warner, Simon Marsden, Transboundary Environmental Governance: Inland, Coastal and Marine Perspectives (Farnham, Surrey, England; Burlington, VT: Ashgate 2012) pg. 307.

46. Council Directive 85/337/EEC of 1985 on the Assessment of the Effects of certain private and public projects on the environment [1985] OJ L175/40.

47. Howard L. Brown, "Expanding the Effectiveness of the European Union's Environmental Impact Assessment Law", (1997) 20(2) Boston College International and Comparative Law Review pg. 314.

48. Case concerning Land Reclamation by Singapore in and around the Straits of Johor (Malaysia v Singapore) (2005) XXVII RIAA 133.

49. Neil Craik, The International Law of Environmental Impact Assessment: Process, Substance and Integration (Cambridge: Cambridge University Press 2008) pg. 118.

50. MOX Plant Case (Ireland v United Kingdom) (Provisional Measures, Order of 3 December 2001) ITLOS Case No 10, ICGJ 343.

51. Neil Craik, The International Law of Environmental Impact Assessment: Process, Substance and Integration (Cambridge: Cambridge University Press 2008) pg. 116, 117.

52. Alan Boyle, "The Environmental Jurisprudence of the International Tribunal for the Law of the Sea", 22(3) The International Journal of Marine and Coastal Law, 2007 pg. 377.

53. Alan Boyle, "The Environmental Jurisprudence of the International Tribunal for the Law of the Sea", 22(3) The International Journal of Marine and Coastal Law, 2007 pg. 375.

54. James Harrison, "Saving the Oceans through Law: The International Legal Framework for the Protection of the Marine Environment" (Oxford: Oxford University Press 2017) pg. 2.

55. MOX Plant Case (Ireland v United Kingdom) (Provisional Measures, Order of 3 December 2001) ITLOS Case No 10, ICGJ 343.

56. Alan Boyle, "The Environmental Jurisprudence of the International Tribunal for the Law of the Sea", 22(3) The International Journal of Marine and Coastal Law, 2007 pg. 376.

57. J. H. Knox, "The Myth and Reality of Transboundary Environmental Impact Assessment", 96(2) American Journal of International Law, 2002 pg. 296–301.

58. Habib M. Alshuwaikhat, "Strategic Environmental Assessment Can Help Solve Environmental Impact Assessment Failures in Developing Countries", 25(4) Environmental Impact Assessment Review, 2005 pg. 308, 309.

Chapter 10

A Journey of Environmental Rights, Justice, and Judicial Trends in India

Issues and Challenges

Ashwani Pant

INTRODUCTION

Environmental jurisprudence, in its essence, consists of such basic fundamental postulates and values that are concerned with the restoration of balance and harmony in the environment by regulating, ordering, preventing, and controlling such human conduct that tends to disrupt, disturb, damage, and destroy the ecology of the Earth. It is indeed a new epoch-making green philosophy which contains a cluster of ecofriendly values concerning human beings, animals, and plants in the present environmental crisis.[1] It envisages the interdependence and coexistence between man and nature and between living and nonliving life systems, reminding us of the ancient Vedic invocation which says, "So long as the earth has mountains, forests, trees etc., the human race will survive." Another Vedic hymn declares: "The Earth is our Mother, we are its children." In the same strand, it considers "Nature as Cosmic Being; Mountain his bones; the earth his flesh; the sea his blood; the sky his abdomen; Air his breath; and Agni (fire) his energy." In this way, ancient Indian sages too had realized the basic environmental imperative that human beings and nature are inseparable and are like mother and child.

Civilized societies can flourish only when there is consistency and harmony among the various members of the community. Earth jurisprudence is a part of legal philosophy and human governance, and it is based on the ideas that the welfare of each member of the community is based on the welfare of the Earth as a whole.[2] Indira Gandhi once said that the essence of Indian Environmental heritage and traditions teaches us that all forms of life, human, animal, and plant are so closely interlinked that disturbance in one gives rise to imbalance in another. It is not merely an extraversion but involves the central issue of human existence and survival and of the future generations. It mirrors the concept of "One World," "Global Family," and "Our Common Future" as supra-parameters to be followed in action by people and governments at both the grassroots and state levels.[3]

Environmental jurisprudence is Kelsen's Grundnorm theory with a series of norms. With a common future or one world as the supra-highest norm, there are subordinate norms such as the right to livelihood, the right to clean environment, sustainable development, prevention of pollution, elimination of poverty, etc.[4] According to Ronald Dworkin, for upholding the rule of law, there must be a balance between moral values, justice, human right, and rights. Today's violations are tomorrow's conflicts. In the context of environmental justice, it is about the intersection of human rights, infrastructure, and how people—equitably and sustainably—access the resources and things they need to survive and prosper. Environmental justice embraces the principle that people and communities are entitled to equal protection of our environment, health, employment, education, housing, transportation, and civil right laws.

CONCEPT OF ENVIRONMENTAL RIGHTS

Environmental rights are the protection of natural resources; the access to and use of natural resources; and how the access to and use of these resources affect surrounding populations, as well as the resources themselves. Environmental rights are an extension of the basic human rights that mankind requires and deserves. In addition to having the right to food, clean water, suitable shelter, and education, having a safe and sustainable environment is paramount as all other rights are dependent upon it. The desire to ensure access for all of Earth's inhabitants to this essential standard of living is the primary concern of environmental rights.

Beyond equal distribution and access to clean and sustainable resources, environmental rights also include an additional obligation from those in the industrialized nations. It requires us to act responsibly in our own use of natural resources, and to regulate our levels of consumption in a more equitable manner. In the global era, the central point of development is sustainable development which increasingly recognizes the importance of human rights. The central point of any social, environmental, or economic program is the protection of human life in relation to life, health, culture, and living standards.

Civil and political rights provide for moral and political order which includes the right to life, equality, political participation, and association for affirming sustainable development. They protect civil mobilization around environmental protection and equity. Economic, social, and cultural rights, also referred to as second-generation rights, provide substantive standards for an individual's well-being. They also provide for self-determination, including the right of all people to manage their own natural resources. In 2008, Ecuador became the first country to recognize the rights of nature in their constitution. It takes the concept of environmental rights to the next logical conclusion by bestowing rights unto nature itself. "Rather that treating nature as property under the law, Rights for Nature articles acknowledge that nature in all its life forms has the right to exist, persist, maintain and regenerate its vital cycles."

Environmental rights basically include

- The right to a clean and safe environment
- The right to act to protect the environment
- The right to information and participate in decision-making

These rights do not exist in isolation and not separate from human rights or other issues linked to poverty and economic and social exclusion. A human rights perspective to sustainable development moves from the "traditional green" issue to a wider approach toward protecting the vulnerable sections of the society. These rights can provide a platform for environmental and sustainable improvements that are likely to benefit the marginalized people, the poor, the women, and minorities. Active involvement and shared control by the people and states most affected by a degraded environment is fundamental at local, national, and global levels.

EVOLUTION OF ENVIRONMENTAL JUSTICE

The concept of environmental justice has been closely linked with the new tide in global environmentalism. The concept of environmental justice has emerged as a new version of justice, and it has been linked, in many ways, with the earlier versions of justice such as philosophical, religious, ethical, social, economic, and political justice.[5]

The theoretical framework of environmental justice can be summed up under the following two broader heads discussed below.

Environmental Justice under Ancient Indian Tradition

The relationship between human beings and nature attracted the seers of the Vedic period in a manner incomparable to any other religious and cultural tradition. The Vedic seers acknowledged that the material causes of this creation happened to be the *Pancha Mahabhutas* (Five Great Elements); traditionally, they are enumerated in the following order: Earth, air, space, water, and light (fire). These five *mahabhutas* are cosmic elements which create, nurture, and sustain all forms of life; thus, they play an important role in preserving and sustaining the environment.[6]

The Atharva Veda (about 2000 BC) is perhaps the first scripture in any spiritual tradition where the respect for the Earth has been propounded. The *Prithvi Sukta* maintains that attributes of the Earth (such as its firmness, purity, and fertility) are for everyone, and no one group or nation has special authority over them. It has been said that human greed and exploitative tendencies have been the main cause of environmental destruction.

According to Hindu scriptures, people must not demand or command domination over other creatures. Eco-spirituality and eco-care require that the entire universe is seen as an extended family, with all living beings in this universe as members of the household. This concept, also known as *Vasudhaiva Kutumbakam* (*Vasudha* means Earth; *Kutumba* means extended family), refers to all human beings as well as other creatures living on the Earth as members of the same extended family. Only by considering the entire universe as a part of our extended family, we can (individually and collectively) develop the necessary maturity and respect for all other living beings.

From the above discussion, it may be said that people of India have a rich religious, social, and cultural heritage of environmental justice. However, it is an irony that despite this rich heritage, India has been considered as one of the most polluted nations. It appears that we the people of India have forgotten their rich ancient religious, ethical, and cultural environmental traditions. Similarly, we have not performed our duties relating to the environment as envisaged in the Constitution of India. Consequently, our natural and human environments have been badly polluted and degraded, and we have also experienced one of the worst industrial disasters in the Bhopal Gas Tragedy, which was comparable to the Chernobyl Nuclear Plant accident.

Modern Environmental Justice

Global environmentalism arises from social conflicts on environmental entitlements, on the burden of pollution, on the sharing of uncertain environmental risks, and on the loss of access to natural resources and environmental services. The modern or contemporary global environmental movements, which have given birth to different versions of environmental justice, grow in reaction to economic growth. Different versions of environmental justice are the result of different clusters of environmental movements. These environmental movements have different levels of relationship with environmental sciences, feminism, state power, religion, business interests, and other social movements. Professor Joan Martinez-Alier separates three main intertwined clusters in the environmental movement.[7] The "cult of wilderness," "the gospel of eco-efficiency," and the "environmentalism of the poor," which are channels of a single river, branches of a big tree, or varieties of the same crop.

ENVIRONMENTAL POLICIES IN INDIA

The concerns of environmental harmony and wildlife protection are found embodied in the ancient scriptures in the Indian subcontinent. Kautilya's Arthashastra and Ashoka's edicts are known to include provisions for safeguarding nature and natural resources. The Vedas also echo the sentiments of environmental ethics and identify harmony as an important prerequisite for human survival and prosperity. Consequently, respect and love for nature is rooted in the Indian civilization.

Contemporary environmental policies began to be framed in India during the British Rule. The Shore Nuisances (Bombay and Kolaba) Act, 1853 was one of the first environment-related acts to be passed. The other legislations include the Elephant's Preservation Act, 1879; the Fisheries Act, 1897; the Factories Act, 1897; the Bengal Smoke Nuisance Act, 1905; the Bombay Smoke Nuisance Act, 1912; Wild Birds and Animals Protection Act, 1912; and the Indian Forest Act, 1927.

The worldwide concern for environmental degradation found its expression in 1972 at the UN Conference on Human Environment. In 1979, a UN symposium identified unsustainable consumption patterns and lifestyles as basic causes of environmental degradation. It was the Brundtland Commission's report titled "Our Common Future" (1987)—a landmark development thinking—that brought environmental issues to the fore. The commission came to the conclusion that the relationship between economic growth and environmental conservation should be one of complementarity and interdependence. The idea of growth at all costs was replaced by the idea of sustainable development.[8]

The Constitution of India provides for certain directives for the states for governance in Part IV as the Directive Principles of State Policy. The Stockholm Declaration of 1972 was perhaps the first major attempt to conserve and protect the human environment at the international level. As a consequence of this declaration, the states were required to adopt legislative measures to protect and improve the environment. Accordingly, the Indian Parliament inserted two articles, namely Article 48A and Article 51A, in the Constitution of India in 1976.[9] Article 48A states that the "State shall endeavour to protect and improve the environment and safeguard forests and wildlife of the country."[10] Article 51A(g) imposes a duty on every citizen of India to protect and improve the natural environment, including forests, lakes, rivers, and wildlife, and to have compassion for all living creatures. Besides these two directives, Article 21, which provides for the fundamental right the right to life and personal liberty, has been interpreted by the courts to include the right to clean environment, right to clean air, and right to clean water as integral parts.

The National Council for Environment Planning and Policy was set up in 1972, which was later evolved as the Ministry of Environment and Forest in 1985 and renamed in 2014 as the Ministry of Environment, Forest and Climate Change (MoFECC). India's Five Year Plans have focused on rapid economic growth, employment generation, poverty alleviation, and balanced regional development. The importance of sustainable development is also being stressed as an objective of public policy.[11] The responsibility of framing and implementing the national environmental policy of India rests with the MoEFCC. It also works to ensure the effective implementation of the Environmental (Protection) Act of 1986. Apart from the constitutional mandates, there are plenty of legislations for the protection of environment that can be classified broadly as

1. Legislation after Independence till the Stockholm Conference (1947–1972)

   During this period, legislations were framed to control deforestation and unplanned town growth, namely, the Factories Act, 1948 and the Mines and Minerals (Regulation and Development) Act, 1957. The Factories Act provides for treatment of liquid effluents, gases, and fumes before final disposal.
2. Legislation Post–Stockholm Conference till Bhopal Disaster (1972–1984)

   The Stockholm Conference had influenced the environmental policies of not only India but of other countries as well. In India, it led to a constitutional amendment in 1976, followed by important legislations such as the Wildlife (Protection) Act, 1972, which provides for prohibition on poaching, establishment of national parks or sanctuaries for protecting, propagating, or developing wildlife and its environment; the Water (Prevention and Control of Pollution) Act, 1974 and the Air (Prevention and Control of Pollution) Act, 1981, both of which provide for the protection of water and air content from pollutants and creation of authorities such as the Central Pollution Control Board (CPCB) and state pollution control boards (SPCBs) in order to ensure the implementation; and the Forest (Conservation) Act, 1980, which prevents deforestation that results in ecological imbalance and environmental deterioration.
3. Bhopal Disaster to 2006 (1984–2006)

   The Bhopal Disaster had a deep impact on the minds of the policymakers, and this led to the enactment of the Environmental (Protection) Act,

1986, which provides for protection and improvement of the quality of environment and preventing, controlling, and abating environmental pollution. The Public Liability Insurance Act, 1991, was enacted to provide immediate relief to persons affected by any accident occurring while handling any hazardous substance. The National Environmental Tribunal Act, 1995, and the National Environmental Appellate Authority Act, 1997 were enacted for the establishment of different redressal forums for environmental cases. The Biological Diversity Act, 2002 is a major legislation for the protection of biological diversity. The new economic policy resulted in the framing of the Environmental Action Plan in 1993 with the objective of improving environmental services and integrating environmental considerations into development programs.

4. Environmental Policy after 2006

   After the World Conference on Sustainable Development, Johannesburg in 2000, the environmental policies were also changed worldwide keeping in view the concept of sustainable development. The National Environmental Policy, 2006 seeks to extend the coverage and fill the gaps that still exist, in light of present knowledge and accumulated experience. Sustainable development concerns in the sense of enhancement of human well-being, broadly conceived, are a recurring theme in India's development philosophy. The National Environmental Policy, 2006 is intended to mainstream environmental concerns in all development activities. The National Environmental Policy, 2006 is framed on three foundational aspirations. These are (i) human beings should be able to enjoy a decent quality of life; (ii) humanity should become capable of respecting the finiteness of the biosphere; and (iii) neither the aspiration for a good life nor the recognition of biophysical limits should preclude the search for greater justice in the world.

   The major objectives with which the National Environmental Policy, 2006 has been framed are

- Conservation of critical environmental resources
- Intragenerational equity: Livelihood security for the poor
- Intergenerational equity
- Integration of environmental concerns in economic and social development
- Efficiency in environmental resource use
- Environmental governance
- Enhancement of resources for environmental conservation

The National Environmental Policy, 2006 establishes some guiding principles for the protection of the environment and conservation of nature and natural resources. These principles are as follows: the principle that human beings are at the center of sustainable development concerns; the right to development; the principle that environmental protection is an integral part of the development process; the precautionary approach; economic efficiency; polluter pays principle; cost minimization; entities with "incomparable" values; equity; legal liability; fault-based liability; strict liability; the public trust doctrine; decentralization; integration; environmental standard setting; preventive action; and environmental offsetting.

The other enactments during this period include the Environmental Impact Assessment Notification, 2006 and the establishment of the National Green Tribunal (NGT) through the act of 2010. The setting up of NGT has been a shot in the arm in the struggle to balance economic growth with environmental protection owing to timely intervention in developmental projects.

JUDICIAL TRENDS TOWARD ENVIRONMENTAL JUSTICE

In interpreting environmental laws and norms, the Supreme Court has largely followed the legislative and internationally accepted measures[12] that are in consonance with our Vedic principles. Likewise, the Gandhian dictum that "Nature has provided everything for our need but not for our greed" is a perpetual source of inspiration for humanistic development of the Indian society and its environmental jurisprudence. In the backdrop of such emotive, holistic, and spiritual environmental heritage, judges have often been confronted with environmental issues of conserving and preserving the environment without hampering developmental processes. The judges environmental jurisprudence is not a static, abstract, grounded, or neutral principle but a dynamic, purposive, and ends-oriented one that balances the right to a clean and healthy environment with the right to livelihood of industrial workers employed in polluting enterprises causing eco-hazards and disasters.

The courts have come across peculiar manifold eco-problems as how to mend nonresponsive and unaccountable administration and expropriated management accountable to those affected directly by an unbridled development spree—be it tribal populations, peasants, forest communities, or poor and whole biotic and nonbiotic species. The judicial engineering on such issues and problems concerning the environment infused by constitutional values and community needs have weaved a new eco-jurisprudence reflecting the goals of eco-justice, human dignity, right to life, and compassion toward Mother Earth by maintaining a delicate balance between human beings and nature. The Supreme Court has made environment a mandatory legal input in business decision-making and has thereby introduced transparency on the issue of environment clearance of projects and environment impact assessment.[13] The Supreme Court has consistently reiterated the imperative need of such a process in the interest of protection of the ecosystem and development consistent with the environment.[14]

Of course, the courts admit that there can be no development without adverse effects on the environment and ecology.[15] However, balance has to be struck between two interests by specialists because public-utility projects cannot be abandoned nor can the environment be degraded and destroyed. The right of a person to a pollution-free environment is a part of basic jurisprudence of the land. Article 21 of the Constitution of India guarantees a fundamental right to life and personal liberty. The Supreme Court has interpreted the right to life and personal liberty to include the right to wholesome environment[16]; moreover, the right to life also includes the right to clean environment, drinking water, and pollution-free atmosphere.[17]

In the famous Taj Trapezium case,[18] the Supreme Court issued directions that coal- and coke-based industries in adjoining areas of the Taj Trapezium damaging Taj Mahal should either change over to natural gas or to be relocated outside the trapezium. In the Dehradun Valley Case,[19] the closing of limestone quarrying in the hills of Mussoorie was ruled by the court. It said, "This would undoubtedly cause hardship to them, but it is a price that has to be paid for protecting and safeguarding the rights of the people to live in a healthy environment with minimal disturbance of ecological balance." The Supreme Court asserted that it would not remain a passive spectator with eyes closed whenever there is an assault on the environment as environment protection is a constitutional mandate.[20] In the Tarun Bhagat case,[21] the court condemned the state government "while professing to protect the environment by means of various notifications and declarations should at the same time permit the degradation of environment by authorising mining operation in a prohibited area," which was a protected area in a wildlife sanctuary. Both development and environment must coexist and run parallel in the interest of social good. The Supreme Court called upon the state to create environmental awareness[22] in the citizenry by showing slides in cinema halls containing information and messages on the environment through radio and television, and by making environment a subject in academic institutions at all levels.

In the case of *M. C. Mehta v. Union of India*,[23] popularly known as the Oleum Gas Leak Case, the Supreme Court evolved a new principle of liability called Absolute Liability. The court held that where an enterprise is engaged in a hazardous or inherently dangerous activity resulting in the escape of a toxic gas, the enterprise is strictly and absolutely liable to compensate all those who are affected by the accident and such liability is not subject to any of the exceptions which operate vis-à-vis the tortious principle of strict liability.[24] The court further pointed out that the measure of compensation must be correlated to the magnitude and capacity of the enterprise because such compensation must have a deterrent effect.[25]

After 1990, the judicial trend in India saw a dip, on account of a nexus between politicians, polluters, and bureaucrats, and lack of transparency and accountability in environmental management. Thus, the poor suffer from both poverty and pollution, while polluters make hay of resources for personal profit or greed under the cover of development. In such situations, the Supreme Court has come to the rescue of the poor and the victims of pollution.[26] For the future generations, the opinions of Justice Jeevan Reddy in the Bichhari[27] pollution case and Justice Kuldip Singh in the Tamil Nadu Tanneries Case[28] would form an essential juristic compendium for an unpolluted environment and safe Earth not only for Indians but for all people of all lands.[29]

The Supreme Court of India, in *Vellore Citizen Welfare Forum v. Union of India*,[30] elaborately discussed the concept of "sustainable development," which has been accepted as part of the law of the land. The precautionary principle and the polluter pays principle are essential features of sustainable development. The precautionary principle makes it mandatory for the state government to anticipate, prevent, and attack the causes of environment degradation.[31] The polluter pays principle demands that the financial costs of preventing or remedying damage caused by pollution should lie with the undertaking which causes pollution. It has been held to be a sound principle, and as interpreted by the Supreme Court of India,[32] it means that the absolute liability for harm to the environment extends not only to compensate the victims of pollution but also the cost of restoring the environment degradation. The above case clearly reveals that the Supreme Court of India has played a vital role in the protection and improvement of the environment. The jurisdiction of the court has been expanded by the way of public interest litigation, which makes the creative role significant and laudable.

ISSUES AND CHALLENGES

A diverse developing society such as ours provides numerous challenges in the economic, social, cultural, and environmental arenas. All of these coalesce in the dominant imperative of the alleviation of mass poverty, reckoned in the multiple dimensions of livelihood security, healthcare, education, empowerment of the disadvantaged, and elimination of gender disparities.[33] The major issues in the effective implementation of environmental policies in India are as follows:

- Land degradation because of soil erosion, alkali salinization, waterlogging, pollution, disposal of waste without any treatment, and use of excessive fertilizers and pesticides
- Effect on the biodiversity of forests and wildlife because of large-scale deforestation; conversion of forests to other land types to be used for agriculture, settlements, infrastructure, and industry; and hunting of wild animals even after a ban and intrusion into protected areas
- Effect on biodiversity, traditional knowledge, and natural heritage because of the advent of genetically modified crops, new pharma products, and environmental pollution
- Depletion of freshwater resources because of pollution
- Increasing levels of pollution of various kinds
- Difficulty in the conservation of manmade heritage because of climate change
- Social factors—poverty, population, urbanization, and unplanned town growth
- Economic factors—nonexistent or poorly functioning markets for environmental goods and services; the manufacturing technology adopted by most of the industries generally based on intensive resource and energy use; expansion of chemical-based industries; growing transport activities; and expansion of port and harbor activities
- Institutional factors—illiteracy, health, and educational awareness

The major challenges faced in the effective implementation of environmental policies are as follows:

- Lack of a legal enforcement authority
- Need for more focus on institutional arrangements and capacity building
- Lack of compliance monitoring, permits, inspections, and self-monitoring
- Non-deterrence factors and enforcement response
- Lack of compliance assistance and data management
- Nonuse of economic and other incentives-based instruments
- Invisibility of indicators to evaluate program success
- Public participation in environmental compliance and enforcement

CONCLUSIONS

The advancement of the relationship between human rights and the environment would enable the incorporation of human rights principles within an environmental scope, such as antidiscrimination standards, the need for social participation, and the protection of vulnerable groups. At the same time, the human rights system would be strengthened by the incorporation of environmental concerns, enabling the expansion of the scope of human rights protection and the generation of concrete solutions for cases of abuses. Of course, one of the most important consequences is to provide the victims of environmental degradation with the possibility of access to justice. The occasional helplessness suffered by the victims of environmental degradation, linking human rights and the environment, brings such victims closer to the mechanisms of protection that are provided for by human rights laws. It is apparent that the environment and human rights are inextricably linked. As the serious impact of a degraded environment on human health and well-being are increasingly recognized, the people are better placed to adjust the policies and cultural practices to reflect their enhanced understanding. As a result, the people should be able to protect human rights and human dignity within their broader social, economic, and cultural contexts by drawing from and contributing to those who are actively engaged in the environmental and public health arenas. This should also facilitate those who arc working in the environmental and conservation fields to develop a better working relationship with those in the human rights arena. This will eventually lead to the articulation of a more integrated approach to dealing with socioeconomic and environmental problems, encouraging the development of a sustainable model for the preservation of biological resources and natural ecosystems, for the use and enjoyment of both present and future generations. Environmental rights are nothing but an extended form of human rights. The journey of environmental rights in the Indian context started particularly after Independence. The Indian journey of environmental protection, right from the beginning, has been an environmentally sensitive and friendly philosophy. In the present scenario, for the protection of environmental rights and affirmation of environmental justice, various efforts have been made nationally and internationally. The active judiciary has also cast obligations from time to time upon various persons to save, protect, and conserve the environment. The environmental jurisprudence in India has expanded enough through the setting of committees, laying down of principles, and thinking creatively and innovatively by judges.

NOTES

1. S.N. Dhyani, *Fundamentals of Jurisprudence- The Indian Approach* 417 (Allahabad: Central Law Agency, Second Edn., 2007).
2. Law Centre's First Case: Saving the planet- Maimi Herald, Available at: http://www.ijariit.com.

3. *Supra Note* 1 at 418.
4. *Ibid.*
5. Shastri, S.C., *Environmental Law* (Lucknow: Eastern Book Company, First Edn. 2002); Martinez-Alier, Joan., *The Environmentalism of the Poor* (New Delhi: Oxford University Press, First Edn. 2005); Guha, Ramacandra (ed.)., *Social Ecology* (New Delhi : Oxford University Press, 2001); Guha, Ramachandra., *Environmentalism : A Global History* (New Delhi: Oxford University Press, 2000).
6. O.P. Dwivedi, 'Classical India' in Dale Jamieson (ed.). *A Companion to Environmental Philosophy* (Massachusetts: Blackwell Publishers Inc, 2001) 37–51 at 38.
7. Martinez-Alier, Joan, *The Environmentalism of the Poor – A Study of Ecological Conflicts and Valuation* (New Delhi: Oxford University Press, 2005, First Indian Edn.) p. 1.
8. Debajit N. Sarkar, "Environmental Policy in India" 3 ARSS 17–20 (2014) available at http://www.trp.org.in/wp-content/uploads/2016/11/ARSS-Vol.3-No.2-July-Dec-2014pp.17-20.pdf.
9. Inserted by the Constitution (Forty-second Amendment) Act, 1976.
10. Part IV – Directive Principle of State Policy, The Constitution of India, 1950.
11. *Supra Note* 8 at 18.
12. *State of H.P. v. Ganesh Wood Product,* AIR 1996 SC 149 ; *Vellore Citizens Welfare Forum v. Union of India,* AIR 1996 SC 2715.
13. *Supra Note 1 at* 419.
14. *Sachidanand Pandey v. State of West Bengal* AIR 1987 SC 1109; *Kinkri Devi v. State of H.P.* AIR 1988 SC 4; *Rural Litigation & Entitlement Kendra Dehradun v. State of U.P.* AIR 1985 SC 653.
15. *Goa Foundation v. Konkan Railway Corp.,* AIR 1992 Bom 471; *General of Public of Sapooran Valley v. State of H.P.* AIR 1993 H.P. 52 ; *Bangalore Medical Trust v. B.S. Muddappa* AIR 1991 SC 1902.
16. *Rural Litigation & Entitlement Kendra Dehradun v. State of U.P.* AIR 1988 SC 1037.
17. *Subhash Kumar v. State of Bihar* AIR 1991 SC 420; *M.C. Mehta v. Union of India* AIR 2000 SC 3192.
18. *M.C.Mehta v. Union of India* AIR 1997 SC 734.
19. *Rural Litigation & Entitlement Kendra Dehradun v. State of U.P.* AIR 1985 SC 653.
20. *Charan Lal Sahu v. Union of Indi,* AIR 1990 SC 1480.
21. *Tarun Bhagat Singh v. Union of India* AIR 1992 SC 514.
22. *M.C.Mehta v. Union of India* AIR 1992 SC 382.
23. AIR 1987 SC 1086.
24. *Supra Note 23 at* 1099.
25. *Ibid.*
26. *M.C. Mehta v. Union of India* AIR 1996 SC 1977; *M.C. Mehta v. Union of India* AIR 1996 SC 2231.
27. *Indian Council for Enviro-Legal Action v. Union of India* AIR 1996 SC 1446.
28. *Vellore Citizens Welfare Forum v. Union of India* AIR 1996 SC 2715.

29. In the meantime Justice Kuldip Singh has given two things: (1) to Delhi government for shifting polluting units outside Delhi; (2) suspend vehicle licences spawning fuel pollution to save Delhi from slow death.

30. AIR 1996 SC 2715.

31. *M.C. Mehta v. Union of India* (1997) 1 Camp L.J. 199 (SC).

32. *Indian Council for Enviro-Legal Action v. Union of India* AIR 1996 SC 1446.

33. Preamble of National Environment Policy, 2006.

Chapter 11

Free Trade

Antithesis to Sustainable Development?

Ashutosh Tripathi

INTRODUCTION

Open, inclusive, and diverse societies are better for business and economic growth of a country.[1] Discriminatory laws hamper economic development and threaten the business stability, which has a jeopardizing effect on the trading concerns of a country. The United Nations Development Programme (UNDP) has recognized certain global sustainable development goals that emphasize the promotion of inclusive economic growth.[2]

According to Kamel, inclusive growth refers to growth that is accessed and shared equitably by all segments of society.[3] Inclusive growth therefore emphasizes holistic economic development of a country by ensuring the inclusion of vulnerable groups of the society. The process of excluding such groups from economic development is known as social exclusion. WHO defines social exclusion as consisting of dynamic, multidimensional processes driven by unequal power relationships interacting across four main dimensions—economic, political, social, and cultural—and at different levels, including individual, household, group, community, country, and global levels.[4] It can be categorized into exclusion based on economic disadvantages and exclusion based on cultural factors. Exclusion is economic when people are denied equal access to resource allocation, whereas it is cultural when the norms of a particular group are considered to be in conflict with the established norms of the society, thereby posing a threat to their group identity. Excluding a particular social group from the economic opportunities precludes full realization of their economic potential, thereby keeping economic growth slow and stagnant.

There are complaints that free trade forces painful economic adjustments for workers and their families because of closure of factories and layoffs.

Charges have also been made that free trade has led to overuse of natural resources, polluted water and air, made workplaces less safe, lessened the number of jobs, and depressed wage levels. Multinational corporations are accused of violating labor and human rights by colluding with the politicians of the host countries, eliminating small family firms, and having no regard for consumer protection.[5]

The goal of development is to improve the well-being of every member of the society. People are not mere tools that can be exploited to produce greater wealth for limited elites, but are the pivot around which development ought to circumscribe. True development roots out and corrects the causes of poverty and generates greater social justice. There has been considerable debate as to whether the right to development can be regarded as a human right. The issue was settled by the Vienna Declaration and Program of Action in 1993 and by subsequent reaffirmations at various intergovernmental conferences since then.

WORLD TRADE ORGANIZATION— A DEVELOPMENT PLATFORM

Development is defined in the preamble to the Vienna declaration as a "comprehensive economic, social, cultural and political process, which aims at the constant improvement of the wellbeing of the entire population and of all individuals, on the basis of their active, free and meaningful participation in development in and the fair distribution of benefits resulting therefrom." The process of development that is recognized as a human right is one "in which all human rights and fundamental freedoms can be fully realized," consequent to the constant improvement of well-being that is the objective of development. Looking at the right to development adds value to the already recognized (economic, social, cultural, civil, and political) rights involved in human development. This means that it not only focuses on realization of those rights individually, but their realization together, taking into account their effects on each other, both with regard to a particular time and over a period of time. It also means that any improvement in the right to development would imply that the realization of some rights has improved while no other right is violated or deteriorated.[6]

The rapid increase in global trade and international integration has accelerated the pace of economic change, causing painful economic adjustments. The workings of World Trade Organization (WTO) have crossed trade barriers overruling all regulatory policies enacted for health, safety, labor laws, and the environment. All those who are disturbed by vigorous changes are raising legitimate concerns in ways commerce and social values are dealt.

To them, it appears sovereignty has shifted from their elected representatives at home to faceless and unaccountable bureaucrats at corporate headquarters in foreign lands.

In this scenario, the following questions generally arise: Why do we need free trade? Do the economic realities of developing countries qualify as free trade? Has free trade caused an adverse impact on the employment, health, and environment? Has the WTO eroded a country's sovereignty?

REASONS FOR RAPID INCREASE IN FREE TRADE

Free trade means that countries can import and export goods without any tariff barriers or other nontariff barriers to trade.

Essentially, free trade enables lower prices for consumers, increased exports, benefits from economies of scale, and a greater choice of goods.

International trade has increased rapidly because costs and facilities that were previously restricting international trade are now much lower, such as transport and transportation costs, transaction costs, and costs imposed by the government. By specializing in goods where countries have a lower opportunity cost, there can be an increase in economic welfare for all countries. Free trade enables countries to specialize in those goods where they have a comparative advantage[7].

If countries can specialize in certain goods, they can benefit from economic advantage and lesser costs overall. It will be much more beneficial for those industries that have high fixed costs or that require high levels of investment.[8] The benefits of economies of scale will ultimately lead to lower prices for consumers and greater efficiency for exporting firms.

NECESSITY OF FREE TRADE

Classic Theory

The classical trade theory, which forms the basis for economic integration theory, has its origins in the literature on political economy from over two centuries ago. These theories gave the early logic that free trade could be advantageous for countries and was based on the concept of absolute advantages in production.

Adam Smith in his magnificent work *The Wealth of Nations*, first published in 1776, specified justifications for free trade, which is applicable even today. Smith explained that "All commerce that is carried on between any two countries must be advantageous to both the countries, and therefore all duties, customs, and excise should be abolished, and free commerce and liberty of exchange should be allowed with all nations."[9]

Smith's absolute advantage is determined by a simple comparison of labor productivities across countries. Nations can manufacture more quantities of goods in which they have absolute advantage with the labor time they save through international trade. Essentially, Smith argued that a firm supplying a larger market would be able to exploit more efficiencies from specialization than could a firm supplying a smaller market. International trade allows such countries to achieve a more refined division of labor and therefore reap a higher real income.[10]

Theory of Comparative Advantages

Comparative advantage is a term associated with nineteenth-century English economist David Ricardo. Ricardo considered what goods and services countries should produce, and suggested that they should specialize by allocating their scarce resources to produce goods and services for which they have a comparative cost advantage. There are two types of cost advantage—absolute and comparative.[11] Comparative advantage means that a country could find it advantageous to import certain goods even if it could itself produce those goods more efficiently than other countries. Conversely, a country would be able to export goods even if other countries could produce them more efficiently. In both cases, countries stand to benefit from trade.

But why would a country ever import goods that it could produce more efficiently than another country? The answer is comparative advantage. Ricardo stated that international trade is not driven by the absolute costs of production, but by the opportunity costs. What determines a country's comparative advantage? It has no single answer. Sometimes specialization is based on climate or natural resources, or skills and capital, or cheap labor or government promotion of a particular industry. Some sources are immutable, while others can evolve over time—based on technology, education, and workers' skills. Entrepreneurship and the business environment are also critical factors. For example, a country may have an ideal climate for producing wine, but without capital and skills necessary for production, that advantage remains unexploited.[12]

GAINS FROM TRADE

John Stuart Mill in his work *The Principles of Political Economy*[13] pointed out three principal gains from trade:

1. Direct economic advantages of foreign trade
2. Indirect effects, which are benefits of a high order
3. Economic benefits of commerce, which are surpassed in importance by effects that are intellectual and moral

DIRECT ECONOMIC ADVANTAGES

"Direct economic advantages" are gains from specialization. Mill stated that by exporting in exchange for imports, a country uses its limited productive resources (such as land, labor, and capital) more efficiently and thus achieves a higher national income. This higher national income makes the country able to afford more goods and services that would not be possible without trade. Free trade allows firms to sell in a larger market. Firms are also able to reduce the average costs of production by expanding output. These economies of scale are passed on to consumers.

Free trade also improves economic performance by increasing competition in the domestic market. This benefit comes through a change in the pricing behavior of imperfectly competitive domestic firms. Without free trade, firms with market power tend to restrict output and raise prices, thereby harming consumers while increasing their own profits. However, international competition forces these firms to behave competitively.[14] Another gain is benefit to consumers from exposure to a large variety of goods. Variety in goods is just as valuable for producers as it is for consumers. Free trade also expands the range of intermediate goods available for domestic firms to use as inputs. These inputs increase the productive efficiency of the industry that produces the final goods.[15]

GAINS IN TERMS OF PRODUCTIVITY

Mill's second gain from trade is its "indirect effects." He stated that trade improves economic performance not only by allocating a country's resources to their most efficient use, but also by making those resources more productive. Extension of the market improves the process of production. A country that produces for a larger market than its own introduces a more extended division of labor, makes greater use of machinery, and makes inventions and improvements in the process of production. Thus, trade promotes productivity growth. The higher an economy's productivity level, the higher that country's standard of living.[16]

Mill mentioned that international trade contributes to productivity gain in two ways:

1. It serves as a conduit for the transfer of foreign technologies that enhance productivity.
2. It increases competition that stimulates industries to become more efficient and improve their productivity. This forces less productive firms out of business and allows more productive firms to expand.[17]

Trade as a conduit for the transfer of foreign technologies operates in several ways. One is through the import of capital goods. Because imported capital goods embody technological advances, they enhance the economy's productivity. Trade barriers raise the prices of imported capital goods and hinder a country's ability to benefit from technologies that could raise productivity. Growth in productivity is also the result of investment in R&D. Import of foreign ideas can be a spur to productivity. Foreign research can be imported directly, or its benefits can be secured by importing goods that embody it. Countries that are open to free tree gain more from foreign R&D expenditures because trade in goods provides knowledge generated by R&D.[18]

Import of specialized intermediate goods that embody new technologies, as well as reverse engineering of such goods are sources of R&D. Developing countries, which do not conduct much R&D themselves, can benefit from R&D done elsewhere because trade makes the acquisition of new technology less costly.[19]

The second channel by which trade contributes to productivity is by forcing domestic industries to become more efficient. Trade increases competition in the domestic market, diminishing the market power of any firm and forcing it to behave competitively. Competition also stimulates firms to improve their efficiency; otherwise, they face risk to go out of business.[20]

John Stuart Mill's third and final principle was that "the economic advantages of commerce are surpassed in importance by those of its effects which are intellectual and moral."[21]

The idea of *doux commerce* observed by Montesquieu in *The Spirit of Laws* is that "commerce cures destructive prejudices."[22] Trade brings people into contact with one another and breaks down the narrow prejudices that come with insularity. Commerce forces merchants to be more responsive to customers. There is a long-standing belief that trade promotes peace among nations because two nations that trade with each other become reciprocally dependent. Most of the research affirms that there is a positive link between trade and peace.[23]

Democracies are more peaceful than autocracies. Overwhelming evidence shows that democracies rarely go to war against one another. Chile, Taiwan, South Korea, and Mexico, after being integrated into the world economy, have moved to more democratic political systems. Thus, trade contributes to peace indirectly by promoting political reforms and democratization. Trade indeed promotes democracy.[24] Countries that are more open to trade also tend to be less corrupt; trade restrictions breed corruption, particularly if bureaucracies are responsible for allocating import licenses.[25]

FREE TRADE AND THE ENVIRONMENT

It has been universally accepted that growth and human happiness, which are necessary for the well-being of the society, cannot be achieved without the preservation and protection of the environment. The twin concerns for nature and for humankind are indivisible, and are a part of a single ecosystem, such that when harm is inflicted on one part, that is, nature or the environment, it ultimately harms the other, that is, humans.

Environmentalists are the most vocal critics of free trade who worry about its impact on the environment. Their argument is that free trade will result in more economic activities that ultimately leads to economic degradation. Environmental degradation is the deterioration of the environment through depletion of resources such as soil, water, and air; the destruction of ecosystems; and the extinction of wildlife.

A couple of questions arise: Is there a relationship between trade and the environment? Does trade lead to environmental damage or does it actually benefit it?

Protectionists of free trade say that environmental damage results from poor environmental policies, not from free trade. Degradation has resulted from an inappropriate use of natural resources. The overuse of these resources has happened because of a lack of well-defined property rights.

When property rights are not well established—meaning no one has ownership rights and control over a resource—then resources are open to all for access. It leads to exploitation beyond the optimal social level. Thus, environmental problems stem from the failure to clearly establish and enforce private or public property rights.[26]

Environmentalists opposes free trade on another ground that it will deteriorate fisheries by overfishing. However, sometimes markets gives solutions for sustainability. For example, some great successes in fisheries management have come from giving individual fishers a "property right" to a share of each year's harvest. Once those rights are established and firmly enforced, fishers have incentives to boost future years' harvests—because an abundant fishery increases the value of their "property"—and also to keep an eye on their neighbors to ensure that they are not taking too much of a shared resource. As it turns out, giving individuals the incentive to act both as stewards and enforcers can be a pretty effective combination.[27]

For dealing with the issue of the climate change, one method is to levy tax on a consumption basis with compensations sought from developed countries in terms of financial aid or generous initial carbon emission quotas.

Ultimately, the world is best off with a uniform carbon price regime administered on a production basis. An initial step is to tax on a consumption basis to help motivate a strong mitigation response by developed countries.

CONCLUSIONS

The benefits of free trade are substantial. The higher real incomes that come with free trade not just allow consumption of more goods, but also help people to afford better food, better access to healthcare and medicines, better education, better affordable housing, and better technologies that improve the environment. Free trade is beneficial as it allows a country to take advantage of the opportunity to trade. However, free trade is not the only determinant of a country's economic prosperity. Free trade is not a magic trick that can solve all economic problems. Many other economic problems such as stable macroeconomic policies, the rule of law, and the protection of property rights enable the market mechanism to function properly, and they are the preconditions for reaping the full benefits of international trade.[28] The thinking that free trade is dangerous for the environment is flawed on many grounds. First, there is little historical evidence of polluting industries migrating to countries where environmental standards are lax. While many developing countries are experiencing rapid industrial growth, this reflects the economic stage that they are going through, rather than environmentally induced migration. Polluting industries, which spend heavily on controls, remain concentrated in the developed countries.

NOTES

1. *The Economic and Business Case for Global LGB&T Inclusion*, Open for Business, 4, available at https://www.open-for-business.org/wp-content/uploads/2016/01/Brunswick_Open_for_Business_full.pdf, last seen on 17/01/2019.
2. Sustainable development goals, UNDP, Goal 8 available at http://www.undp.org/content/undp/en/home/sustainable-development-goals.html, last seen on 17/01/2019.
3. *Linking Inclusive Growth and Trade and Investment*, www.unescap.org, http://www.unescap.org/sites/default/files/Linking%20Inclusive%20Growth%20and%20Trade%20and%20Investment,%20Identifying%20Transmission%20Channels.PDF, last seen on 19/11/2016.
4. J. Reinaud. Trade, Competitiveness and Carbon Leakages: Challenges and Opportunities. *Energy, Environment and Development Programme Paper*, Department for International Development, Chatham House, London, 09/01.
5. Nader & Ralph, The Case Against Free Trade: GATT, NAFTA, and the Globalization of Corporate power I (Earth Island Press. ed. 1993).

6. Cullet, Philippe "Definition of an Environmental Right in Human Rights, Context," International Environmental Law Research Center, p. 2. Available online at http://www.ielrc.org/content/a9502.pdf, Accessed 6 January, 2019.

7. https://www.economicshelp.org/trade2/benefits_free_trade/

8. Carroll A.B and Shabana, K.M., "The Business Case for Corporate Social Responsibility: A Review of Concepts, Research and Practice", *International Journal of Management Reviews* 85–105, 85, 2010

9. Adam Smith, Lectures on Jurisprudence 511–514 (Clarendon Press ed., 1901.

10. Douglas A. Irwin, Against the Tide: An Intellectual History of Free Trade 214 (1st ed., 1996.

11. Ruffin & Roy J, *David Ricardo's Discovery of Comparative Advantage,* 34 HPE 727, 727–748, 2000.

12. Ibid.

13. John Stuart Mill, Principles of Political Economy 580 (Longman Publisher 25th 1990.

14. www.fao.org/docrep/v4360E08.htm (Last visited on 10/07/2019).

15. John Stuart Mill, Principles of Political Economy 580 (Longman Publisher 25th 1990.

16. John Stuart Mill, Principles of Political Economy 580 (Longman Publisher 25th 1990.

17. Mill (1909), 583.

18. https://wirtzbill.com/2016/10/11/the-essence-of-free-market-environmentalism/ accessed on 20.8.2019.

19. Ibid.

20. See Sivadasan Jagadeesh, "Barriers to Entry and Productivity: Micro-evidence from Indian Manufacturing Sector Reforms," Working Paper, University of Chicago Graduate School of Business, November, 2003

21. Mill (1909), 581.

22. Montesquieu, The Spirit of Laws 338 (A. M. Cohler trans., Cambridge University Press rev. ed 1904.

23. Bruce Russett, Michael L. Berbaum & Oneal, John, *Causes of Peace: Democracy, Interdependence, and International Organizations*, 47 ISQ 91, 91–271, 1895.

24. B. Peter Rosendorff, Edward D.; Helen V. Milner & Mansfield, *Free Trade: Democracies, Autocracies, and International Trade*, 94 APS Rev. 21, 21–31 , 2000.

25. Ades, Alberto & Rafael Di Tella, *Rents, Competition, and Corruption*, 89 AE Rev. 982, 982–983, 2000.

26. The legitimate objection that efficient global trade in permits requires effective monitoring of emissions—so permits sold are not replaced by extra unrecorded emissions—is a separate issue, albeit one that might compound other incentive concerns. All effective emission control policies rely on some monitoring technology.

27. https://www.sightline.org/2011/02/21/the-coase-isnt-clear/ accessed on 20.08.2019.

28. Ibid.

Chapter 12

Are Organic Foods Truly Environment Friendly?

Jayshree Sharma

INTRODUCTION

Access to food is an inalienable right. Although food production has increased in recent years, particularly in developing countries, more than one billion people suffer from chronic malnutrition. Models predict that average global temperatures will increase between 1.8 degrees and 4.0 degrees Celsius at the end of the twenty-first century and will be accompanied by random alterations, both temporal and geographic, in precipitation patterns. Agriculture is a sector where mitigation action has strong potential cobenefits for sustainable development—food security, poverty reduction among the 70 percent of the poor living in rural areas, environmental services, and climate change adaptation, that is, improving agroecosystem resilience. With the growth of the health and wellness industry, organic food has emerged as preferred food among the health-conscious people. But navigating the maze of organic food labels, benefits, and claims can be confusing. One might have questions regarding organic food and whether it is really better for one's mental and physical health.

MEANING OF "ORGANIC" FOOD

Organic is primarily a labeling term used on various food products formulated through specific methods and practices approved by the US Department of Agriculture (USDA) and its National Organics Program (NOP). The focus centers on farming practices and food production steps that are monitored and controlled in order to decrease risk of food contamination and improve food quality.[1]

The USDA sets, defines, and regulates the use and meaning of "organic" on food labels pertaining to raw or processed agricultural products and ingredients that have been

(a) Organically grown (farmed), and
(b) Handled in compliance with the standards of April 2001, which have been fully enforced since October 2002.

These standards pertaining to organic food prohibit the use of

- Most synthetic fertilizers and pesticides
- Sewer sludge fertilizers
- Genetic engineering
- Growth hormones
- Irradiation
- Antibiotics
- Artificial ingredients
- Many synthetic additives

Organically grown crops are certified as such when the following criteria get fulfilled:

- The crop must be produced on land without the use of synthetic substances (pesticides, herbicides, fertilizers) except those provided in the standards.
- The land must be free of prohibited substances for three years prior to harvest.
- The land must have defined boundaries and buffer zones preventing the crop to have contact with prohibited substances from adjoining land.
- Soil fertility and crop nutrient management must be done in a manner to improve soil conditions, minimize soil erosion, and prevent contamination of crops, soil, or water by plant nutrients, pathogenic organisms, or heavy metals.

Management methods may include

- Use of crop rotation
- Use of composted animal manure with specified carbon to nitrogen ratios and temperature readings
- Use of uncomposted plant materials

Seeds, seedlings, and planting stock used for crops must be organically grown except as provided in the law. Crop-related pest problems must be controlled by mechanical and physical methods including

- Introduction of predators or parasites of the pest species
- Development of habitat for natural enemies of the pests
- Use of lures, traps, and repellants

Weed problems must be controlled by

- Mulching
- Hand weeding and mechanical cultivation
- Mowing
- Flame, heat, or electricity
- Grazing livestock
- Plastic or synthetic mulches that are removed at the end of the harvest

Disease problems must be controlled by

- Management practices to suppress the spread of disease
- Application of nonsynthetic biological, botanical, or mineral inputs

There are also criteria for organically grown meat, poultry, eggs, and dairy, including conditions such as

- Livestock must be fed rations composed of agricultural products, pasture, and forage that are organically produced and, if applicable, handled.
- Prohibitions regarding animal feed include
  - Administering of animal drugs in the absence of illness
  - Use of hormones to promote growth
  - Use of supplements in amounts above those for adequate nutrition
  - Use of mammal or poultry slaughter byproducts for feed
  - Excessive use of feed additives
  - Routine administration of synthetic parasiticides
- The producer must provide conditions to maintain and promote the health and welfare of livestock including
  - Sufficient nutritional feed rations
  - Appropriate housing, pasture, sanitation conditions
  - Conditions allowing for exercise, freedom of movement, and minimal stress for the animals
  - Administration of veterinary care

- Origin of livestock
  - Organic livestock must be from livestock under continuous organic management from the last third of gestation or hatching.
  - Organic poultry must be under continuous organic management beginning no later than the second day of life.
  - Milk or milk products must be from animals that have been under continuous organic management beginning no later than one year prior to milk production.

Thus, organic production is managed with the intent to integrate cultural, biological, and mechanical practices to promote the cycling of resources, ecological balance, and biodiversity. These practices help to protect the soil and groundwater, provide health-promoting conditions for animals, and ultimately help promote the health of the consumer. Mechanical or biological methods are used to process an organically produced agricultural product for the purpose of retarding spoilage or otherwise preparing the agricultural product for market. This includes acceptable processing aids and ingredients, appropriate packaging materials and labeling, cleaning methods, waste disposal, and pest management at processing facilities.

CERTIFICATION OF ORGANIC PRODUCTS

When the US Congress passed its 1990 Farm Bill, a congressional mandate was included in the bill (Title 21) instructing the USDA to create a national legal definition of organic that would provide reliable, uniform, and enforceable standards for any food bearing the term "organic." The development of organic standards was designed to provide consumers with a food-labeling process that they could trust to reflect high-quality standards in food production. Certification is the process by which the consumer is assured that a product marketed as "organic" is in compliance with production and handling requirements set forth in USDA regulations. All producers of organic food, livestock, and fiber crops, as well as handlers or organic products must be certified (except growers who gross less than US$5000 and retailers).

Growers and handlers first submit an organic farm plan or an organic handling plan to a USDA-accredited certifying agent detailing their growing and handling methods. Then, on-site inspections are conducted by certifying agents to verify submitted plans. To qualify as organic, methods and materials used in production must meet standards set in the new regulations. Moreover, clear documentation of methods and materials must be kept. In addition, there must be a paper trail tracing a product back to its production site, enabling verification of production methods and materials.

IDENTIFICATION OF ORGANIC FOODS

Organic foods can be identified through four different types of label information:

i. The least common but most reliable method is the claim "100 percent organic" on the front of any certified organic food. This claim requires all ingredients in the food (without exceptions) to be produced in compliance with organic regulations.
ii. Much more common in the marketplace is the presence of the USDA organic logo on the front of a certified organic food. Certified organic foods bearing the USDA logo must contain at least 95 percent (by weight or fluid volume, excluding water and salt) approved ingredients. Up to 5 percent of the food may contain prohibited ingredients, if those ingredients are not available in an organic form.
iii. A third way to identify certified organic foods is through "Made With" labeling claims on the front of the packaging. For example, a certified organic pasta sauce may say "Made with Organic Tomatoes" on the front of the packaging. In the case of "Made With" claims, at least 70 percent of all ingredients (by weight or fluid volume, excluding water and salt) must be in compliance with all organic regulations. As such, 30 percent of ingredients may contain prohibited ingredients, provided that those ingredients are not available in an organic form. Just like use of the organic logo, however, there is one important caveat to this "30 percent" rule for certified organic foods showing "Made With" claims: the 30 percent "nonorganic" portion of the food ingredients must not be genetically engineered, fertilized with sewage sludge, or irradiated.
iv. A final way to identify certified organic foods is through individual ingredient entries on the ingredients list on the side or back of the packaging. If a food contains less than 70 percent of its ingredients (by weight or fluid volume, excluding water and salt) as organic, no labeling claims are permitted on the front of the packaging. However, individual organic ingredients that comply with USDA regulations may be listed on the side or back of the packaging in the product's ingredients list.

INDIA AS AN EMERGING MARKET FOR ORGANIC FOOD PRODUCTION

On January 1, 2019, India joined a group of roughly fifty countries that mandates clear and legible consumer-friendly labeling for organic products.

Henceforth, manufacturing, packing, marketing, distribution, or import of any organic food is prohibited unless the package is labeled with complete and accurate information regarding the organic status of the product. Organic products should carry a government-quality assurance mark and the new Jaivik Bharat logo, which is meant to distinguish organic products from non-organic ones.[2]

The new regulations could transform a nascent and important market segment in significant ways. In addition to businesses that sell organic products, India also has an estimated 800,000 organic farmers—the largest in the world. In addition, the regulations could minimize the pesticide residue to zero levels, which is also a major issue in Indian organic products.

Regulations are needed to control and monitor Indian organic products, as it is difficult to trace whether a food item that is claimed to be organic is actually free of pesticides all along the value chain. Besides, organic foods that are marketed through direct sales to the end consumer by small producers or producer organizations (annual turnover less than □12 lakhs) are currently exempted from stringent inspection.

The USDA has caught several products—including ones exported from India—with fake organic certificates. For instance, according to the USDA, Nainital-based Indian Herbs Extraction, Kannauj-based Lala Jagdish Prasad & Co., and Tamil Nadu–based Green India Herbs have been caught with fraudulent organic certificates in the past. Since organic labeling is at a more advanced stage in many other countries, export-oriented products from India have been under a regime of rules for some time. Earlier, USDA had suspended the licenses of New Delhi–based Aryan International and the Lucknow branch of Organic India Pvt. Ltd. Four more Indian companies have surrendered the licenses which allowed them to sell products claimed to be organic in the US.

The most common fraudulent actions include mislabeling of nonorganic agricultural products as organic, for example, using the USDA organic seal without being certified organic, using the word "organic" on the front of the package when the ingredients are organic but the entire product is not certified organic. Another fraudulent action is using the USDA organic seal on a multi-ingredient product that only has a small number of organic ingredients (less than 95 percent of the total product). Using fraudulent documents to market, label, or sell nonorganic agricultural products as organic is punishable by fines of up to US$11,000 for each violation.

It is necessary to ensure that nonorganic and organic agricultural products produced for human consumption meet food safety requirements and pass inspections. Both nonorganically grown and organically grown foods should be safe to consume. In India, most companies in the organic food business are located in tier 1 and tier 2 cities.

The Indian Council for Research on International Economic Relations (ICRIER) in 2017 surveyed over 100 companies in the sector, located in major cities. According to the ICRIER report, nearly all the firms pointed out that there is a prevalence of fraud and malpractices in the organic business. These malpractices can be of different types, the most serious of which is mixing organic products with conventional products. Given India's realities, that could hurt certain well-intentioned players. A Ministry of Agriculture survey in 2015 had found traces of pesticides in samples collected from various outlets across India, including organic ones. Litigating such finer points on quality would become a significant issue for the regulators.

THE HARMFUL EFFECTS OF ORGANIC FARMING: CLIMATE CHANGE

International researchers from the Chalmers University of Technology looked at the impact of organic and conventional food production on the climate. The team found that organic crops produce much lower yields, mainly because chemical fertilizers are not used to boost the crops. As a result, in order to produce the same amount of organic food as conventional crops, much more land is required.

In a study published in *Nature*, a team of researchers found that organic peas farmed in Sweden have about a 50 percent bigger impact on the climate than peas farmed using conventional methods. For other foodstuffs, there was an even bigger difference, with Swedish winter wheat being close to 70 percent.

The researchers also evaluated the effect of greater land use on carbon dioxide emissions, which they call "Carbon Opportunity Cost." They took into account how much carbon is stored in forests that will be released as a result of deforestation, when assessing the impact of organic food on the environment and arrived at the following conclusion: organic food has a bigger impact on the climate than conventional food, owing to the extra carbon dioxide emissions produced through the deforestation required as a result of less-efficient organic production.[3]

"The greater land-use in organic farming leads indirectly to higher carbon dioxide emissions, thanks to deforestation," Stefan Wirsenius, one of the authors of the study, said in a press release. "The world's food production is governed by international trade, so how we farm in Sweden influences deforestation in the tropics. If we use more land for the same amount of food, we contribute indirectly to bigger deforestation elsewhere in the world."

The team said that the findings apply to organic meat production too, for example, organic dairy cows that are fed organic grains. "The type of food is often much more important," Wirsenius says. "Eating organic beans or organic chicken is much better for the climate than to eat conventionally produced beef." While organic farming can be better for farm animal welfare, "when it comes to the climate impact, our study shows that organic food is a much worse alternative."

Another study by German researchers came to a similar conclusion that organic farming is inefficient. They compared what they considered to be a typical organic diet with a typical standard diet on two measures—carbon footprint and overall land use.[4] They found that the carbon footprints of organic and conventional diets were same, with no significant difference. However, this includes the fact that the conventional diet contains 45 percent more meat, and meat consumption is the main driver of the carbon footprint. Therefore, if you eliminate the meat variable, organic produce has a much higher carbon footprint than conventional produce, but this higher organic carbon footprint is offset by reduced meat consumption. Further, the organic diet (which again includes the meat variable) uses 40 percent more land than the conventional diet. That is a huge difference. That is in line with other studies which show organic farming uses 20–40 percent more land than conventional farming.

ALTERNATIVE FARMING PRACTICES AND WORKING

With the world's population nearing 7.5 billion—and global prosperity and the desire for more resource-intensive foods rising steeply too—it is clear that farming needs to become more productive. One way of meeting future food needs could be hydroponics—growing plants without soil and instead using a nutrient-rich solution to deliver water and minerals to their roots. It is already being used to increase farming outputs and grow plants in habitats that would not normally sustain them.[5]

Despite sounding like something out of science fiction, it is nothing new. The Aztecs built floating farms around the island city of Tenochtitlan, and the explorer Marco Polo wrote about seeing floating gardens during his travels through thirteenth-century China. By the 1930s, Pan American Airways had established a hydroponic farm on a remote Pacific island to allow its flights to top up with food en route to Asia.

Today, farmers are slowly increasing their use of hydroponics, and researchers are looking more closely at how it could solve future food problems. In the future, some of its applications could be out of this world.

Hydroponics is described as the process of growing plants or crops in water without the use of soil, while organic farming involves choosing not to use inorganic fertilizers in the growing process. In order to be considered certified organic, a plant can be grown using only unrefined minerals. The issue, however, is that a number of these unrefined minerals, although natural, can be toxic in nature. For example, mined phosphate contains excessive amounts of fluoride and radioactive radium, both of which can be extremely harmful to humans. Even the use of organic fertilizers such as manure poses the risk of E-coli and salmonella outbreaks. On the other hand, hydroponic plants are grown in nutrient solutions usually indoors, completely free from chemicals and pesticides, making them much safer. Plants also grow quicker in hydroponic farming thanks to the controlled environment. In turn, the crop yield is significantly increased, leading to more production from the same amount of space.

There is a growing body of evidence that seems to indicate that closed-loop water recirculation systems such as hydroponics and aquaponics (the coupling of fish production with vegetable production) may in fact offer an advantage over soil-based organic growing since the water chemistry of both these systems can be manipulated to boost natural plant bioactives for health benefits. Thus, plants grown through hydroponics have better nutritional value. It has been proven that the vitamin content is 50 percent more in hydroponically grown plants as compared to conventional ones.[6]

Dubai-based Pegasus Agriculture Group highlights that the similarities between organic farming and hydroponics boil down to the fact that both farming practices aim to protect the Earth's fragile environment. However, there are some ways in which hydroponics manages to triumph over organic agriculture in environmental protection endeavors. It uses 90 percent less water than traditional agriculture, hence conserving the world's most important resource from depletion. It also manages to prevent soil from degradation, preserving valuable topsoil for plants that cannot be hydroponically grown.

Given all the added benefits of hydroponics, the bottom line when it comes to the organic farming and hydroponics debate is the fact that hydroponics manages to be better than the former in numerous ways, making it a considerably more attractive agricultural method of growing plants.

In conventional agriculture, soil supports a plant's roots—helping it to remain upright—and provides it with the nutrients it needs to grow. In hydroponics, plants are artificially supported, and a solution of ionic compounds provides nutrients instead.

The thinking behind this is simple. Plant growth is often limited by environmental factors. By applying a nutrient solution directly to a plant's roots in a controlled environment, a farmer can ensure that the plant always has an optimal supply of water and nutrients. This nutritional efficiency makes the plant more productive.

The solution can be delivered in a number of ways. A plant may be

- placed in an inert substance (such as volcanic glass perlite or rock wool) and have its roots periodically flooded with solution
- placed in an inert substance and rained on by a solution dripper
- suspended with its roots in the air, with these then sprayed with solution mist
- placed on a slightly sloping film that allows solution to trickle over its roots

All of these systems are mechanized in one way or another, usually using either a pump or a mister to deliver the solution from a separate store. The solution is also usually aerated to ensure that the roots are supplied with adequate oxygen. Mineral absorption requires energy and is powered by respiration.

The cons of hydroponics are that running and maintaining a hydroponic system can be complex. Plants require over a dozen essential nutrients, with the optimal amount of each varying according to species, growth stage, and local conditions, such as water hardness.[7]

Moreover, some nutrients get absorbed quicker than others, which can cause a build-up of positive or negative ions in the solution, affecting its pH. This can then hinder the absorption of other nutrients—partly because their uptake is pH-dependent, but also because excess quantities of some will prevent the uptake of others. Too much ammonia, for instance, decreases calcium uptake. Too much calcium prevents magnesium absorption.

CONCLUSIONS

Organic foods have emerged as a healthier alternative to conventional food products. As stringent international standards are adapted to organic products, they ensure good health and longevity. Organic farming has emerged as a lucrative sector for Indian farmers and other food producers as they are highly in demand. On the downside, organic farming is less productive than conventional farming as it requires substantial land compared to conventional farming in the absence of pesticides, sewer sludge fertilizers, genetic engineering, growth hormones, irradiation, antibiotics, artificial ingredients, and many synthetic additives, and leads to mass deforestation and thereby increases the carbon footprint.

The organic farming brand is counterproductive. It is based on the ideology of being Earth-friendly and creates a false dichotomy. In comparison to organic food practices, other alternate farming practices such as hydroponics rely less on land and thereby minimize the need for deforestation. While it has its own drawbacks, it creates a much lower carbon footprint compared to organic farming methods.

As the human population is expected to further rise in the coming decades, it is necessary to find new food resources, but not at the cost of natural resources. Proper planning and management ensures distribution of food without compromising in terms of quality or carbon footprint. Studies from European countries indicate the ill effects of organic farming at its present stage. Therefore, there is a serious need for Indian farmers and horticulturists, as well as the industries connected with organic food to take notice of climate change and look at alternate farming practices like hydroponics as well. Care for the environment includes supporting any practice that minimizes land use in food production and ensures ecological balance.

NOTES

1. George Mateljan Foundation, *Everything you need to know about organic foods*, accessed at <http://www.whfoods.com/genpage.php?tname=faq&dbid=17> on 29th January, 2019 at 10:00 a.m.
2. Neetu Chandra Sharma, *The new food factories: Inside India's organics trade,* accessed at <https://www.livemint.com/Industry/RoxfUb6XwV2Qbq7qDaLhqL/The-new-food-factories-Inside-Indias-organics-trade.html> on 28th January, 2019 at 11:00 a.m.
3. Chrissy Sexton, *Organic food is actually much worse for the environment,* accessed at <https://www.earth.com/news/organic-food-worse-environment/ > on 30th January, 2019 at 10:05 a.m.
4. Steven Novella, *Organic Farming Is Bad for the Environment*, accessed at <https://www.earth.com/news/organic-food-worse-environment/> on 30th January, 2019 at 10:09 a.m.
5. Big Picture, Hydroponics and the future of farming, accessed at <https://bigpictureeducation.com/hydroponics-and-future-farming> on 30th January, 2019 at 10:15 a.m.
6. Pegasus Agriculture: *"Hydroponics a more superior option to organic farming"*, accessed at <https://www.hortidaily.com/article/35604/Hydroponics-a-more-superior-option-to-organic-farming/> on 30th January, 2019 at 10:18 a.m.
7. Big Picture, Hydroponics and the future of farming, accessed at <https://bigpictureeducation.com/hydroponics-and-future-farming> on 30th January, 2019 at 10:15 a.m.

REFERENCES

Big Picture, Hydroponics and the future of farming, accessed at https://bigpictureeducation.com/hydroponics-and-future-farming.

George Mateljan Foundation, *Everything you need to know about organic foods*, accessed at < http://www.whfoods.com/genpage.php?tname=faq&dbid=17>.

Novella, Steven *Organic Farming Is Bad for the Environment*, accessed at <https://www.earth.com/news/organic-food-worse-environment/>.

Pegasus Agriculture: *"Hydroponics a more superior option to organic farming"*, accessed at <https://www.hortidaily.com/article/35604/Hydroponics-a-more-superior-option-to-organic-farming/>.

Sexton, Chrissy *Organic food is actually much worse for the environment,* accessed at https://www.earth.com/news/organic-food-worse-environment/; https://commerce.gov.in/writereaddata/uploadedfile/MOC_636016030908099515_Indian_Organic_Sector_Vision_2025_15-6-2016.pdf; https://www.researchgate.net/publication/227207095_Alternative_Farming_Techniques_for_Sustainable_Food_Production.

Sharma, Neetu Chandra *The new food factories: Inside India's organics trade*, accessed at <https://www.livemint.com/Industry/RoxfUb6XwV2Qbq7qDaLhqL/The-new-food-factories-Inside-Indias-organics-trade.html>.

Chapter 13

Green India

A Legal Perspective

Aadarsh Anand and Dalima Arora

INTRODUCTION

The environment encompasses all living and nonliving things occurring naturally on earth. The Supreme Court recognizes environment as a difficult word to define. Its normal meaning relates to the surroundings, but obviously, that is a concept which is relatable to whatever object it is which is surrounded. Environmental degradation is a polycentric and multifaceted problem affecting the human existence. It is interesting to note that natural resources which had been literally untouched in the past are now being exhausted so rapidly because of industrialization that it has led to scarcity of some resources. The overexploitation of the resources for industrialization and urbanization, explosion of population, disruption of natural ecological balances, and destruction of a multitude of animal and plant species for economic reasons have focused our attention on the need for environmental protection and ecological preservation. An expected 60 percent of developed land experiences soil erosion, waterlogging, and salinity. Additionally, it is assessed that in the vicinity of 4.7 and 12 billion tons of topsoil are lost every year from soil erosion. From 1947 to 2002, normal yearly per capita water accessibility declined by about 70 percent to 1822 cubic meters, and the overexploitation of groundwater is severe in Haryana, Punjab, and Uttar Pradesh. The different types of pollution—viz. water pollution, air pollution, land pollution, noise pollution, and so on—that takes place in the environment are well understood and need not be explained. The release of the toxic wastes on the land or throwing of garbage has led to land pollution. Unprecedented changes in climate, resulting in floods, droughts, and storms, are responsible for major natural disasters, the worst of which are famines, epidemics, and immigration. Increase in global warming has been melting glaciers and receding snowlines. The world is entering a phase wherein the environment would get tangled in a barrel of degradation, affecting the availability of water, food, and energy in a big way.

The word "environment" relates to surroundings. It includes virtually everything. It can be can defined as anything which may be treated as covering the physical surroundings that are common to all of us, including air, space, land, water, plants, and wildlife.[1] According to the Webster's Dictionary, environment is defined as the "aggregate of all the external conditions and influences affecting the life and development of an organism."[2] Section 2(a) of the Environment (Protection) Act, 1986 defines environment as something that "includes water, air and land and the inter-relationship which exists among and between water, air and land, and human beings, other living creatures, plants, micro-organism and property."

ENVIRONMENTAL LEGISLATION IN INDIA

The Stockholm Declaration of 1972 was perhaps the first real effort to monitor and safeguard the human environment at the international level. As a result of this declaration, the states were required to have authoritative measures to secure and enhance the environment. The Indian Parliament too embedded two articles—48A and 51A—in the Constitution of India in 1976.[3] Article 48A of the Constitution appropriately guides that the state should attempt to secure and enhance the environment and protect forests and wildlife of the nation.

Additionally, proviso (g) of Article 51A forces an obligation on each resident of India, to secure and enhance the common habitat, including forests, lakes, waterways, and wildlife, and to have empathy for living animals. The total impact of Articles 48A and 51A(g) is, by all accounts, that both the state and citizens are under a constitutional commitment to ration, see, secure, and enhance the environment. Each era owes an obligation to the succeeding eras to create and save the regular assets of the country in the most ideal way.[4] The expression "ensure and enhance" showing up in both Articles 48A and 51A(g) appears to suggest a confirmed government action to enhance the nature of the environment and not simply to save the environment in its corrupted shape.

Aside from the constitutional mandate to ensure and enhance the environment, there are numerous legislations regarding the matter. Some of the more important of these for our motivation are as follows:

- Water (Prevention and Control of Pollution) Act, 1974
- Water (Prevention and Control of Pollution) Cess Act, 1977
- Air (Prevention and Control of Pollution) Act, 1981

- Environment (Protection) Act, 1986Public Liability Insurance Act, 1991
- National Environment Tribunal Act, 1995
- National Environment Appellate Authority Act, 1997
- Wildlife (Protection) Act, 1972
- Forest (Conservation) Act, 1980

The Water Act deals with the prevention and control of water pollution and the maintenance or increase in the health of water bodies. The act restricts any toxic, harmful, or dirtying matter from going into any stream or well. The act paved the way for the development of the Central Pollution Control Board (CPCB) and state pollution control board (SPCBs). New ventures are required to obtain the endorsement of these boards before releasing any effluents or sewage into water bodies. No individual, without the prior assent of the boards, should bring into utilization a new or changed outlet for the release of sewage or effluents into a stream, well, sewer, or on land. The assent of the boards might likewise be required for proceeding with the current release of sewage or effluents into a stream, well, sewer, or on land.

In the Ganga water pollution case,[5] the owners of a few tanneries near Kanpur were releasing effluents from their factories in the river Ganga without setting up essential treatment plants. The Supreme Court held that the money-related limit of the tanneries ought to be considered as immaterial while expecting them to set up essential treatment plants. The court ordered to stop the running of these tanneries and additionally not to let out effluents from the tanneries either straightforwardly or in a roundabout way into Ganga without subjecting the effluents first to a changeless process by setting up essential treatment plants as affirmed by the SPCB. The Water (Prevention and Control of Pollution) Cess Act, 1977 is aimed at collecting a cess on water used by people running certain businesses to increase the assets of the CPCB and SPCBs constituted for the prevention and control of water pollution. The argument is to collect the money from those whose activities cause pollution and who must bear the costs of the upkeep and running of such boards. The enterprises may apply for a refund to the tune of 25 percent[6] if they set up a treatment plant for sewage and effluents. The Air Act is intended to counteract, control, and reduce air pollution. The real wellsprings of air pollution are ventures, vehicles, residential flames, and so on. Air pollution adversely affects the heart and lungs in humans, and reacts with hemoglobin in the blood. The Air Act characterizes an air toxin as any "strong, fluid or vaporous substance incorporating commotion show in the air in such focus as might be or have a tendency to be harmful to individuals or other living animals or plants or property or environment." The act states that without the prior assent of the SPCB, no individual should construct or run any mechanical plant in an air-pollution control zone. The CPCB and SPCBs constituted under the Water Act might likewise wield the power and capacities under the Air Act. The principal goal of the boards under the Air Act is to enhance the quality of air and to avert, control, and lessen air pollution in the nation. It is explicitly mentioned that people running industries should not allow air contamination in excess of standards set by the boards.

In Delhi, the public transport framework, including transport and maneuvers, is working on a solitary fuel CNG mode on the headings given by the Supreme Court.[7] Initially, there was considerable resistance from transport unions and taxi administrators. Later, they themselves understood that the utilization of CNG is environment friendly as well as cost-effective. Noise has been considered as an air toxin in the Air Act. Sound becomes noise when it causes inconvenience or aggravation. There are many wellsprings of noise pollution such as factories, vehicles, and careless use of amplifiers at events, religious functions, religious spots, and so on. The utilization of loudspeakers during celebrations, winning celebrations by groups during recreational activities, and other such events causes both noise and air pollution. The Air Act aims to avoid and control both these types of pollution.

The Environment (Protection) Act, 1986 was enacted to protect the environment and to forestall, control, and reduce environmental pollution. The act was an immediate outcome of the Bhopal Gas Tragedy. The expression "environment" has been characterized to incorporate water, air, and land, and the relationships that exist among and between water, air, and land, and individuals, other living animals, plants, microorganisms, and property. The definition is sufficiently broad to incorporate in its domain every single living animal, plant, and microorganism, as well as their association with water, air, and land. The act has given tremendous power to the Central Government to bring measures for planning and executing countrywide programs for the prevention, control, and reduction of environmental pollution. It enables the government to set standards for the environment, emanation or release of environmental contaminations; to direct mechanical areas; to endorse method for overseeing dangerous substances, to set up shields for avoiding mishaps; and to gather and spread data with respect to environmental pollution. Any repudiation of the arrangements of the Act, standards, requests or bearings made thereunder is culpable with detainment for a term which may stretch out to five years or with fine up to one lakh rupees or with both. The Act is an "umbrella" enactment intended to give a frame work to Central Government coordination of the activities of different Central and State specialists built up under past laws, for example, the Water Act and the Air Act[8].

The Indian Parliament passed the Public Liability Insurance Act 1991 to accommodate public liability insurance with the end goal of giving prompt alleviation to the people influenced happening while at the same time handling any unsafe substance and for issues associated therewith. The Act deals with mandatory public liability insurance for establishments handling any unsafe substances to give least alleviation to the casualties (other than workers) through the component of the gatherer's choice. Such an insurance will be founded on the rule of "no blame" liability as it is restricted to just alleviation on a constrained scale.[9] Such insurance separated from protecting the interests of the casualties of mischances would likewise give cover and empower the business to release its liability to settle expansive cases emerging out of significant mishaps.[10] In any case, accessibility of prompt alleviation under this law would not prevent the casualties from going to courts for asserting vast pay.

The National Environment Tribunal Act, 1995 was enacted to accommodate strict liability for harms emerging out of any mishaps occurring while handling any unsafe substances. The act accommodates the formation of a National Environment Tribunal for viable and quick transfer of cases emerging from such mishaps. It forces liability on the proprietor of an endeavor to pay remuneration if there should arise an occurrence of death or damage to any individual, or harm to any property or environment because of a mishap. Such mishaps more likely than not happen while handling any perilous substances. An inquirer may likewise make an application before the tribunal for such alleviation as is given in the Public Liability Insurance Act, 1991.

The National Environment Appellate Authority Act, 1997 has been enacted to accommodate the formation of a National Environment Appellate Authority to hear claims regarding confinement of regions in which any ventures, operations, or processes might not be completed or should be done subject to certain criteria under the Environment (Protection) Act, 1986. The authority was formed so that no civil court or other authority should have to engage on issues on which the authority was so enabled under the act. It is clear that this act was enacted with the target to enable fast decision-making on environmental issues.

The Wild Life (Protection) Act, 1972 was enacted with a view to accommodate the protection of wild creatures, winged animals, and plants. The act disallows picking, evacuating, harming, decimating, and so on of any predefined plant from any forest. The act accommodates the State Wildlife Advisory Board to inform the state government in formulating strategies for the protection and conservation of wildlife and indicated plants, as well as in identifying regions to be proclaimed as sanctuaries, national parks, and so on. The act is controlled by a director of wildlife preservation with assistant directors, and a chief wildlife warden with other wardens and their staff. The Forest (Conservation) Act, 1986 was passed with a view to check deforestation. The act provides that no destruction of forests or utilization of forestland for non-forest purposes can be allowed without the prior endorsement of the central government. The conservation of forests involves safeguarding and protection of existing forests, as well as reforestation. Reforestation ought to go ahead to supplant the vanishing forests. It is a ceaseless and incorporated process.[11] The act is planned for a commendable reason, and it must be implemented entirely for the advantage of the overall population.

It is obviously evident that there is no lack of enactments on environment protection in India. Be that as it may, the implementation of these enactments has been a long way from satisfactory. What is required is the viable and effective authorization of the constitutional mandate and other environmental enactments.

CASES ON ENVIRONMENTAL PROTECTION

On Constitutional Interpretation of Environment

The 42nd Amendment to the Constitution of India included Article 48A and 51A(g) which come under the Directive Principles of State Policy and fundamental duties, respectively. The Supreme Court of India in *Sachidananda Pandey v. State of West Bengal*[12] stated that the court is bound to tolerate as a top priority the aforementioned articles whenever a case identified with environmental problems is brought to the court. Article 48A states: "The State shall endeavor to protect and improve the environment and to safeguard the forest and untamed life of the country." Further, Article 51A(g) imposes an obligation upon every subject of India to protect and improve the common habitat and confers ideals to come before the court for appropriate alleviation. The Supreme Court in *Damodar Rao v. S. O. Municipal Corporation*[13] held that the environmental pollution and spoliation slowly poisoning and polluting the atmosphere should also be viewed as amounting to the violation of Article 21 of the Indian Constitution.

On Sustainable Development

The bench of Justices P. N. Bhagwati and Ranganath Mishra in *Rural Litigation and Entitlement Kendra, Dehradun v. State of Uttar Pradesh*[14] presented the idea of "feasible development." An NGO named RLEK recorded an argument against limestone quarrying in the valley in 1987. It was stated that the lasting resources of humanity are not to be depleted in one era. The normal assets ought to be utilized with imperative consideration and care, so nature and conditions may not be influenced in any harmful way.

On Animal Welfare

The Supreme Court restricted *Jallikattu* and other animal races and battles. It was ruled that bulls cannot be treated as performing animals on account of

Animal Welfare Board of India v. A. Nagaraj and Ors.[15] The court alluded to sections 3 and 11 of the Prevention of Cruelty to Animals Act, 1960 and declared that animal battles effected by humans are illegal, even those carried out under the appearance of tradition and culture. The court recorded various recommendations and overhauled the penalties and discipline in the Prevention of Cruelty to Animals Act, 1960 to work viably.

On Wildlife and Forest Protection

The occupation of forest inhabitants in the Nilgiris area of Tamil Nadu was influenced by the demolition of backwoods. The Supreme Court in *T. N. Godavarman Thirumulpad v. Union of India and Ors.* passed a progression of headings since 1995, till the last judgment in 2014. The court chose to set up a Compensatory Afforestation Funds Management and Planning Authority (CAMPA) to screen afforestation endeavors, to regulate the compensation to those who endured because of deforestation, and to quicken exercises for conservation of normal timberlands. A writ petition was recorded by the NGO Tarun Bharat Sangh in the Supreme Court to quit mining exercises in Sariska Wildlife Sanctuary. The court on account of *Tarun Bharat Sangh v. Union of India and Ors.* (1991) restricted all the mining exercises in the sanctuary.

The Taj Mahal Case

In the Taj Mahal case,[16] the Supreme Court issued headings that coal- and coke-based ventures in Taj Trapezium (TTZ) which were harming the Taj Mahal should either change over to flammable gas or migrate outside TTZ. Further, the Supreme Court coordinated to ensure the plants around the Taj Mahal were relocated by the forest department:

> The Divisional Forest Officer, Agra, is directed to take immediate steps for seeing that water is supplied to the plants. . . . The Union Government is directed to release the funds immediately without waiting for receipt of the proposal from the UP Government on the basis of the copy of the report. Funding may be subsequently settled with the UP Government, but in any set of circumstances for want of funds the officer is directed to see that plants do not wither away.[17]

On Smoking in Public Places

In 2001, the Supreme Court of India forced prohibition on smoking of tobacco in public places everywhere throughout the country.[18] Smoking causes harm not just to the smokers but to nonsmokers as well, who are compelled to inhale secondhand smoke. More than three million individuals die each year in India as a result of smoking tobacco, including bidis and cigarettes.[19] One lakh Indians get lung cancer consistently because of smoking. Moreover, lung cancer kills 95 percent of its victims.[20] That is the reason the Supreme Court decision has massive social value. Be that as it may, there is no enforcement agency for ensuring the ban is observed. Cigarettes and bidis are openly sold at railway stations, bus stands, cinema halls, and so forth. The statutory warning "smoking is injurious to health" is printed on cigarette packets in such little print and shading that it is hardly intelligible. Indeed, in the event that it is intelligible, it has not served its purpose. Therefore, only social awareness can help in stopping smoking.

CRITICISM

The issue of air pollution in India is as complex and diverse as the nation itself. Broadly speaking, handling air pollution in India is not just the responsibility of the government but is both an incentive and punishment for businesses as well as individuals if the environment is taken into consideration.

The state government of New Delhi, India's national capital, which has a population of over 16 million, devised a radical plan of cutting down traffic and controlling air pollution. On odd and even dates, only those private cars with odd- and even-numbered licensed plates, respectively, were allowed to ply on the roads. This unique idea of having odd–even-numbered vehicles off the roads on alternate days failed badly.[21] Many people stepped out of their comfort zone and ditched cars to opt for public transport. This strategy, however, was not so effective because it affected only 5–6 percent of vehicles in Delhi; moreover, traffic police department did not have the manpower to enforce this decision. The odd–even plan delivered extremely frustrating outcomes in terms of checking air pollution. Distinctive inquiries were led by heads of establishments such as TERI and IIT Kanpur, which confirmed the poor results of the two-phased 15 days' plan. The first phase gave acceptable outcomes, but in the second phase, the pollution increased by 23 percent despite having nearly equal number of vehicles out and about. The investigation revealed that the amount and number of fines issued to violators decreased in the second phase. This became an advantage for people who could afford to pay the fines and travel in their own cars for the whole week. The other disadvantage of the odd–even rule was the monopoly gained by cab drivers wherein they charged exorbitant tariffs from the passengers. This was quite evident in Delhi when auto-rickshaw owners took advantage of people's helplessness and charged much more than regular fares.[22]

Swachh Bharat Abhiyan was India's prime minister, Mr. Narendra Modi's first major project brand. The purpose of the mission is still not clear; we have to understand that this whole campaign is to clean India. But the people who have made this country clean have been left behind. People are not using toilets because they either do not have access to one or do not have the resources to install one. As indicated by recent government information, 1.42 lakh tons of solid waste was produced every day in urban regions in July 2019, and just 15.33 percent of it was properly disposed of, showing how underprepared urban civic bodies are to deal with the mammoth task. Additionally, there is a dearth of committed city units that can bring qualified business analysts, public policy graduates, preservationists, and specialists into city organizations. Just 31.83 lakh toilets could be constructed between April 2016 and January 2017 under the mission, which was around 25 percent of the objective set for 2016–2017.[23] In order to put an end to open defecation and achieve better solid waste management, the one-year goal for urban zones was to build 25 lakh individual toilets, build 1 lakh public toilets, and accomplish 100 percent collection and transport of waste in 1000 urban communities and in 100 urban areas. Moreover, these numbers represent only one-fourth of the mission's objective. By 2019, the government intends to build 12 crore toilets across India, which appears to be an exceptionally difficult assignment, judging by the execution till now. It is not just that the execution has been poor, even the nature of execution has come into question. An evaluation of the effects of the mission, conducted by the National Sample Survey Organization (NSSO), found that toilets built in rural areas were lying unused, as the villagers had a few issues with using them and the government or panchayats had neglected to address these issues.

According to the 2017 State of Global Air Report, India is home to 13 of the 20 most polluted cities in the world. In Delhi, half of the about 4.4 million children have lung damage that they will never recover fully from.[24] The report showed that the pollution-related death rate in India increased by 150 percent in the 1990–2015 period. Today, in India 14.7 people in every 100,000 die of an ozone-related illness. Are the environmental laws really applicable in India? To achieve our goals, we need to go beyond the environmental ministry and involve the other ministries of finance, agricultural, industry, urban, transport, energy, and health. There is also a need to engage the local government, civil society organizations, business leaders, trade unions, and citizens at large.

CONCLUSIONS

Environment is the place or surroundings where we live; to keep it clean is a fundamental prerequisite for our survival. Degradation of the environment is serious threat to our planet, be it in the form of air, water, or land pollution. Urbanization, industrialization, overpopulation, and overexploitation of resources are some of the issues that have led to environmental degradation. Environmental pollution has become a global issue, and India is no exception. Every living being requires nourishment, clean water, and clean air to survive. It would be safe to say that there are enough laws in India and the entire world to conserve the environment. However, it is the fault of the people and their governments that the former are not aware of such laws while the latter have made no serious attempts to make the former aware of them. It is not just awareness; people are increasingly lacking common sense too with regards to the need for a clean, green environment. In the past few decades, the government of India has shown keen interest in protecting the environment and has consequently enacted various environmental laws, such as like the Environment (Protection) Act, 1986; the Forest (Conservation) Act, 1980; the Wildlife Protection Act, 1972; Water (Prevention and Control of Pollution) Act, 1974; Air (Prevention and Control of Pollution) Act, 1981; and the Indian Forest Act, 1927. Moreover, the government has made several attempts to save the environment in the recent past through initiatives such as the Swachh Bharat Abhiyaan or the odd–even rule in Delhi. While these initiatives show that the government is involved in several plans to protect the environment, the failure of these plans demonstrates that the public is not cooperating enough. It may be safe to say that

To see a world in a grain of sand
And a heaven in a wild flower,
Hold infinity in the palm of your hand
And eternity in an hour—William Blake

NOTES

1. Dr. Jai Ram Upadhyay, 'Environmental Law' 2 (3rd Edition Central Law Agency 2005.
2. R. M. Lodha, Environmental Ruin: The Crises of Survival 365 (2nd Edition Indus Publishing).
3. Inserted by the Constitution (Forty-second Amendment) Act, 1976.
4. *State of Tamil Nadu v. Hind Store*, (1981) AIR SC 711.
5. *M. C. Mehta v. Union of India*, (1988) AIR SC 1037. See also *Bhavani River v. Sakthi Sugar Limited* (1998) AIR SC 2059.
6. Substituted for '70%', w.e.f. 26.1.1992.
7. *M. C. Mehta v. Union of India*, (1998) AIR SC 2963.
8. Supra note 2, p. 68.
9. Public Liability Insurance Act, 1991.
10. V. K. Agarwal, Environmental Laws in India: Challenges for Enforcement 4 (Bulletin of the National Institute of Ecology 2005).

11. *Anupama Minerals v. Union of India & Others*, (1986) AIR A.P. 225.
12. AIR 1987 SC 1109.
13. AIR 1987 AP 171.
14. AIR 1987 SC 2187.
15. (2014) 7 SCC 547.
16. *M. C. Mehta v. Union of India*, (1999) AIR S.C. 3192.
17. *M. C. Mehta v. Union of India*, (2001) 9 SCC 520.
18. *Murli S. Deora v. Union of India* (2001) 3 SCC 765.
19. V. K. Agarwal, Environmental Laws in India: Challenges for Enforcement 7 (1st ed. 2005).
20. *Dr. B. L. Wadehra v. Union of India*, (1996) AIR SC 2969.
21. 'Delhi odd-even: Exemptions for VIPs, bikes face criticism', Hindustan Times https://www.hindustantimes.com/delhi-news/delhi-odd-even-exemptions-for-vips-bikes-face-criticism/story-AZns3sPNuTKsrygV5DRQtN.html.
22. IndiaSpend Team, 'How successful was odd-even really? After all, Delhi's PM 2.5 levels rose 15% during trial period', Firstpost https://www.firstpost.com/india/was-odd-even-really-successful-delhis-pm-2-5-levels-rose-15-percent-during-trial-period-2587526.html (Nov 09, 2017).
23. Dipak K. Dash, '71% in survey say Swachh Bharat a flop in cities', The Times of India https://timesofindia.indiatimes.com/india/71-in-survey-say-Swachh-Bharat-a-flop-in-cities/articleshow/49005371.cms? (visited on: May 01, 2018).
24. Joseph Jones, '2017 State of Global Air Report: Air Pollution in India', The National Law Review https://www.natlawreview.com/article/2017-state-global-air-report-air-pollution-india , April 13, 2017.

Chapter 14

Ocean Fertilization as a Method to Mitigate the Climate Change

Issues, Interests, and Concerns

Vedant Dikshit

INTRODUCTION

One of the major environmental concerns today faced by the international community is climate change. Owing to the presence of an excessive amount of greenhouse gases, solar radiation gets absorbed in the lower atmosphere. This results in an increase in the global temperature and eventually leads to disruption in weather patterns across the world.[1] The effects of climate change are evident in the form of shrinking of ice caps, submergence of land, harm to marine biodiversity, storms, droughts, lowered crop yields, and extinction of a large number of species.[2] It has been a continuous move by the world community to devise new methods of scientific research that can effectively mitigate the effects of climate change and reestablish the balance between the atmosphere and the Earth. Several conventions to that effect such as the United Nations Framework Convention on Climate Change, 1992; Kyoto Protocol, 1997; and subsequent Doha (2012) and Paris (2015) amendments have been signed by several states.[3] In furtherance of the research to mitigate climate change, John Martin, in the early 1990s suggested a new process knows as ocean fertilization.[4] In this process, a few nutrients such as iron, urea, and phosphorus are added to the ocean in order to increase its sinking capacity. The addition of these nutrients compensates for the nutrient deficiency of the ocean and leads to an algal bloom. These developed algae then absorb carbon dioxide (CO_2) from the atmosphere and sink under the seabed where they remain buried for centuries. This absorption leads to reduction in the level of CO_2 in the atmosphere and thus helps to mitigate global warming and climate change. This process of addition of nutrients to increase the CO_2-absorbing capacity of the oceans and subsequent sequestration of CO_2 is termed ocean fertilization.[5]

When proposed, this process seemed highly beneficial to climate change activists; however, serious concerns were raised by marine environmentalists. It was pointed out that the process artificially intervenes in the marine biology, and thus can have a disastrous and irreparable impact on marine biodiversity. Further, the efficiency level and the outcomes of the process are also uncertain.[6] With extreme benefits and equally adverse impacts attached to the process, it brought climate change activists in conflict with marine environmentalists. Therefore, it is a point of analysis through research as to how ocean fertilization, which involves two competing interests, should be regulated under the regime of international environmental law, and whether the existing international conventions and treaties can effectively regulate it. The urgency for the mitigation of climate change and the danger of irreparable loss to the marine environment make it necessary for the world community to establish international regulations and scientific research with respect to ocean fertilization.

Until now, about thirteen experiments on ocean fertilization, including LOHAFEX by India and Germany in 2009, have been conducted.[7] This essay covers the examination of the legal aspect of ocean fertilization. It has been divided into four parts. The first part provides an introduction, research question, and the scope of the essay. The second parts explains the process of ocean fertilization, and the benefits and issues associated with it, while the third part examines the international regulations under various treaty obligations to regulate ocean fertilization. Finally, the essay is concluded with suggestions and recommendations by the author.

This chapter primarily relies on conventions, treaties, case laws, and legal articles to examine the controversy. The conventions include the United Nations Convention on Law of Seas, 1982 (UNCLOS);[8] Convention on Biological Diversity, 1992 (CBD);[9] London Convention on the Prevention of Marine Pollution by Dumping of Wastes and Other Matter, 1972 (LC);[10] Protocol to the London Convention on the Prevention of Marine Pollution by Dumping of Wastes and Other Matter, 1996 (LC-LP);[11] and International Convention for the Prevention of Pollution from Ships, 1973 as modified by the Protocol of 1978 (MARPOL).[12] Judgements of the International Court of Justice (ICJ) and other courts are also referenced. Further, reference has been made to commentaries and research articles published by scientists and legal academicians. However, local agreements and the municipal regulations have been kept out of the purview of this chapter.

CLEAN FERTILIZATION: BENEFITS, INTERESTS, AND CONCERNS

Climate change is considered a serious threat which can have several irreversible consequences. The two methods widely recognised to mitigate the effects of climate change are (i) decreasing the production of greenhouse gases and (ii) increasing the sequestration of such greenhouse gases by other resources.[13] By the twentieth century, under sequestration techniques, land sequestration methods such as afforestation were considered as the only available procedures. However, a dramatic shift came in the late 1990s with the introduction of techniques for the oceanic absorption of CO_2.[14]

Oceans are one of the largest biological carbon sinks.[15] There are two processes by which the oceans absorb CO_2—first, by the method of partial pressure, and second, by photosynthesis.[16] There always exists an equilibrium between the atmosphere and the oceans, and hence, according to the principles of thermochemistry, any increase in the partial pressure of CO_2 within the air results in the dissolution of CO_2 from the atmosphere into the oceans, which have comparatively lower partial pressure.[17] Another process by which the ocean absorbs CO_2 is through photosynthesis.[18] The phytoplankton present in the ocean undergo photosynthesis and absorb CO_2 from the atmosphere. These planktons then sink into the ocean and bury the CO_2 for several hundred years under the ocean bed. A natural balance in this manner is thus maintained between the atmosphere and oceans.[19] However, this natural atmosphere–ocean balance has been disrupted by an extraordinary increase in CO_2 levels in the atmosphere owing to human activities, to the extent that oceans are not able to dissolve any further CO_2. This surplus carbon traps the sunlight and is the core reason for climate change.[20]

Ocean fertilization is a process by which the sequestration capacity of the ocean is enhanced by inflating the amount of phytoplankton present in the ocean, so that the surplus CO_2 can be further absorbed by it.[21] In this process, a micronutrient such as iron, phosphorus, or urea, which is limited in the ocean, is added to it. The region preferred for such experiments is generally a high-nutrient and low-chlorophyll area that has a good amount of other nutrients.[22] This addition of matter stimulates the growth of phytoplankton in the ocean and leads to a phytoplankton bloom. This bloom accelerates the process of photosynthesis which subsequently increases the absorption rate of CO_2 by the phytoplankton in the ocean. These phytoplankton then sink to the ocean bed, burying the CO_2 under the ocean bed for several hundred years.[23] In international legal parlance, ocean fertilization is described as "any activity undertaken by humans with the principal intention of stimulating primary productivity in the oceans, not including conventional aquaculture, or marine culture, or the creation of artificial reefs." [24]

The major benefit of the process is the depletion of CO_2 from the atmosphere, which reduces global warming and thus helps to mitigate climate change. Apart from CO_2 reduction, other advantages include stimulation of fisheries production,[25] algal bloom,[26] lowering of oceanic temperature,[27] etc. As per the United Nations Framework on Climate Change, under Sections 3(a) and 4, states should undertake responsibility to conduct research and discover different methods to mitigate climate change.[28] The Kyoto Protocol signed in 1997 prescribes for a reduction in greenhouse gases of 8 percent below the 1990 level within the period 2008–2012.[29] The Doha Amendment signed in 2012 further increased the level to 20 percent below the 1990 level in the time period 2013–2020.[30] This level was further increased to 50 percent by 2030 below the 1990 level in the Paris Agreement, signed in 2016.[31] Thus, there has been a significant move by the international community to mitigate the effects of climate change. Under such obligations, states are not to just work on the existing methods such as afforestation and creation of land sinks, but are also advised to develop new methods which could help in mitigating climate change.[32] In this context, ocean fertilization is seen as a method that is both effective and cost efficient, and could be easily undertaken even by developing nations to fulfil their obligations under the abovementioned conventions.[33]

Marine environmentalists, however, argue that such projects can have serious and irreversible consequences on the oceans and marine biodiversity.[34] It is stated that these projects can lead to ocean acidification,[35] asphyxia,[36] production of greenhouse gases,[37] toxic chemicals,[38] harmful algal growth, and so on in the oceans.[39] Also, several concerns have also been raised with respect to the feasibility of such projects.[40] In essence, the concerns raised are against the artificial human intervention in the natural processes of the marine environment and biological ecosystem that could have an irreversible impact.

On the one hand, there exists an immediate need to mitigate climate change, while on the other, there exist issues relating to the scientific uncertainty involved with the ocean fertilization project that may lead to irreversible consequences on the oceans and the biodiversity they sustain. This conflict between two competing environmental claims under climate change conventions and marine preservation principles has become a concern for the international legal community. It is thus crucial to draw a line where these interests and concerns can be effectively balanced, and the process can be effectively regulated under various environmental principles and conventions.

REGULATING OCEAN FERTILIZATION: PRINCIPLES AND CONCERNS

In the development of environmental laws, several principles such as the precautionary principle and the principle of sustainable development have emerged and have been key in the framing of conventions and the treaties.[41] The major challenge against ocean fertilization comes from the precautionary principle as it has been widely accepted as a customary international law in the regime of marine environmental law.[42] The precautionary principle has several versions; however, in the field of marine environmental law, it is understood as a principle which requires that states must take appropriate precautions when there is a scientific uncertainty attached with an activity, which can have the potential to cause substantially irreversible harm to the marine environment.[43] The ocean fertilization project, as discussed above, involves huge scientific uncertainty and can have serious consequences on the marine environment. Until now, only about thirteen experiments have been conducted, and the results of these experiments were largely vague and incapable of providing a common inference.[44] In addition, none of the experiments suggested the long-term consequences of the project. In some experiments, huge algal blooms were observed, whereas some others proved to be futile with several negative effects.[45]

The issue was heavily discussed at the 30th Meeting of the Contracting Parties to London Convention on Dumping. In the meeting, it was decided that it is essential to develop a new method to mitigate climate change; however, this cannot be at the cost of destruction of the marine environment.[46] In 2008, a resolution was passed which prohibited all ocean fertilization activities, but allowed only those for marine scientific research.[47] The discussions further developed, and in 2010, an assessment framework was adopted by the parties. It prescribed for a nonbinding procedure to be followed while conducting an ocean fertilization project, and laid down strict chemical, biological, and technical assessment requirements before conducting such projects. It is only when a project follows the assessment framework can it be regarded as one for a legitimate scientific purpose and can thus be allowed.[48]

Although the assessment framework after considering potential risks allows for ocean fertilization, it is only a temporary instrument and is nonbinding. It only allows the scope for research and does not prescribe ocean fertilization as an independent tool to achieve certain objectives. The 2013 resolution further provides for several proposals to amend it to include ocean fertilization.[49] These amendments allow ocean fertilization as a tool to mitigate climate change, subject to the precaution procedure prescribed by them. However, it is not easy in the international legal sphere to attain consensus over any new amendment. Hence, it becomes crucial to examine that within the existing paradigm of international law, how far, and to what extent, can the existing treaties and conventions regulate such activity.

The treaties and conventions which are most pertinent to ocean fertilization are UNCLOS,[50] the London Convention,[51] the London Protocol,[52] and CBD.[53] The following section discusses how far these preestablished conventions can regulate ocean fertilization, what are the problems associated with these conventions, and finally, how can the international community move forward toward establishing a balance to regulate ocean fertilization.

The United Nations Convention on Law of Seas, 1982

UNCLOS encompasses several provisions that are pertinent in regulating ocean fertilization, such as marine scientific research,[54] preservation of the marine environment,[55] regulation of dumping in the oceans,[56] provisions relating to high seas,[57] and exclusive economic zones.[58] It further entails the provisions for environmental impact assessment,[59] transboundary harm,[60] and adoption of international standards of precaution into domestic laws.[61] Thus, UNCLOS seems to be a wide-ranging convention covering all the limbs of the ocean fertilization activity. However, the manner in which these provisions are framed within UNCLOS raises several issues and difficulties in the actual implementation of these provisions. On perusal, it is evident that these provisions are loosely worded and therefore only set a general framework with precautionary objectives rather than specifically enforceable obligations.[62]

Part XIII of UNCLOS, which deals with marine scientific research, provides for the right of the coastal state with respect to the researching state; however, it does not in effect imposes any obligation or environmental standard to be maintained by the coastal state during research. It further complicates the issue by providing that a coastal state shall have the sovereign right to conduct and regulate any marine scientific research within its territory.[63] The provisions related to high seas as enumerated within Part VII of UNCLOS are restricted to security, freedom of navigation, safe passage, etc., and do not cover the issue of preservation of the high seas.[64] The dumping provision as contained in UNCLOS are aspirational and merely provide for the state to adopt such laws to regulate dumping and per se does not restrict dumping.[65] The other provisions of UNCLOS which involve transboundary harm, economic zone rights, etc. are contingent on the occurrence of damage and operate only when harm is established.[66]

The only provisions that are proximate to the concerns as raised against ocean fertilization are provided in Part XII of UNCLOS under the preservation of marine environment from pollution. As provided under Articles 192–196, states are obliged to take all possible actions to prevent and control pollution in the marine environment.[67] Article 1 of UNCLOS defines pollution as "any introduction of any substance in the ocean, which may be likely to have deleterious consequences on the marine environment."[68] Further, UNCLOS describes pollution as the release of toxic, harmful, or noxious substances from land-based sources, vessels, or by dumping into the marine environment.[69] Thus, UNCLOS controls the substances that can potentially cause harm to the marine environment; however, it does not regulate the addition of the materials in the oceans. Hence, the obligation under UNCLOS will only govern ocean fertilization if the substance added can potentially cause pollution or produces a substance that may potentially lead to pollution in the marine environment. The substances that are used for ocean fertilization, such as ferrous sulfate, phosphorus, and urea, are harmless and are not pollutants per se.[70] However, concerns have been raised that the addition of such substances can lead to ocean acidification and production of certain toxic chemicals which have the potential to affect the environment. Thus, the addition of such chemicals and micronutrients can be classified under pollution. However, to regulate such an activity, a strong causal link is required to be established between the materials added and the substances produced. Since the establishment of a clear causal link is subject to scientific uncertainty and is under research, the strict enforcement of provisions and the extent to which such provisions can regulate the entire ocean fertilization process are speculative.

The London Convention, 1972 and the 1996 London Protocol on Dumping[71]

The 1972 Convention on Prevention of Pollution by Dumping of Wastes and Other Matter and the subsequent 1996 protocol, extending the obligations present in UNCLOS, regulate the dumping of materials in the oceans. The convention provided a list of materials that are prohibited from dumping in the oceans; however, it is not effective in regulating ocean fertilization, as none of the materials used in ocean fertilization is restricted by the annexure.[72]

The London protocol, unlike the convention, takes a progressive step and provides for a reverse list, restricting any dumping, except for the materials which are prescribed in the annexure to the protocol.[73] Thus, as none of the materials which are involved in ocean fertilization is provided in the annexure, the London protocol seems to be an effective tool to regulate ocean fertilization. However, a major hurdle is the definition of "dumping" in the protocol.

Article 1 of the London protocol defines dumping as "deliberate" disposal of "waste" in the ocean. However, it excludes the placement of materials, other than for mere disposal, which is not contrary to the aims of the protocol.[74] Much debate has occurred on how far iron or any other micronutrient involved in ocean fertilization can be considered as "waste." The absence of any precise definition of waste in the protocol and the low toxicity of these materials tend to put such materials outside the scope of waste.[75] This situation further gets complex as the protocol in its annexure provides for "inert, inorganic geologic material" which can be dumped in oceans.[76]

Thus, the effectiveness of the London protocol in regulating ocean fertilization is contingent on the understanding of the terms "waste" and "inert organic material." Further, the protocol, while regulating dumping, does not clarify the scope of it and in the present form does not provide for a clear space to include ocean fertilization. In order to regulate ocean fertilization, the contracting parties to the London convention and protocol in 2008 and 2010 passed two resolutions. These resolutions are aimed to bring ocean fertilization under the purview of the London protocol, and to develop (i) an assessment framework which can be used as a procedural barrier and (ii) a determinative method to test the environmental consequences of the project.

Assessment Framework

In 2010, the contracting parties to the London convention and the protocol developed an assessment framework to establish a regulatory procedure for conducting ocean fertilization.[77] This framework has two limbs: initial assessment and environmental assessment.[78] The initial assessment determines if the project can be classified as "ocean fertilization." The environmental assessment, on the other hand, provides for the environmental impact and whether the activity violates the aims and objectives of the convention. It also determines, by way of scientific peer review and publication, if the project has scientific attributes. Further, a report with respect to site selection has to be made. The next step involves the examination of movement of the substances to be added to the ocean. Then, an effect assessment is to be carried out, which takes into consideration the biological and chemical impact of the project on the ocean and marine biodiversity. Afterward, a risk assessment and risk management are carried out which assess the risks involved in the project and the ways in which the parties can mitigate such risks.[79]

Though the framework takes into consideration all the possible impacts that the ocean fertilization project can have on the ocean, marine biodiversity, and neighbouring states, it has several limitations. As discussed above, the framework is a nonbinding procedure and is therefore dependent on the wish of the states. Further, as the environment across the world is not uniform, a uniform standard cannot be considered feasible. Certain places such as Arctic and Antarctic oceans have fragile environments and require different consideration and thus cannot be brought under one set of overarching blanket standards. In addition, different oceans have different thresholds with respect to particular nutrients. Thus, by prescribing a uniform standard, the assessment framework fails to take into consideration these factors of variance in the biological diversity of the oceans. Hence, it is intended by the contracting parties that Annexure I, which provides for the list of substances that may be dumped in oceans, be amended in accordance with the London protocol, and that the substances involved in ocean fertilization should be included within it.[80] It is aimed to establish a harmonious regime regulating ocean fertilization taking into consideration the local environmental conditions.

The Convention on Biological Diversity 1992

One of the major contentions raised against ocean fertilization is the potential harm caused to the marine biodiversity. The CBD covers this aspect. It provides for the conservation of the biodiversity and in situ habitat protection of the marine species. Thus, this convention becomes most important in terms of examining and regulating the consequences of ocean fertilization on the marine living ecosystem.

Article 8(d) of the CBD requires states to undertake measures for the protection of the habitat and natural environment of marine species.[81]As reflected in its preamble, and in the UN General Assembly resolutions,[82] the convention prioritizes in situ conservation over other measures,[83] such as development of natural parks, sanctuaries, etc. Further, Article II of the Convention on Migratory Species imposes a similar obligation, in the context of in situ conservation of migratory species, especially for the species which are endangered.[84] In 2008, when the deliberations on the assessment framework were going on, an important decision was taken by the Conference of Parties (COP) to CBD which completely prohibited ocean fertilization for carbon exchange or commercial activities.[85] Furthermore, it presented in its report that if the primary contention is that ocean fertilization should not be conducted owing to a lack of research, it is crucial to conduct ocean fertilization for research and must have minimum restraints in such research, which does not seem to be the stand of the international community.[86] It also raised serious concern with respect to ambiguity in the definition of small and large scale in the assessment framework.[87]

The CBD thus seems to be an efficient treaty for the conservation of species; however, similar to UNCLOS, the major issue with CBD is its loose wording and aspirational provisions rather than specific enforceable obligations. Article 7 only requires the parties to identify the process and categories of activities that are likely to have significant adverse impacts on the conservation and sustainable use of biological diversity, without laying down any obligation.[88] Further, Article 14 requires the parties to document the changes; Article 8 requires the parties to promote the in situ conservation of biodiversity.[89] Thus, the CBD does not prescribe a real enforcement mechanism, but only sets the general objective. Hence, the effectiveness of the CBD to regulate ocean fertilization is highly speculative. Further, as highlighted in several CBD decisions,[90] its provision is limited to the activities in territorial seas, and since the places considered as feasible for ocean fertilization are high seas and exclusive economic zones, the feasibility of CBD in controlling ocean fertilization is highly doubtful.

Procedural Ambiguity within the Treaties and Conventions

Another issue involved is the dispute settlement procedure as provided by these conventions. UNCLOS provides for a compulsory dispute settlement procedure,[91] whereas the London protocol specifies an arbitral tribunal as the settlement body.[92] Moreover, the CBD requires mediation as a prior dispute settlement procedure before moving to compulsory dispute settlement.[93] Hence, the conflicting position is not only with respect to the obligations, but also with the procedure for the settlement of disputes. As seen above, UNCLOS, London protocol, and CBD do not cover disputes in entirety, and since the matter is fragmented and treaties provide for different settlement procedures, it would not be possible to reconcile the issue in one case where it can be collectively heard and decided by one court or any other body.[94] The International Court of Justice in the case of *Australia-New Zealand v. Japan* (the Southern Bluefin Tuna case) held that "it is a commonplace of international law for a dispute to arise in more than one treaty.[95]There is frequently a parallelism of the substantive obligation and the procedural requirement within the treaties and conventions."[96] This case, however, does not settle what dispute settlement procedure should be followed, and also does not clarify whether a tribunal formed under one treaty can interpret the obligations under another treaty or separate tribunals have to be formed for different treaties. The Southern Bluefin Tuna case to some extent provides an inclination toward the former proposition; however, ITLOS in the Mox Plant case[97] upheld the latter contention. Thus, there exists no single understanding to resolve the fragmentation of the matter of ocean fertilization. It will lead to different courts or similar bodies hearing the same matter, and might result in conflicting decisions. Hence, the overlap of treaties and the probability of fragmentation of the dispute makes it crucial to develop a separate legal regime for ocean fertilization with an established dispute settlement mechanism.

CONCLUSIONS

It seems nowhere the intention of the world community that one kind of pollution is transformed into another kind of pollution. The conservation of atmosphere must not have adverse consequences on the marine biodiversity. Thus, the competing interests of marine conservation in the form of the precautionary principle have to be balanced with the compelling need to mitigate climate change. In this process, certain steps in the form of prescribing ocean fertilization for legitimate scientific purposes seem to be a balanced interlocutory approach. However, as pointed out in the analysis, this process has its own drawbacks and gives a weak regulatory control over the ocean fertilization activity. The other concern is the lack of any binding convention to prevent ocean fertilization from commercial abuse. Further, preexisting conventions such as UNCLOS, LC-LP, and CBD only cover certain aspects of ocean fertilization, and no treaty covers the entire process. In addition, the aspirational wording and lack of clarity of terms make the competence of these conventions and treaties to regulate ocean fertilization speculative.

As India also possesses a huge costal border and has similar concerns, the role of India shall be crucial in the process. It is suggested that to exercise effective control on ocean fertilization, amendments should be made to the preexisting treaties. The entries within the London protocol must be extended to include particulate matter involved in ocean fertilization. Further, the definition of the word "waste" must be specified in the protocol. It will ensure that the state follows the proper procedure and carries out an assessment before conducting any such activity. An amendment should be made in the Kyoto Protocol to exclude the carbon credits obtained from ocean fertilization. It will prevent the commercial abuse of ocean fertilization, and for the time being, it can be within the purview of scientific research. It would further the research objectives under climate change conventions, considering the preservation of the marine environment. In addition, it should be tried to come to an agreement to club the relevant provision of these treaties, to establish a uniform regime, with its own substantive and procedural setup covering the entire ocean fertilization process. Keeping in the view the immediacy and urgency to mitigate climate change and the increasing number of ocean fertilization projects undertaken without necessary steps, such development is crucial and indispensable for the conservation of atmospheric as well as marine environments.

NOTES

1. Philippe Sands, Principles of International Environmental Law, 279, 3rd edition, 2003
2. R K Pachauri & L.A. Mayer, Climate Change: Synthesis Report, *Climate Change : Synthesis Report. Contribution of Working Groups I, II and III to the Fifth Assessment Report of the Intergovernmental Panel on Climate Change*, at 17, 2014
3. *Supra note 1 at 280.*
4. Hugh Powell, *Fertilizing the Ocean with Iron,* 46 OCEANUS, 30 (2008).
5. *Id.*

6. Oceanographic Commission, *Ocean Fertilization A Scientific Summary for Policy Makers,* UNESCO 1, 2010

7. Randall S. Abate, *Sowing Seeds Uncertain: Ocean Iron Fertilization, Climate Change, and the International Environmental Law Framework,* 27(2) PACE ENVIRONMENTAL LAW REVIEW, 558, 2010

8. United Nations Convention on the Law of the Sea, 1833 U.N.T.S. 397. [Hereinafter UNCLOS], December 10, 1982

9. 1992 Convention on Biological Diversity, 1760 U.N.T.S. 79. [Hereinafter CBD], June 5, 1992

10. Convention on Prevention of Marine Pollution by Dumping of waste and other matters, 1046 U.N.T.S. 120. [Hereinafter London Convention], December 29, 1972

11. Protocol to Convention on Prevention of Marine Pollution by Dumping of wastes and Other matter 2006 ATS 11. [Hereinafter London Protocol], November 7, 1996

12. International Convention for the Prevention of Pollution from Ships, 2 Nov, 1973. [Hereinafter MARPOL], November 2, 1973

13. Jennie Dean, *Iron Fertilization: A Scientific Review with International Policy Recommendations,* 32ENVIRONS,ENVIRONMENTALLAW&POLICYJOURNAL,321,2008.

14. *Ibid.*

15. Christine Bertram, *Ocean Iron Fertilization in the Context of the Kyoto Protocol and the Post-Kyoto Process,* 38 ENERGY POLICY1135, 2010.

16. *Ibid.*

17. Howard Herzog, Ken Caldera & John Reilly, *An Issue of Permanence: Assessing the Effectiveness ofTemporary Carbon Storage,* CLIMATIC CHANGE, NO. 59, 302, 2003.

18. Suzuki, *Combined Effects of Photosynthesis and Calcination on the Partial Pressure of Carbon Dioxide in Seawater, Journal of Oceanography,* NO. 54, 5, 1998.

19. *Ibid.*

20. *Supra note 17.*

21. Oceanographic Commission (IOC), *Ocean Fertilization A Scientific Summary for Policy Makers,* UNESCO 1, 2010.

22. *Ibid.*

23. *Supra note 21.*

24. International Maritime Organisation (IMO), *Report of the 30th Consultative Meeting to London Convention and the 3rd Meeting of Contracting Parties to the London Protocol, 2008.*

25. R. E. Thomson, *Bottom-Up Ecosystem Trophic Dynamics Determine Fish Production in the Northeast Pacific,* 308 SCIENCE, 1280, 2005.

26. P. W. Boyd et al., *Mesoscale Iron Enrichment Experiments 1993-2005: Synthesis and Future Directions,* 315 SCIENCE 612, 2007.

27. Maurice Levasseur, *DMSP and DMS Dynamics During a Mesoscale Iron Fertilization Experiment in the Northeast Pacific Temporal and Vertical Distributions,* 53 ELSEVIER, 2360 , 2010.

28. United Nations Framework Convention on Climate Change, Article 3(a) r/w aArt. 4, 9 May, 1992, 1771 UNTS 107.

29. Article 3, Kyoto Protocol to the UN Framework Convention on Climate Change, 11 December, 1997, 2303 UNTS 148.

30. Article 1, Doha Amendment to Kyoto Protocol, 8 December, 2012, 2303 UNTS 148.

31. Paris Agreement, to the UN Framework Convention on Climate Change, 5 October, 2016, 2303 UNTS 148.

32. *Supra note 28.*

33. Christine Bertram, *Ocean Iron Fertilization in the Context of the Kyoto Protocol and Post-Kyoto Process,* Energy Policy, 1135, 2010.

34. Jennie Dean, *Iron Fertilization: A Scientific Review with International Policy Recommendations*, 32 Environs Environmental Law & Policy Journal 321, 2008.

35. Karen N. Scott, *The Day After Tomorrow: Ocean C02 Sequestration and the Future of Climate Change,* 18 GEO INTERNATIONAL LAW REVIEW 57, 2005.

36. Phillip Williamsona, *Ocean Fertilization for Geoengineering: A Review of Effectiveness, Environmental Impacts and Emerging Governance*, 90 ELSEVIER 475, 2012.

37. Fuhrman, J.A., *Possible Biogeochemical Consequences of Ocean Fertilization,* Limnol Oceanogr, 36 , 1991.

38. *Ibid.*

39. Glibert, P.M, *Ocean Urea Fertilization for the Carbon Credits Poses High Ecological Risks,* 56 Marine Pollution Bulletin, 1049, 2008.

40. *Ibid.*

41. Philippe Sands, Principles of International Environmental Law, 279, 3rd ed., 2003.

42. *Ibid.*

43. North Sea Continental Shelf. (Federal Republic of Germany/Denmark), Judgement, 1969 I.C.J. Rep. 3 (Feb 1969) ("North Sea Case"); Legality of the Threat or Use of Nuclear Weapons case, Advisory opinion, 1996 I.C.J Rep. 226, (July 1996). ("Nuclear Weapons Case").

44. Randall S. Abate, *Sowing Seeds Uncertain: Ocean Iron Fertilization, Climate Change, and the International Environmental Law Framework,* 27(2) Pace Environmental Law Review, 558, 2010.

45. *Ibid.*

46. International Maritime Organization, Report of the 30th Consultative Meeting and the 3rd Meeting of Contracting Parties, LC 29/17, November, 2008.

47. Resolution LC-LP.1, 2008.

48. Resolution LC-LP.2 On the Assessment Framework for Scientific Research Involving Ocean Fertilization, 2010.

49. Resolution LP.4(8), 2013.

50. United Nations Convention on the Law of the Sea, 1833 U.N.T.S. 397, December 10, 1982.

51. Convention on Prevention of Marine Pollution by Dumping of Waste and other Matters, 1046 U.N.T.S. 120, December 29, 1972

52. Protocol to Convention on Prevention of Marine Pollution by Dumping of wastes and Other matter, 2006 ATS 11, November 7, 1996

53. 1992 Convention on Biological Diversity, 5 Jun, 1992, 1760 U.N.T.S. 79.

54. UNCLOS 1982 Part XIII.

55. UNCLOS 1982, Part XII.

56. *Id.*

57. UNCLOS 1982 Part VII.

58. UNCLOS, 1982 Part VI.

59. UNCLOS 1982 art. 206.

60. UNCLOS 1982 art. 194(5).

61. UNCLOS 1982 art. 210(6).

62. R G Rayfuse, M G Lawrence, K Gjerde, *Ocean Fertilization and Climate Change: The Need to Regulate Emerging High Sea Uses,* 23(2) The International Journal of Marine and Coastal Law, 313, 2008.

63. UNCLOS 1982 art. 246.

64. *Supra note* 44.

65. *Ibid.*

66. Xue Hanqin, Transboundary Damage in International Law, Cambridge University Press, 2, 2003.

67. UNCLOS 1982 art. 192.

68. UNCLOS 1982 art. 1.

69. *Supra note 44.*

70. R G Rayfuse, M G Lawrence, K Gjerde, *'Ocean Fertilization and Climate Change: The Need to Regulate Emerging High Sea Uses'* 23(2) The International Journal of marine and Costal Laws, 313, 2008.

71. *Supra note 37.*

72. London Convention 1972, Annexure II.

73. Philomine Verlaan, *Current Legal Developments London Convention and London Protocol, The International Journal of Marine and Coastal Law*, 185, 2011.

74. London Protocol art. 1.

75. R G Rayfuse, M G Lawrence, K Gjerde, *'Ocean Fertilization and Climate Change: The Need to Regulate Emerging,* The International Journal of Marine and Coastal Law 313, 2008.

76. London Protocol, Annex. I.

77. International Maritime Organization, Report of the 31st Consultative Meeting and the 5th Meeting of Contracting Parties, LC 29/17, October 2010.

78. Resolution LC-LP.2, On the Assessment Framework for Scientific Research Involving Ocean Fertilization, 2010

79. *Id.*

80. *Supra note 62.*

81. CBD art. 8(d).

82. G.A. Res. 37/7, October 30, 1980.

83. A Guide to the Convention on Biological Diversity 11 (IUCN: Gland and Cambridge, 1994.

84. CMS art. II.

85. COP 9 Decision IX/16, 2008. CBD, COP 9, Decision IX/20, 2008.

86. *Ibid.*

87. *Ibid.*
88. CBD Art. 7.
89. CBD Art. 14.
90. *Supra note 85.*
91. UNCLOS 1982, Art. 287.
92. London Protocol 1996, Art. 16.
93. CBD Art. 27.
94. Rosemary Rayfuse, *The Future of Compulsory Dispute Settlement Under the Law of The Sea Convention*, 36 VUWLR 683, 2005
95. Southern Bluefin Tuna (New Zealand-Japan, Australia-Japan), Objection to Jurisdiction, 52, R.I.I.A. 23, 2000.
96. *Ibid.*
97. MOX Plant, Provisional Measures (Ireland v. U. K), Case No. 10, Order of Dec.3, 2001.

Chapter 15

A Legal Appraisal on Liability and Compensation Logic to Address the Impact of Climate Change

Sharaban Tahura Zaman and M. Hafijul Islam Khan

INTRODUCTION

In recent years, there has been a growing need to address loss and damage resulting from climate change through international processes.[1] This discourse involves the issue of state liability and compensation as a means to address climate change–induced loss and damage. The aim of this chapter is to analyze legal questions arising from the application of a liability and compensation logic to address climate change and how it can be resolved. The question of state liability for climate change involves international, domestic, and tort law.[2] However, to explore all these avenues, more comprehensive research is required. Therefore, the chapter only explores the avenue that falls under the public international law. The chapter focuses solely on key legal questions that are critical in this regard. And to resolve these unprecedented questions, the chapter explores innovative interpretations of existing rules under customary international laws, judicial precedents, and scholarly articles, including the judgment in the *Urgenda Foundation v. Government of the Netherlands*[3] case (the decision by the Dutch District Court prevailed and was upheld in the Hague Court of Appeal in 2018 with the rule that failure to reduce greenhouse gas emission is violation of Dutch citizens' rights).

The chapter in its first two sections elaborates two preliminary issues: (1) the nature of loss and damage resulting from climate change impacts and (2) basis of liability and compensation logic under international law and climate regulatory regime. In the third section, the chapter attempts to identify the key legal questions and associated challenges to address liability and compensation. This section analyzes six complex issues (duty of care or due diligence, effect of compliance with climate regulation, liability in case of multiple wrongdoers, retrospective effect, causation uncertainties, and effective remedies) and the legal questions related to them, as well as their resolution. The section ends with identifying the key findings and concluding remarks.

NATURE OF LOSS AND DAMAGE RESULTING FROM CLIMATE CHANGE IMPACTS

Climate change and its adverse impacts and vulnerabilities are now a reality.[4] According to the Intergovernmental Panel on Climate Change (hereinafter referred to as IPCC) Fourth Assessment Report, 2007, "mitigation would not prevent all climate change impacts"[5] and adaptation too has its limit beyond which it cannot provide adequate and sustainable outcomes.[6] Therefore, focusing efforts solely on collective mitigation and adaptation will not suffice and irreplaceable losses and acute damages will take place owing to the effect of historical and current anthropogenic emissions.[7] And no country can escape from the loss and damage associated with climate change impacts.[8] Now the point is what "loss and damage associated with climate change impacts" actually denotes.

Unfortunately, an agreed upon definition of loss and damage is yet to emerge. However, the Cancun Decision adopted in 2010 at the Conference of the Parties (known as COP 16) gives a guideline in this regard by asserting that "loss and damage associated with the adverse effects of climate change include impacts related to extreme weather events and slow onset events."[9]

What are slow onset events? This is clarified by a footnote stating that they include rising sea level, increasing temperatures, ocean acidification, glacial retreat and related impacts, salinization, land and forest degradation, loss of biodiversity, and desertification.[10] Based on this proposition, the Subsidiary Body for Implementation (SBI) broadly defines loss and damage as "The actual and/or potential manifestation of impacts associated with climate change in developing countries that negatively affect human and natural systems."[11]

The review report characterizes loss as "negative impacts in relation to which reparation or restoration is impossible such as loss of freshwater resources"[12] and considers damage as "negative impacts in relation to which reparation or restoration is possible such as windstorm damage to the roof of a building, or damage to a coastal mangrove forest as a result of coastal surges."[13] Based on field research, scholars also suggest that such loss and damage is beyond being able to cope with or adapt to.[14]

Reflecting the above discussion, a definition set forth by Doreen Stabinsky and Juan P. Hoffmaister is given below, which adequately underpins the nature of loss and damage:

> The phrase "loss and damage" refers broadly to the entire range of damage and permanent loss "associated with climate change impacts in developing countries that are particularly vulnerable to the adverse effects of climate change" that can no longer be avoided through mitigation nor can be avoided through adaptation.[15]

The Paris Agreement, adopted in 2015 by the international community, in its Article 8 recognizes the definitional analysis and declares that loss and damage associated with the adverse impact of climate change includes slow onset events, extreme weather events that may cause irreversible and permanent loss and damage, or even noneconomic losses to the community's livelihood.

However, it is noteworthy that developing countries are not only most vulnerable and least responsible for climate change but also least capable to deal with the actual loss and damage, which includes loss of life, traditional livelihood, property, territory, culture; ecological damage; displacement; and migration.[16] Historically, global emissions of greenhouse gases originated in developed countries.[17] These disproportionate contributions to climate change and suffering from the consequences bring up the serious legal question of liability and compensation for the damage caused.[18] The next section of the chapter will explore the basis of liability and compensation under international law and climate regulation to address loss and damage associated with climate change.

LIABILITY AND COMPENSATION APPROACHES TO ADDRESS LOSS AND DAMAGE

Under international law, liability essentially serves two purposes: prevention and compensation.[19] The primary aim of liability is to secure adequate redress for victims through compensation or other forms of reparation,[20] and the secondary aim is to prevent or change the wrongdoer's behavior.[21] However, the state liability in environmental cases usually arises because of the violation of one or more customary international laws or the violation of a treaty.[22] Based on this proposition, the current section will explore the basis of liability and compensation under customary international laws and climate regulatory regime.

State Liability and Compensation under International Law

States have a duty to ensure that activities within their territory or control do not affect the environment of other states.[23] The origin of this obligation of conduct to prevent transboundary environmental harm can be traced in the well-known *Trail Smelter Arbitration* case.[24] According to the judgment,

> No state has the right to use or permit the use of its territory in such a manner as to cause injury by fumes in or to the territory of another or the properties or persons therein when the case is of serious consequence and the injury is established by clear and convincing evidence.[25]

The judgment of the International Court of Justice (ICJ) in the *Corfu Channel* case denotes a similar proposition by asserting that every state has an "obligation not to allow knowingly its territory to be used for acts contrary to the rights of other States"[26] Similar connotation is also found in the *Nuclear Tests* case[27] and *Lac Lanoux Arbitration* case.[28] The significance of such older judicial or arbitral precedence was later on referred to in a number of legal instruments.[29] The Stockholm Declaration, adopted in 1972, in its Principle 21 not only affirmed the sovereign right to exploit natural resources but also imposed the duty "to ensure that activities within their jurisdiction or control do not cause damage to the environment of other states." The UN General Assembly affirmed Principle 21 as the reflection of customary international laws.[30]

Principle 2 of the Rio Declaration adopted in 1992 also affirmed sovereign rights over a state's own resources and established responsibility to avoid transboundary environmental harm. However, Principle 2 of the Rio Declaration has a significant contribution in transboundary environmental harm issues as it set forth a groundbreaking norm for the further elaboration of international environmental law.[31] In the *Advisory Opinion on the Legality of the Threat or Use of Nuclear Weapons* case, ICJ for the first time affirmed that

> The existence of the general obligation of states to ensure that activities within their jurisdiction and control respect the environment of other states or of areas beyond national control is now part of the corpus of international law relating to the environment.[32]

Thus, Principle 2 of the Rio Declaration on transboundary environmental harm is not a soft law or a mere aspiration[33] but the corpus of international environmental law. Therefore, taking the view mentioned above, it can be firmly concluded that the states' duty to prevent, minimize, and control transboundary pollution and environmental harm resulting from activities within their jurisdiction or control is an obligation of conduct to be followed and the basis of state liability under international law.

On the remedy issue, the general international law determined adequate redress measures for the violation of an environmental obligation.[34] When the state responsibility is established, the first obligation is to avoid the wrongful act, and if that fails, "full reparation" should be secured for the damage caused.[35] Article 34 of the International Law Commission (ILC) 2001 defines that the remedy for violating the state responsibility is "full reparation" as "restitution, compensation, and satisfaction either singly or in combination"; further, what would be the most suitable remedy will depend on the nature of the case and injury suffered.[36]

However, compensation or restitution is likely to be the normal remedy where the claimant state has suffered an injury to its people or damage to its property, natural resources, or the environment.[37] In the matter of restitution, the key issue is what is lost and what needs to be restored. In this regard, often the restoration of the damaged environment or its equivalent is not possible.[38] Moreover, state practices and ILC's work suggest that such restoration of environmental damage is often not adequate or even appropriate.[39] In these circumstances, compensation becomes the "main and central remedy."[40] In this regard, the judicial precedents of the *Trail Smelter* case can be the best reference wherein for transboundary air pollution, the arbitral tribunal awarded compensation to Canada for the damage caused. However, such award of compensation can only be declared if a "clear and unbroken causal link" can be established between the wrongful action and the injury/damage actually suffered.[41]

State Liability and Compensation under Climate Change Regulatory Regime

As mentioned above, state liability can be based either on the breach of a treaty obligation or customary international law. As to the second option, this part of the chapter will explore the potential basis of liability to address loss and damage under the obligation of three key legal instruments of climate regulatory regime: the United Nations Framework Convention on Climate Change (UNFCCC) 1992, the Kyoto Protocol 1997, and the Paris Agreement 2015.

UNFCCC is the first legal instrument in history that architected a governing regime to prevent anthropogenic emission interfering with the climatic system, which achieved universal ratification. Considering UNFCCC without the Kyoto Protocol, there are two provisions specifically applicable to the issue of liability.[42]

The first is Article 2 which asserts that the objective of the convention is to "stabilize greenhouse gas concentrations in the atmosphere at a level that would prevent dangerous anthropogenic interference with the climate system," and such level should be achieved within a specific time frame in a sustainable manner. The article represents the objective of UNFCCC specifically in the realm of customary international laws.[43] Moreover, according to the Vienna Convention 1969, a signatory state which did not ratify a convention is still under an obligation not to frustrate the object and purpose of a treaty to which it is a signatory.[44] Some scholars have argued that the failure of the state in national policy to uphold the objectives given in the text of UNFCCC raises the issue of liability.[45] However, the argument is highly contentious as the provision is considered nonbinding and ambitious in nature.[46]

The second provision is Article 4(2), which deals with the commitment issue. The article requires industrial states to commit to mitigating greenhouse gas (GHG) emissions within their territory to the 1990 level by the year 2000. However, every state eventually failed to meet its commitment.[47]

Now the question is whether these articles are adequate enough to maintain an action of liability for loss and damage, especially against those states that are parties only to UNFCCC but not to Kyoto Protocol, such as the USA and Canada. The most agreed upon scholarly legal answer is no, as the articles are too vague.[48]

However, the situation is different under the Kyoto Protocol as the instrument is legally binding on the parties. Annex B of the protocol provides a specific quantified emission reduction commitment for every industrialized country. Article 3(1) of the Kyoto Protocol mandates countries listed in Annex I of the protocol to individually or jointly fulfill their assigned emission criteria within the specified time frame. According to the said article, it is a specific obligation and failure to comply with it would be a violation of the express treaty obligation,[49] which potentially could give rise to state liability.[50]

But the binding commitment of the Kyoto Protocol only applies to its parties that ratified the protocol and not to major GHG emitters such as the US, China, and India that did not ratify it. Therefore, to address loss and damage, the prospects of establishing liability against the largest emitters' countries which are not a party to the Kyoto Protocol are limited under the Kyoto governing regime.[51]

The Paris Agreement, adopted in 2015 and entered into force in 2016, gives a breakthrough by recognizing loss and damage in a separate article—Article 8. Under Article 8.1, parties recognized the sole importance and obligation to minimize, avert, and address loss and damage associated with the adverse impact of climate change. However, Article 8.3 clarifies that parties' obligations to address loss and damage associated with climate change will be "cooperative and facilitative" in character. Furthermore, Paris Decision (adopted in the same conference of the parties with the Paris Agreement, 2015 for interpreting the agreement) in its paragraph 52 explicitly and unambiguously states that Article 8 will not provide, involve, or give basis to any liability or compensation. So the Paris Agreement explicitly excludes the scope of liability or compensation as a step to address loss and damage. However, when UNFCCC was signed in 1992, small island states made a declaration by stating that

> Signature of the convention shall in no way constitute a renunciation of any rights under international law concerning state responsibility for the adverse effects of climate change and that no provisions in the convention can be interpreted as derogating from the principles of general international law.[52]

Small island countries, by making this declaration, retained a space open for establishing liability. Moreover, the preamble of UNFCCC affirms the states' responsibility not to cause harm under customary international laws.[53] Therefore, based on state responsibility and declaration of small island countries, a basis of liability for loss and damage can be established against major emitters' countries.

However, what should be the redress measures for the victims of atmospheric pollution is not clear under UNFCCC, the Kyoto Protocol, and the Paris Agreement. The conventions did not recognize the polluter pays principle; moreover, the legal content of this principle remains unclear.[54] Though developing countries strongly put stress on compensation and rehabilitation to redress loss and damage, on the climate negotiation table (as was evident at the time of the Paris Agreement adoption), these words are considered a discomfort for industrialized countries.[55] Therefore, on the compensation issue, victims need to rely more on customary international laws than the climate-governing regime. The next section of the chapter will explore the key legal questions and challenges arising from the application of liability and compensation logic to address climate-induced loss and damage.

ISSUES AND CHALLENGES TO ADDRESS LIABILITY AND COMPENSATION IN THE CLIMATE REGIME

The discussion in the last two sections reflects the proposition that it is evident the adverse impact of climate change causes environmental harm and that there is a basis for the liability and compensation logic largely under customary international laws and to some extent under the climate regulatory regime. However, such application of the liability and compensation logic to address climate-induced loss and damage often raises the number of fundamental legal questions which need to be addressed adequately to bring an effective liability claim for climate victims. This section will identify and analyze these legal hurdles to find an effective solution.

Duty of Care or Due Diligence

Under customary international laws to establish a breach of state liability to prevent transboundary harm, the claimant needs to prove a lack of due diligence or duty of care.[56] It means that state liability can only occur if the respective state has not acted with duty of care, and such standard of care must be determined according to the actual circumstances and obligation in question.[57] It is noteworthy that if the damage is unforeseeable or unavoidable despite the states' exercise of due diligence, it will not be counted as a breach of obligation.[58] Now the question is what the duty entails.[59]

Here the general duty is to act reasonably to address the foreseeable risks under the existing circumstances.[60] Now from a climate change perspective, the key questions are: Is the risk associated with climate change foreseeable? If a state adopts some mitigation policies and measures, is it sufficient to comply with the duty? The answers are contentious. However, the most precise answer in this regard can be found in the judgment given in the recent *Urgenda Foundation v. Government of the Netherlands*[61] case where the Hague District Court affirmed governmental duty of care for GHG mitigation, which was later affirmed by the Hague Court of Appeal. The district court considered five questions to determine the scope of the government's duty of care[62]:

a. the nature and scope of the damage caused by climate change;
b. the foreseeability of the damage;
c. the likelihood of dangerous anthropogenic climate change;
d. the nature of the government's actions (and omissions); and
e. the discretion that the government may exercise based on public law."[63]

To address foreseeability, the court took into consideration current scientific consensus and held that owing to the increasing scientific evidence, climate change impacts are more probable and foreseeable.[64] Considering the nature, foreseeability, and likelihood of damage, the court held that in the matter of climate change, the government's duty of care is far-reaching, as the risk of climate change is extreme and the consequential damage is severe.[65] The government's duty to control emissions within its jurisdiction means that it must ensure the legal and institutional framework for mitigation.[66] And as mitigation is essential to prevent climate change, the court found that the government's policy discretion to address this issue is therefore restricted.[67] Under the existence and scope of the government's duty of care,[68] "sufficient" mitigation[69] effort is required to prevent dangerous anthropogenic climate change,[70] and the court found that current Dutch policies are insufficient and cannot be justified.[71]

Taking the judgment as a groundbreaking decision, it can be set forth that a lack of due diligence or duty of care can validly establish in a climate change context a breach of state liability to prevent transboundary harm.

The Effect of Compliance with Climate Regulation

Under the climate regulatory regime, mitigation and adaptation are the key tools to tackle climate change. However, as mentioned in the first section, focusing efforts solely on mitigation and adaptation cannot prevent loss and damage, and such harm is unavoidable owing to historical and current anthropogenic emissions. Now the question is: if states comply with regulatory conditions and obligations, will they preclude from state liability for climate change–related loss and damage? In other words, can larger emitters take "regulatory compliance defense"?[72]

The question is highly contentious in legal doctrine.[73] There are views which strongly support this regulatory compliance defense; in contrast, there are also arguments that such compliance defense could completely diminish the efficiency of environmental liability.[74] However, the question is applicable to those countries that accept the Kyoto Protocol's obligations and comply with the regulatory provisions, such as Germany and the Netherlands.[75] To address the question, the victim state can argue that the protocol only provides a minimum standard which does not free an Annex I country to take further measures if it is necessary.[76] A similar proposition is found in the judgment of *Urgenda Foundation v. Government of the Netherlands* where the court held that Dutch policies are insufficient and required an extensive duty of care based on circumstances, as the risk of climate change is high and the consequential damage is severe.[77]

Moreover, against the "regulatory compliance defense," there are arguments that along with the Kyoto obligation, the party needs to comply with other obligations such as the obligation to prevent transboundary harm under customary international laws.[78] Contrary to this view, it can be argued that the Kyoto obligation replaced the preexisting customary rule.[79] But the argument is not convincing, and the question of whether preexisting legal obligations overlap with the protocol's requirements is still contentious.[80] However, according to Faure and Nollkaemper, the general proposition is that the argument "compliance with the Protocol does not necessarily present a defense to liability claims seems reasonable."[81]

Causal Uncertainty

Under international laws in a liability claim, a "clear and unbroken causal link" needs to be established and the state is liable to compensate only for that damage which is caused by its wrongful act.[82] However, in climate change liability claims, establishing a causal link between emissions, climate change, and harmful effects is challenging.[83] Here the key question is whether a clear causal link exists between anthropogenic GHG emissions and climate change.[84] Well, a conclusive link is yet to be established, though scientific evidence provides convincing proof about anthropogenic GHG emissions and their effect to cause loss and damage associated with climate change.[85]

On the causality issue, the other key question is whether the specific damage suffered by one victim is effectively caused by GHG emissions from one particular source.[86] Moreover, climate change resulted from a combination of natural sources and GHG emissions, and it can be caused by many sources.[87]

The causal link is primarily determined by normality and foreseeability.[88] However, the issues are modestly proved by IPCC scientific evidence that climate change is caused by anthropogenic emissions and its adverse impact is scientifically predictable.[89] GHG emissions from each state are also well known and documented owing to the inventories drafted for implementing UNFCCC.[90]

In the *Urgenda Foundation v. Government of the Netherlands* case, on the basis of the scientific consensus, the court accepted that a "sufficient causal link can be assumed to exist between the Dutch GHG emissions, global climate change and the effects (now and in the future)."[91] Additionally, the court affirmed that the evolving risk of future harm is sufficiently concrete which can trigger the government's duty of care.[92] By stating this, the court effectively applied the precautionary principle to interpret and address causality.

The precautionary principle has a significant role in causal uncertainty because it requires regulatory action without causal certainty to prevent irreversible harm. According to Professor Boyle, the state's responsibility of not causing harm is simply not one of the responsibilities for ex post facto injury. It is an obligation of "diligent prevention and control of foreseeable risks,"[93] and in this regard, it can be set forth that under the state responsibility, international law includes the precautionary principle.[94] The principle is acknowledged in the preamble and Article 3(3) of UNFCCC. Therefore, with causal uncertainty, a liability claim may be set forth for climate change under the rule of not to cause harm along with the precautionary principle. But more legal research in this regard needs to be done. However, the precautionary principle is also a viable basis to determine the compensation for the damage caused by the emitter state.[95]

Multiple Wrongdoers

Climate change is caused by the cumulative effect of historical and current GHG emissions from various industrialized countries. Therefore, along with the issue of uncertainty in causal link and contribution of each state, a related question arises: Should states be held liable individually based on their own contribution to GHG emissions, or would a joint and several liabilities rule be applicable? As discussed above, issues of causal uncertainty may be tackled based on scientific evidence, and the contribution of each state is now well documented owing to the inventories drafted for implementing UNFCCC.[96]

However, even if the contribution of a particular state can be determined, the question still remains as to whether the liability should be held jointly or separately, as the problem originated because of the cumulative effect of global emissions.

According to the general international law, if one or more states commit a wrongful act in concert or simultaneously which cause a single injury, each state will be liable for its actions under the principle of joint and several liabilities.[97] Here the liability would be "joint" for each other's wrongful act, and "several" as each state can be held separately liable.[98] But this rule is normally not examined in a situation where the causal link is uncertain.[99]

According to some legal scholars, instead of applying the principle of joint and several liabilities, the same can be achieved under the rule of attribution.[100] For example, in the *Corfu Channel* case, the ICJ did not hold that Albania's liability for failure to warn was reduced because of the concurrent responsibility of a third state (Yugoslavia).[101] Therefore, based on this proposition under the rule of attribution, the victim state could obtain the full damage from one state.[102] However, whether this rule is applicable or not in climate change liability claims is questionable because establishing attribution is also challenging here. But it is also not rational to exclude liability of states in climate change on the ground that conclusive proof of attribution is yet to emerge and multiple actors are involved. According to the Dutch district court, "lack of individual responsibility in the Dutch government for the harm of climate change does not negate its duty of care."[103]

Therefore, to make the major emitter state liable under the rule of joint and several liabilities or rule of attribution, more conclusive scientific evidence needs to be developed to adequately establish the attribution and causal link, and then hope IPCC plays an effective role to ensure climate justice.

Retrospective Liability

Climate change and its adverse impact is the result of accumulated past and current anthropogenic emissions. Therefore, constructing state liability for climate change may raise the question of retrospective liability. Retrospective liability denotes that the emissions which were lawful in the past would be considered wrongful today.[104]

According to Article 13 of the ILC 2001 Draft Articles on State Responsibility, "an act of a State does not constitute a breach of an international obligation unless the State is bound by the obligation in question at the time the act occurs." A similar proposition is found in the *Island of Palmas* case where arbitration held that "a juridical fact must be appreciated in the light of the law contemporary with it."[105] Moreover, in the matters of state responsibility, there is a guarantee against retrospective effects in international law.[106]

Yet, liability under climate change does not involve a retrospective effect.

From 1990, after the IPCC first assessment report, the global community knew that GHG emissions may cause climate change.[107] Now the key task is to assess when liability comes into existence and when the adverse impact of climate change was foreseeable.[108] Historical emissions may only be relevant here to assess the proportional contribution to the damage, where contribution of industrialized states will be larger than that of developing countries that recently started to emit, such as China and India,[109] though both can be validly held liable here.

COMPENSATION AND/OR RESTORATION

In the matter to determine redress measures, the legal question is: what would be the effective remedy for climate-induced loss and damage—restitution, redress, or prevention?

An effective remedy specifically for transboundary environmental damage is yet to be developed.[110] However, in the *Factory at Chorzow* case, the Permanent Court of International Justice held that the redress measures should have the capacity to remove all consequences which result from the illegal act. It can be restitution in kind or payment of compensation.[111]

Taking the above view, a victim state can claim restitution or payment of compensation for damage. As states' contribution to GHG emissions is proportional, the liability will arguably be equal to their contribution.[112] Therefore, monetary compensation would be more accurate as restitution in kind would be more difficult for liable states[113] because they contribute only proportionally to climate change causing loss and damage.[114] Besides compensation, compulsion for mitigation can also seek to prevent continuing and future harm.[115] However, the assessment of noneconomic loss such as loss of livelihood, cultural value, and identity would be critical here to determine the accurate amount of compensation. Moreover, how the issue of resettlement/relocation and rehabilitation of climate-induced migration will be settled is another complex issue to settle.[116]

CONCLUSIONS

It has been twenty-six years of struggle in climate negotiation to architect an effective governance regime to address the climate change issue.[117] However, the efforts are falling short with mitigation and adaptation tools, and the scientific evidence indicating that loss and damage are now the reality.[118] Therefore, it is high time to address the question: Who will take the burden of such loss and damage? As mentioned before, in the Paris Agreement 2015, although parties adopted a separate provision to recognize (Article 8) loss and damage resulting from the adverse impact of climate change, para 52 of the Paris decision excludes the clause of liability and compensation.[119]

However, as the chapter discussed before, under customary international laws (which are equally applicable to all states) as well as under the climate regulatory regime (binding only on its parties), there is a basis of liability and compensation logic to address loss and damage associated with climate change. But the basis is intricate with many legal questions and scientific uncertainties yet to be answered or resolved, for example, due diligence strain; attribution and causal uncertainty; complexities of multiple actors and joint or several liabilities; proportional contribution and retrospective effect; and difficulties in the assessment of noneconomic loss and damage. Moreover, there is a lack of suitable avenues to seek the claim. Though Article 14 of UNFCCC provides various dispute settlement options (negotiation, arbitration, conciliation, or submission to the ICJ), only two states (Cuba and Solomon Islands) accept the mode. But states can still present interstate claims; in fact as mentioned before, some small island countries reserve the right to make such claims.[120] In this regard, a suitable forum needs to be found, and here ICJ's jurisdiction is only possible if both states accept ICJ's compulsory jurisdiction.[121] Such consent is very unlikely from major emitters such as the United States, China, and India. Besides interstate suits, private individuals who are injured or likely to be injured can file suits against own or emitter state. This has already happened in the Inuit Petition to the Inter-American Commission on Human Rights[122] and *Urgenda Foundation v. Government of the Netherlands* case, though the former did not succeed and the latter won on appeal in the appellate court. However, specific liability claims require decisive evidence and legal reasoning.[123] In climate change liability claims, even though there are still lack of conclusive scientific evidence and legal reasoning, it should not necessarily wipe out the opportunity of a claim for state liability and compensation[124] to redress climate victims. As the chapter has discussed before, to resolve legal questions and uncertainties, there are various scopes under customary international laws, judicial precedents, and climate-governing regimes. Moreover, science and technology are developing each day. Additionally, scholarly articles are providing a new interpretation of the existing rules to support liability claims. Therefore, we just need to dig these sources further with extensive legal and scientific research to find a definite answer to all the legal questions and uncertainties.

NOTES

1. K. E. McNamara, 'Exploring Loss and Damage at the International Climate Change Talks', 5:3, International Journal of Disaster Risk Science (2014), 242.
2. M. G. Faure and A. Nollkaemper, 'International Liability as an Instrument to Prevent and Compensate for Climate Change' 26: A, Stanford Journal of International Law (2007) 123, 126.
3. The Hague District Court 24 June 2015, Urgenda Foundation v. Government of the Netherlands (Ministry of Infrastructure and the Environment, case number / cause list number: C/09/456689 / HA ZA 13-1396, 2015.
4. According to Fourth Assessment Report of the Intergovernmental Panel on Climate Change (IPCC), 2007, "Warming of the climate system is unequivocal, as is now evident from observations of increases in global average air and ocean temperatures, widespread melting of snow and ice, and rising global average sea level." See also OC Ruppel, C Roschmann & K Ruppel Schlichting (Eds), *Policy and Legal Responses to Loss and Damage associated with Climate Change: Legal Responses and Global Responsibility* Vol. I (Nomos Publishers Germany, 2013) 843.
5. K. E. McNamara, Supra note 1, 242.
6. W. N. Adger, 'Are there social limits to adaptation to climate change?' 93:335, Springer Science and Business Media B.V. (2008), 335, 350.
7. K. E. McNamara, Supra note 1, 242.
8. IPCC, 2014. 'Climate Change 2014: Impacts, Adaptation and Vulnerability; IPCC Working Group II Contribution to AR5. Summary for Policymakers. Intergovernmental Panel for Climate Change. Available at <http://www.ipcc .ch/>(accessed 20.12.15).
9. Para 25, Decision 1/CP.16, The Cancun Agreements: Outcome of the Work of the Ad Hoc Working Group on Long-term Cooperative Action under the Convention (UN Doc. FCCC/CP/2010/7/Add.1, 15 March 2011).
10. *Ibid.*
11. Para 2, Note by the secretariat, 'A literature review on the topics in the context of thematic area 2 of the work programme on loss and damage: a range of approaches to address loss and damage associated with the adverse effects of climate change' (UN Doc. FCCC/SBI/2012/INF.14, 15 November 2012).
12. *Ibid.*
13. *Ibid.*
14. K. Warner and K. Geest; 'Loss and damage from climate change: local-level evidence from nine vulnerable countries', 5:4 International Journal Global Warming (2013) 367,369.

15. D. Stabinsky and J. P. Hoffmaister, 'Loss and Damage: Some key issues and considerations', 23 July 2011, TWN Briefing Paper on Loss and Damage (2011), 1.

16. OC Ruppel, C Roschmann & K Ruppel Schlichting (Eds), Policy and Legal Responses to Loss and Damage associated with Climate Change: Legal Responses and Global Responsibility Vol. I (Nomos Publishers Germany, 2013), 98.

17. United Nation Framework Convention on Climate Change (Rio, 11th December 1992; in force 21 March 1994), Preamble.

18. OC Ruppel, C Roschmann & K Ruppel Schlichting (Eds), Supra Note 16, at 201.

19. I. Brownlie; The Rule of Law in International Affairs 79–80 (Kluwer Law International, 1998), at 79–80.

20. M. G. Faure and A. Nollkaemper, Supra note 2, at 123, 139.

21. Ibid.

22. P. W. Birnie, A. E. Boyel and C. Redgwell; International Law & the Environment, 3rg edn. (Oxford University Press, 2009), 214.

23. Ibid, 137.

24. Ibid, 143.

25. Trial Smelter Arbitration 16 April 1938 and 11 March 1941, Trail smelter case (United States v. Canada), pp. 1905–1982.

26. ICJ 15 December 1949, Corfu Channel ((United Kingdom of Great Britain and Northern Ireland v. Albania) ICJ Reports (1949), 22.

27. ICJ 20th December 1974, Nuclear Tests (Australia v. France), ICJ Reports (1974), 253.

28. Arbitral Tribunal 16 November 1957, 1 Lake Lanoux Arbitration (France V. Spain), ILR Report 1957, 101; See also I. Brownlie and J. Crawford, Principles of Public International Law, 6th edn. (Oxford University Press, 2003), 182.

29. P. W. Birnie, A. E. Boyel and C. Redgwell, Supra Note 22, at 144.

30. UNGA Res 2996 (XXVII) (1972); See also UNGA Res 2995 XXVII (1972); 2996 XXVII (1972); 3281 XXIX (1974); 34/186 (1979); P. W. Birnie, A. E. Boyel and C. Redgwell, International Law & the Environment, 3rg edn. (Oxford University Press, 2009), 145.

31. P. W. Birnie, A. E. Boyel and C. Redgwell, International Law & the Environment, 3rg edn. (Oxford University Press, 2009), 138.

32. ICJ 8 July 1996, Legality of the Threat or Use of Nuclear Weapons, Advisory Opinion, ICJ Reports 1996, 226, para 29.

33. P. W. Birnie, A. E. Boyel and C. Redgwell, Supra Note 22, at 138.

34. Ibid, 225.

35. Ibid. See also Article 1-30, ILC 2001 Articles on State Responsibility.

36. ICJ 31 March 2004, Case Concerning Avena and Other Mexican Nationals (*Mexico V. United States of America*), ICJ Reports (2004), 12, para 119 S.

37. P. W. Birnie, A. E. Boyel and C. Redgwell, Supra Note 22, at 228.

38. *Ibid*, 229.

39. *Ibid*, 228.

40. Year Book of International Law Commission 1993, Vol. II, Part.1 Document of the forty-fifth session, (UN Doc. A/CN.4/SER.A/1993/Add.l (Part 1)) 63, 76.

41. P. W. Birnie, A. E. Boyel and C. Redgwell, Supra Note 22, at 229.

42. J. Kilinski, 'International Climate Change Liability: A Myth or A Reality?' 18:2, Journal of Transnational Law & Policy (2009), 378, 388.

43. J B. Smith, R. J. T. Klein and Saleemul Huq (eds), Climate Change, Adaptive Capacity and Development (Imperial College press, 2003), 182.

44. Ibid.

45. J. Kilinski, Supra Note 42, at 378, 389.

46. D. Bodansky, The United Nations Framework Convention on Climate Change: A Commentary', 18 Yale International Law Journal. (1993), 451, 516; See also P. Sands, Principles of International Environmental Law, 2nd edn, (Cambridge University Press, 2003), 361–365.

47. J. Kilinski, Supra Note 42, at 378, 389.

48. D. Bodansky, Supra Note 46, at 216.

49. J. Kilinski, Supra Note 42, at 378, 390.

50. M. G. Faure and A. Nollkaemper, Supra note 2, at 123, 144.

51. J. Kilinski, Supra Note 42, at 378, 392.

52. United Nations Framework Convention on Climate Change (UNFCCC), (Rio, 9 May 1992; in force 1994) 1771 U.N.T.S. 107, 31 I.L.M. 849 (1992) Declaration 1–2.

53. The preamble of UNFCCC declares the following: "States have, in accordance with the Charter of the United Nations and the principles of international law, the sovereign right to exploit their own resources pursuant to their own environmental and developmental policies, and the responsibility to ensure that activities within their jurisdiction or control do not cause damage to the environment of other States or of areas beyond the limits of national jurisdiction."

54. R. S. J. Tol and R. Verheyen, 'State responsibility and compensation for climate change damages—a legal and economic assessment', Energy Policy 32 (2004), 1109–1130.

55. K. E. McNamara, Supra note 1, 242, 243.

56. L. Rajamani, 'Addressing Loss and Damage from Climate Change Impacts', 30:1, Economic & Political Weekly (2015), 19.

57. R. S. J Tol and,R. Verheyen, Supra Note, at 1109–1130, 1113.

58. L. Rajamani, Supra Note 56, at 19.

59. H. David, S. James, 'Negligence in the Air: The Duty of Care in Climate Change Litigation' 155:6, University of Pennsylvania Law Review (2007), 1741–1794, 1746.

60. Ibid.

61. Urgenda Foundation v. Government of the Netherlands, Supra Note 3.

62. J. Zeben, 'Establishing a Governmental Duty of Care for Climate Change Mitigation: Will Urgenda Turn the Tide?', 4:2, Transnational Environmental Law(2015), 339–357, 347.

63. Ibid.

64. Urgenda Foundation v. Government of the Netherlands, Supra Note 3, at para 4.63.

65. Ibid, para 4.52.

66. Ibid, para. 4.66.
67. Ibid, para. 4.64.
68. The Dutch government did not contest its responsibility to take mitigation or adaptation measures, but rather questioned the required scope of the measures before 2020, para. 4.64.
69. Ibid. para. 4.73.
70. Ibid., para. 4.83.
71. Ibid., paras 4.84–4.85.
72. M. G. Faure and A. Nollkaemper, Supra note 2, at 123, 151.
73. Ibid.
74. Ibid.
75. Ibid, 152.
76. R. S. J. Tol and R. Verheyen, Supra Note, at 1109–1130, 1122.
77. Urgenda Foundation v. Government of the Netherlands, Supra Note 3, at paras 4.65, 4.84–4.85.
78. M. G. Faure and A. Nollkaemper, Supra note 2, at 123, 152.
79. M. E. Villiger, 'Customary International Law and Treaties', Martinus Nijhoff Publisher (1985), 183.
80. M. G. Faure and A. Nollkaemper, Supra note 2, at 123, 152.
81. Ibid.
82. P. W. Birnie, A. E. Boyel and C. Redgwell; Supra Note, at 158.
83. L. Rajamani, Supra Note 56, at 19.
84. M. G. Faure and A. Nollkaemper, Supra note 2, at 123, 157.
85. IPCC, 2014. Supra Note 8.
86. M. G. Faure and A. Nollkaemper, Supra note 2, at 123, 158.
87. Ibid.
88. Ibid.
89. P. K. Thornton *et al.*, 'Climate variability and vulnerability to climate change: a review', 20:11, Global Change Biology (2014), pp. 3313–3328, 3319.
90. M. G. Faure and A. Nollkaemper, Supra note 2, at 123, 165.
91. Urgenda Foundation v. Government of the Netherlands, Supra Note 3, para 4.90.
92. Ibid, para 4.89.
93. P. W. Birnie, A. E. Boyel and C. Redgwell; Supra Note, at 153.
94. Ibid.
95. M. G. Faure and A. Nollkaemper, Supra note 2, at 123, 159.
96. Ibid, 165.
97. Ibid, 166.
98. J. Crawford, 'The Third Report on State Responsibility', UN Doc. A/CN.4/507 (15 March 2000), para 31.
99. M. E. Villiger, Supra Note 79, at 185; See also Ibid.
100. J. Crawford, Supra Note 98, at para 33.
101. ICJ 15 December 1949, Corfu Channel ((United Kingdom of Great Britain and Northern Ireland v. Albania) ICJ Reports 1949, p. 244; See also Ibid.
102. M. G. Faure and A. Nollkaemper, Supra note 2, at 123, 167.

103. Urgenda Foundation v. Government of the Netherlands, Supra Note 3, at paras 4.79 and 4.90.

104. M. G. Faure and A. Nollkaemper, Supra note 2, at 123, 171.

105. International Arbitral Awards 4 April 1928, Island of Palmas case (*Netherlands v. USA*), Report of International Arbitral Awards 829–827(1928), 829.

106. M. G. Faure and A. Nollkaemper, Supra note 2, at 123, 172.

107. R. S. J. Tol and,R. Verheyen, Supra Note, at 1109–1130, 1114.

108. M. G. Faure and A. Nollkaemper, Supra note 2, at 123, 172.

109. Ibid.

110. C. Gray, Judicial Remedies in International Law, Oxford: Clarendon publication (1987), 250.

111. Permanent Court of International Justice 26th July 1927, Case Concerning The Factory At Chorzow (Claim for Indemnity), Report of Permanent Court of International Justice, 9(1927), 47.

112. M. G. Faure and A. Nollkaemper, Supra note 2, at 123, 174.

113. Ibid.

114. Ibid.

115. Ibid.

116. O. C. Ruppel, C Roschmann & K Ruppel Schlichting (Eds), Supra Note 16, at 202.

117. S. T. Zaman, 'Paris COP21: Time to make a difference', The Dhaka Tribune (27th November 2015).

118. IPCC, 2014. Supra Note 8.

119. Ibid.

120. M. G. Faure and A. Nollkaemper, Supra note 2, at 123, 129.

121. The Statute of the International Court of Justice, Article 36(2).

122. Inuit Petition Inter-American Commission On Human Rights To Oppose Climate Change Caused by the United States of America (2005).

123. M. G. Faure and A. Nollkaemper, Supra note 2, at 123, 177.

124. Ibid., 178.

Chapter 16

Waste Management Mechanism

Challenges and Implementation

Riya Gulati

INTRODUCTION

Waste management is the process that involves the management of detritus right from its origin to its eventual disposal. It encompasses activities such as conglomeration, conveyance, treatment, and disposal of chaff, along with monitoring and modulation of the waste management process. Waste can be in solid, liquid, or gaseous form, and each type has its own procedure of disposal and management. Owing to the advent of industrialization and unsought population growth, a large amount of waste has been generated, which has caused impediments in its disposal. Some waste and even waste disposal processes pose threat to animate beings and environment.

To overcome such challenges, the government must ensure to adopt a proper disposal technique by embracing the 3R principles: reduce, reuse, and recycle the waste. This will not only reduce the amount of waste ejection, but it will also save space in landfills and preserve the natural resources. Apart from the government, individuals must also be held accountable in case of noncompliance to the rules with regards to waste management.

TAXONOMY OF WASTE

Solid Detritus

It is explicated as any discarded matter that is abandoned by being disposed of, incinerated, recycled, or deemed "waste-like." Solid debris can physically be a solid, semisolid, liquid, or a container of a gaseous substance.[1] It comprises of plastic, paper, tins, metals, ceramics, glass, and organic waste.[2]

It spawns from residential, commercial, agricultural, mining, and industrial activities and can be managed in assorted ways.[3] Solid waste management can encompass source reduction, recycling, collection, processing, storage, transportation, and disposal. Solid waste provisions incorporate landfills, transfer stations, composting sites, processing facilities, and incinerators.[4]

Liquid Dross

It refers to any form of liquid remnant that is deleterious for living organisms and the environment.[5] It can be expounded as such liquids as wastewater, oils, fats, grease, sludge, used oil, solids, liquids, gases, or hazardous household liquids. They can also be discarded mercantile substances such as pesticides, cleaning fluids, or byproducts of manufacturing processes.[6] Liquid wreckage can come from domestic, industrial, and commercial activities.[7] It includes filthy water, wash water, organic liquids, waste detergents, and even rainwater. Dealing with liquid dross is one of the biggest challenges of citified sanitation as it requires skilled personnel, huge capital investment, coordination between different authorities and organizations, and public awareness.[8]

Gaseous Waste

It refers to waste products in the gaseous form resulting from various human activities such as biological processes, manufacturing, processing, and material consumption.[9] It is generated in the environment predominantly because of anthropogenic activities. It includes carbon dioxide, carbon monoxide, methane, chlorofluorocarbons, and oxides of nitrogen and sulfur. Gaseous waste is the chief source of air pollution and cause grave environmental menaces.[10] Employing filters, scrubbers, electrostatic precipitators, and catalytic converters can help in the management of gaseous waste.[11]

RAMIFICATION OF IMPROPER WASTE DISPOSAL

Improper waste disposal annihilates the natural environment as it seriously endangers flora and fauna.[12] Improper waste disposal is responsible for causing (i) soil contamination—the dross that ends up in landfills excretes perilous chemicals that emanate into the soil, which not only affects plant growth but also humans and animals that feed on those plants; (ii) air contamination—the trash that is burned in landfills emits hazardous gases that are dangerous for the ozone layer and pose great health risks because they diffuse into the air that we breathe; and (iii) water contamination—the hazardous waste that leaches into the ground affects groundwater which is used for multifarious purposes such as drinking and irrigation. Moreover, the toxic liquid chemicals from waste also seep into water bodies and affect marine habitats and humans who consume fish and other marine life. As perceptible, improper waste disposal can adversely affect human health, animals, and marine life. It causes skin irritation, respiratory problems, blood infection, reproductive issues, and growth problems. Furthermore, mosquitoes, insects, and rats have the tendency to breed in sewage, landfills, and wreckage. They carry life-threatening diseases such as malaria, dengue, leptospirosis, and salmonellosis. Moreover, the moisture produced from waste is a breeding ground for microbes. Improper decomposition of waste emits gases that are responsible for causing extreme climate changes. Improper waste management is regarded as an important contributor to global greenhouse gas emissions. For example, owing to the emission of greenhouse gases, the environment is facing threats from extremely vigorous storms, tornadoes, and smoldering heat. Hence, recklessness in handling waste is slowly pushing the planet toward extinction.[13]

CHALLENGES IN WASTE MANAGEMENT

The management of waste is still a pervasive issue in the twenty-first century. As an outcome of growing populace, ongoing relocation from rural to urban areas and palpably ineluctable increase in waste per capita as economies flourish, many cities in the lower-income countries, especially in Asia and Africa, are set to double their municipal solid waste within 10–15 years. At the same time, globalization is actuating a shift in production, and hence, there has been a displacement of hazardous and industrial waste generation from developed to developing nations. Waste management has become a pressing issue that affects many aspects of the economy. If the different types of waste are not managed properly, it will not only impact public health but will also cause lamentable damage to the environment.[14] Owing to noxious waste generation and inadequate waste collection, conveyance, treatment, and disposal, India has faced major environmental challenges. There are numerous encumbrances that are associated with proper waste disposal such as lack of availability of qualified waste management professionals, production of a large quantity of pernicious waste, reliance on outdated technologies to deal with waste disposal, insufficient budget to cover the costs, and regulations on waste management based on vested interests[15] and lack of environmental awareness.[16] Also, developed countries are exporting their waste to India that has caused disarray and impediments in its disposal.

The key challenges with regards to waste management are dearth of collection and segregation of waste at source, dumping of e-waste, scarcity of land, and lack of awareness. Even the new Municipal Solid Waste Management Rules 2000 failed to manage waste in a cyclic process. Also, the use of latest and exorbitant technologies to tackle the urban waste problem ignores their social and environmental implications. The use of technologies in the process of incineration, gasification, pelletization, and pyrolysis for the treatment of thermal waste poses risk to the community, and therefore, they are being widely opposed.[17]

REGULATIONS ON WASTE MANAGEMENT IN INDIA

In India, waste management is governed by Ministry of Environment, Forest and Climate Change that works together with state pollution control boards (SPCBs). There are numerous laws and enactments which provide provisions for waste (disposal) regulation.[18]

The Environmental Protection Act, 1986

This act places an interdiction on harming the environment by expounding that no person who is operating any industry, activity, or process should emit or discharge environmental pollutants in violation of the prescribed standards.[19] The act also provides that if any incidence occurs that harms the environment through any foreseen or unforeseen event, then the person responsible for such harm is under obligation to intercept or alleviate the pollutant discharged as a result of such event. The person is also duty bound to apprise the concerned authorities about the event that may harm the environment.[20] The act also encapsulates the "polluter pays principle" which enunciates that any cost that has been incurred to reinstate the environment to its natural state shall be indemnified by the person who is liable for such degradation.[21]

Bio-Medical Waste (Management and Handling) Rules, 1998

The fundamental objective of these rules is to ensure a safe mode of disposal of biomedical waste which encompasses byproducts generated during treatment, diagnosis, immunization, or research activities.[22] These rules apply to everyone who produces, accumulates, receives, reserves, transports, treats, discards, or handles biomedical waste of any sort.[23] The rules set out an obligation on the occupier of an institute producing biomedical waste to take all the necessary measures so as to ensure that such waste is handled cautiously without causing any adverse effects on human health and environment.[24] These rules proscribe blending of biological waste with any other type of waste. The general rule provides that biomedical waste cannot be kept stored beyond a period of 48 hours without being treated. But if it becomes necessary to store the waste beyond 48 hours, permission from the prescribed authority is required to ensure that the waste does not adversely affect the environment and human health.[25]

Municipal Solid Wastes (Management and Handling) Rules, 2000

The prime aim of the these rules is to hold the municipal authority within the territorial region of the municipality accountable for the execution of the provisions of these rules and for any infrastructure progression for collection, storage, separation, conveyance, processing, and ejection of municipal solid waste.[26] SPCBs are responsible for conceding permission to set up waste disposal facilities and supervising to ensure that the municipal solid waste disposal concurs with the compliance criteria given in the rules set by the Central Pollution Control Board (CPCB).[27] The Union Ministry of Environment, Forest and Climate Change revamped the Municipal Solid Wastes (Management and Handling) Rules, 2000 and introduced the new Solid Waste Management Rules, 2016 as the compliance of 2000 rules was limited and vacillating.[28]

The Batteries (Management and Handling) Rules, 2001

These rules were notified to set up a mechanism for the disposal of lead acid batteries. The rules are applicable to anyone who is involved in the manufacturing, processing, purchase, sale, and use of batteries or components thereof. Hence, it applies to every manufacturer, dealer, recycler, assembler, reconditioner, auctioneer, importer, consumer, and bulk consumer (organizations/departments purchasing more than 100 batteries).[29] The rules set out the responsibility of a manufacturer, assembler, reconditioner, and importer to establish collection centers at various places for the purpose of collection of used batteries from dealers or consumers and to use the international sign of recycling on the batteries.[30] They make it obligatory for every consumer to deposit the used batteries back with the manufacturer, dealer, designated collection centers, and recycler. The same obligation to deposit the used batteries applies for bulk consumers, but they are also required to file half-yearly returns with the SPCB about the usage.[31]

The Hazardous Wastes (Management, Handling and Transboundary Movement) Rules, 2008

These rules place responsibilities on the occupier for a safe and environmentally sound handling of perilous waste produced in their establishment. The rules provide that the occupier must vend or send the hazardous waste to a recycler or reprocessor who is permitted by the government to dispose of the waste in a cautious manner.[32] The occupiers, reusers, recyclers, and reprocessors can keep the hazardous waste for storage for a maximum duration of 90 days.[33] The transfer or sale of hazardous waste for recycling can only be done after procuring a valid registration from the CPCB.[34] The use of perilous waste for energy recovery or as a supplementary resource also requires an approbation from the CPCB.[35] The transboundary shipment of perilous waste is modulated by the Basel Convention of which India is a signatory. The cardinal aim of the convention is to reduce the movement of perilous waste between countries, especially the transfer of hazardous waste from developed to the less developed countries.[36] The import of perilous waste for disposal to India is proscribed by law. Although the import for reuse, recycle, or recovery purposes is permissible, it is subjected to certain restrictions. However, India permits the export of hazardous waste but only with a prior informed consent of the importing nation.[37]

The Plastic Waste (Management and Handling) Rules, 2011

These rules have been laid down to regulate the use, manufacture, and reprocessing of plastic waste. These rules provide that the recovery, recycling, and disposal of plastic waste must be carried out as per the rules and standards specified by the central government. It has laid down obligations on the part of the municipal authority to set up, operationalize, and coordinate the waste management system. The municipal authority must not only ensure safe collection, segregation, storage, processing, transportation, and disposal of plastic waste, but it should also set up collection centers for plastic waste and ensure that the open burning of plastic waste is interdicted.[38] It is obligatory on the part of manufacturers and recyclers of plastic products to procure a grant for registration or renewal of registration from the SPCB. This registration is valid up to three years.[39] In order to ensure that people use plastic bags judicially, explicit pricing of the plastic bags depending upon their size, quality, and waste management costs has been laid down. It also restricts the retailer to provide plastic bags free of cost.[40] Recycling of plastic commodities and waste is to be done through a firm procedure laid down by the Bureau of Indian Standards specifications.[41]

The E-Waste (Management and Handling) Rules, 2011

The chief objective of these rules is to put into place a system that manages e-waste in an environment-friendly manner by modulating the issue of reprocessing and disposal of e-waste. Owing to the advancement of new technologies and (illegal) import of e-waste, India has faced dire challenges in the disposal of e-waste. Hence, these rules delineate the responsibilities of the producers, collection centers, dismantlers, consumers or bulk consumers, and reprocessors for effective e-waste management. The rules state that the producer of electronic equipment is responsible for accumulating the e-waste produced during the manufacture of such equipment and from the "end of life" of their commodities, which is in line with the principle of "extended producer responsibility." It is the duty of the producers to ensure that e-waste is channelized to a registered recycler or dismantler. They must also make sure that the proper collection and channelization of e-waste by authorized collection agencies takes place. They can either set up collection centers or a take-back system either independently or collectively.[42] These rules patently set out the responsibilities of the collection centers. They provide that the collection centers must make sure that the e-waste accumulated by them is stowed in a secured way until it is sent to registered dismantlers or recyclers. They must also ensure that no harm is caused to the environment during the storage and transportation of the e-waste.[43] The rules provide that every dismantler is responsible for making sure that the facility and dismantling processes are according to the guidelines or standards published by the CPCB. They must also ensure that the dismantled e-waste is segregated, separated, and redirected to registered recycling facilities for the restoration of usable materials. They must send the nonrecoverable/nonrecyclable components and materials to authorized treatment, storage, and disposal facilities. They must not process any e-waste for refining or recovery of substances unless the dismantler is registered with the SPCB as a recycler for recovery and refining of materials. They must take necessary steps so as to make sure that the dismantling processes do not have any untoward effect on human health and the environment.[44] These rules state that the consumers or bulk consumers of electronic equipment must ensure that the e-waste produced by them is channelized to authorized collection centers, recyclers, or registered dismantlers, or is returned to the pick-up or take-back services provided by the manufacturers.[45] The rules have also laid down responsibilities for the reprocessor or recycler. They must ensure that the facility and recycling processes are in compliance with the standards laid down in the guidelines published by the CPCB. They must also ensure that the remnants generated are discarded in a hazardous waste treatment storage disposal facility.[46]

GOVERNMENT INITIATIVES TO COMBAT THE ISSUES PERTAINING TO WASTE MANAGEMENT

India is one of the countries where most of the waste is disposed. As per the reports of Associated Chambers of Commerce and Industry, India engendered

130 million tons of e-waste in 2018, a substantial increase from the 93.5 million tons in 2016. India is anticipated to produce 260 million tons of e-waste by 2020. The market size of waste management in India is estimated to be worth USD 14 billion with an annual increase hovering around 7 percent by 2025.[47]

To overcome the issues of waste management, the government has assigned responsibilities to various departments, ministries, local authorities, and boards. The government from time to time had undertaken many nationwide clean-up projects such as Swachh Bharat Abhiyan, Mahatma Gandhi Swachhata Mission, Municipal Solid Waste (MSW) Management Projects, and zero waste management projects that had involved active public participation.[48] In big cities, there has been a provision of daily doorstep collection of waste. Also, there are ragpickers (*kabadiwala*) and street sweepers employed in every district to maintain high level of cleanliness by ensuring that the domestic waste is disposed of properly. In order to regulate the waste management mechanism in the country, the government has initiated some key programs such as Jawaharlal Nehru National Urban Renewal Mission, Total Sanitation Campaign, MNRE's waste-to-energy programs, and National Biogas and Manure Management Programme.[49]

SOLUTIONS TO THE PROBLEM

It is not just the duty of the government to ensure a clean environment, it is also a fundamental obligation of every individual to maintain a clean and healthy environment for themselves and others. Hence, it is necessary to understand the mechanism of proper waste disposal.

For domestic waste, a procedure similar to that of European countries' waste disposal must be adopted. The curbside collection method (wherein the bin collection trucks come and collect the waste from households) must be espoused in India. Although India does have this system in a few states, there are other states which must adopt such a system. It should be the duty of every individual to segregate their waste in three bins (of different colors). For example: a green wheelie bin container for recyclable materials, a brown one for biodegradable waste (kitchen waste), and a black one for other general waste. This technique of waste collection is not only considered to be environmentally friendly, but it has also generated public awareness on waste production and waste reduction. In order to facilitate such services, households must pay for the bin services. They must also be levied fine if they throw waste on the road.

In case of industrial waste, it must be the duty of the industrialists to ensure proper waste disposal techniques such as incineration, pyrolysis, or prior treatment of waste before releasing it into water bodies. They must be charged or brought before the court if they dispose any deleterious substances without treating them beforehand.

More number of dustbins must be introduced on roads and at public places. Anyone throwing waste on the ground must be fined. Similar to foreign countries, it must be the duty of the owner of a pet to clean up after them.

Also, there is a need to keep pace with the emerging technologies. Scientific research must be carried out, public awareness must be generated, and new technologies must be adopted in order to ensure proper waste management.

CONCLUSIONS

Indeed, a person is influenced and affected by not only their social environment but also their physical environment. The cleaner the environment, the healthier the person. It is high time that our country has stringent laws for environmental protection by taking the air and water quality of major cities into consideration. However, there are many factors which contribute to air and water pollution. One such factor is improper waste disposal. The more stringent the law, the easier it is to have compliance. Hence, it is the collective duty of the government and individuals to keep the environment clean by adopting proper waste management techniques.

NOTES

1. *Solid Waste*, Idaho Public Health, <idahopublichealth.com/environmental-health/solidwaste>, last seen on 10/01/2019.
2. *There are 5 types of waste, do you know them all?,* 4 Waste, https://4waste.com.au/rubbish-removal/5-types-waste-know/, last seen on 10/01/2019.
3. *An Introduction to Solid Waste Management*, The Balance Small Business, https://www.thebalancesmb.com/an-introduction-to-solid-waste-management-2878102, last seen on 10/01/2019.
4. Supra 1.
5. Anonymous, *What is Liquid Waste Disposal?* Nitschke Liquid Waste, < https://www.nitschkeliquidwaste.com/about/>, last seen on 10/01/2019.
6. *What is Liquid Waste?,* eWaste Disposal Inc, < https://www.ewastedisposal.net/liquid-waste/>, last seen on 10/01/2019.
7. Liquid Waste, IWMA, < http://iwma.ie/commercial-waste/liquid-waste/>, last seen on 10/01/2019.
8. *Liquid Waste Management and Treatment*, Open University, < http://www.open.edu/openlearncreate/mod/oucontent/view.php?id=80563&printable=1>, last seen on 11/01/2019.

9. *What is the Definition of "Gaseous Waste"?*, Reference < https://www .reference.com/science/definition-gaseous-waste-ed12462e35a6d11d>, last seen on 11/01/2019.

10. *Waste Management: Management of Solid, Liquid and Gaseous Wastes*, Environmental Pollution < http://www.environmentalpollution.in/waste-management /waste-management-management-of-solid-liquid-and-gaseous-wastes/377>, last seen on 11/01/2019.

11. *Disposal of Liquid Wastes and Disposal of Gaseous Wastes*, Biology Discussion < http://www.biologydiscussion.com/difference/disposal-of-liquid-wa stes-and-disposal-of-gaseous-wastes/7078>, last seen on 11/01/2019.

12. *The Effect of Waste on Our Natural Environment*, Groupe Bouffard, http:// www.groupebouffard.com/en/effect-of-waste/#top, last seen on 12/01/2019.

13. *10 Negative Effects of Improper Rubbish Removal*, Skipthetip, < https://ww w.skipthetip.com/10-negative-effects-of-improper-rubbish-removal/>, last seen on 12/01/2019.

14. David C Wilson & Costas A Velis, *Waste Management- Still a Global Challenge in the 21st Century: An Evidence- based Call for Action*, 33[12] SAGE 1049, 1049–1050 (2015), available at https://journals.sagepub.com/doi/pdf/10.1177/ 0734242X15616055, last seen on 12/01/2019.

15. Rinkesh, *What is Waste Disposal?,* Conserve Energy Future, available at https ://www.conserve-energy-future.com/various-waste-disposal-problems-and-solutions. php, last seen on 12/01/2019.

16. Lilliana Guerrero, Ger Mass & William Hogland, *Solid Waste Management Challenges for Cities in Developing Countries*, 33[1] Elsevier 220, 220–232 (2013), available at https://www.sciencedirect.com/science/article/pii/S0956053X12004205, last seen on 12/01/2019.

17. Raveesh Agarwal, Mona Chaudhary & Jayveer Singh, *Waste Management Initiatives in India for Human Well Being*, European Scientific Journal, 105, 120–121 (2015), available at < http://home.iitk.ac.in/~anubha/H16.pdf>, last seen on 13/01/2019.

18. Pramit Bhattacharya, *Waste Management Laws in India*, iPleaders, available at https://blog.ipleaders.in/waste-management-laws-india/, last seen on 13/01/2019.

19. Section 7, The Environmental Protection Act, 1986.

20. Section 9, The Environmental Protection Act, 1986.

21. Section 9(3), The Environmental Protection Act, 1986.

22. Rule 3, Bio-Medical Waste (Management and Handling) Rules, 1998.

23. *Bio-Medical Waste (Management and Handling) Rules, 1998*, Wealthy Waste, available at http://www.wealthywaste.com/bio-medical-waste-management -and-handling-rules-1998, last seen on 13/01/2019.

24. Rule 4, Bio-Medical Waste (Management and Handling) Rules, 1998.

25. Rule 6, Bio-Medical Waste (Management and Handling) Rules, 1998.

26. Rule (4) (1), Municipal Solid Waste Management Rules, 2000.

27. *Compliance to rules governing municipal solid, bio-medical and plastic waste*, Columbia.edu, available at < http://www.seas.columbia.edu/earth/wtert/sofos/india _nationwide_survey.pdf>, last seen on 14/01/2019.

28. Swati Singh Sambyal, *Government notifies new solid waste management rules*, Down To Earth (19/09/2016), available at < https://www.downtoearth.org.in/news/waste/solid-waste-management-rules-2016-53443>, last seen on 14/01/2019.

29. *Batteries (Management and Handling) Rules, 2001*, India Environment Portal, available at < http://www.indiaenvironmentportal.org.in/content/453217/batteries-management-and-handling-rules-2001/>, last seen on 14/01/2019.

30. Rule 4, The Batteries (Management and Handling) Rules, 2001.

31. Rule 10, The Batteries (Management and Handling) Rules, 2001.

32. Rule 4, The Hazardous Wastes (Management, Handling and Transboundary Movement) Rules, 2008.

33. Rule 7, The Hazardous Wastes (Management, Handling and Transboundary Movement) Rules, 2008.

34. Rule 9, The Hazardous Wastes (Management, Handling and Transboundary Movement) Rules, 2008.

35. Rule 11, The Hazardous Wastes (Management, Handling and Transboundary Movement) Rules, 2008.

36. *Basel Convention*, Wikipedia, available at < https://en.m.wikipedia.org/wiki/Basel_Convention>, last seen on 14/01/2019.

37. Rule 13, The Hazardous Wastes (Management, Handling and Transboundary Movement) Rules, 2008.

38. Rule 6, The Plastic Waste (Management and Handing) Rules, 2011.

39. Rule 9, The Plastic Waste (Management and Handing) Rules, 2011.

40. Rule 10, The Plastic Waste (Management and Handing) Rules, 2011.

41. *Indian Standard Guidelines for Recycling of Plastics*, Internet Archive, available at < https://archive.org/details/gov.in.is.14534.1998/page/n3>, last seen on 14/01/2019.

42. Rule 4, E-Waste (Management and Handling) Rules, 2011.

43. Rule 5, E-Waste (Management and Handling) Rules, 2011.

44. Rule 7, E-Waste (Management and Handling) Rules, 2011.

45. Rule 6, E-Waste (Management and Handling) Rules, 2011.

46. Rule 8, E-Waste (Management and Handling) Rules, 2011.

47. *Waste management in India*, Wikipedia, available at https://en.wikipedia.org/wiki/Waste_management_in_India, last seen on 15/01/2019.

48. Hardik Patel & Hitesh Solanki, *Government Initiatives and Activities to Combat the Issues of Municipal Solid Waste Management in India*, ResearchGate 1 (2018), available at https://www.researchgate.net/publication/325857651_Government_Initiatives_and_Activities_to_combat_the_issues_of_Municipal_Solid_Waste_Management_in_India, last seen on 15/01/2019.

49. Supra 17.

Chapter 17

Challenges to Realizing the Human Right to Clean Water in the Slums of Mumbai

Ritika Chauhan

INTRODUCTION

Sustainable development is a desirable state of development. Although several definitions exist, the most often used definition of sustainable development is that proposed by the Brundtland Commission according to which the "needs of the present are met without compromising the ability of future generations to meet their own needs."[1] It has been defined as a scheme of such social and economic transformation wherein the optimization of current economic and societal benefits is focused on, without posing any threats to the potential benefits likely to be enjoyed in future.[2] The principle underlying the processes of such development is integration of economic, environmental, and societal concerns while making decisions.[3]

EVOLUTION OF THE CONCEPT OF SUSTAINABLE DEVELOPMENT

Sustainable development, as a concept, was first discussed in 1972 in Stockholm where representatives from more than ninety countries met for the United Nations Conference on Human Environment.[4] Sustainable development was seen as a global objective, a bridge between the extreme views of developing and developed countries on economic growth, development theories, and environmental issues. Principle 14 of the resultant declaration[5] recognized the need to amicably settle conflicts related to development, as well as the need to protect and preserve the environment.

Soon after, there was an increase in debates between the developed and developing economies. While the former argued that economic growth was of primary importance and nothing should hamper the process of development in their countries, the latter stated that development meant much more than mere economic growth. They believed that it was imperative the countries designed their policies in such a manner that improved the quality of life of the human population in general. In response to these debates, the World Commission on Environment and Development published a report that is commonly known as the Brundtland Commission Report[6] on sustainability. The report acknowledged that in order to deal with the environmental issues around the world, it was important to focus on the quality of life of the people. This meant that there was a direct relationship between poverty, population, unequal distribution of wealth, and the environmental pressure. The report enlisted broad remedies and recommendations for a sustainable way of growth and development.

In 1992, a global conference was convened in Rio De Janeiro, the United Nations Conference on Environment and Development, also known as the Earth Summit. The outcomes of this conference included the 1992 Rio Declaration, Agenda 21, and international treaties such as the 1992 UN Framework Convention on Climate Change, United Nations Convention on Biological Diversity, and United Nations Convention to Combat Desertification of 1994. It was at this conference that twenty-seven principles were laid down to help countries achieve sustainable development. Agenda 21 was drafted that served as a global plan of action.

In furtherance of discussions held in Rio, the United Nations Commission for Sustainable Development (UNCSD) was created on November 25, 1992. UNCSD was active between the years 1997 and 2002 and held numerous conferences globally. The World Summit on Sustainable Development was held in Johannesburg, South Africa where a plan of implementation was drafted in reference to sustainable development.

When Rio+20, "The Future We Want," was held in 2012, discussions on sustainable development were at their peak. This conference is credited with generating a stronger momentum for accomplishing goals of sustainable development. A primary interagency mechanism was established to provide a common direction to various committees and programs working toward sustainable development.[7] This is known as the Executive Committee of Economic and Social Affairs Plus (ECESA Plus). Other agencies that are also instrumental in providing issue-specific collaborations include UN-Water, UN-Oceans, UN-Energy, the High Level Task Force on Food Security, the Interagency Committee of the UN Decade of Education for Sustainable Development, to mention a few.[8] ECESA Plus acts as coordinating platform for all the abovementioned agencies, carrying out the directions from Rio+20.

SUSTAINABLE DEVELOPMENT IN INDIA

The concept of sustainable development in India has existed long since it was given importance by the UN and continues to be incorporated in the country's national development goals. The expression "*sabka saath sabka vikas*," frequently used by the current prime minister, Mr. Narendra Modi, encompasses the ideology behind sustainable development accurately. India has shown significant progress in sustainably developing and growing. There are various indicators that support the above contention.

In addition to being a signatory to the 2030 Agenda for Sustainable Development, India is known to have played an important role in shaping these seventeen Sustainable Development Goals (SDGs) at the Sustainable Development Summit of the United Nations in September 2015.

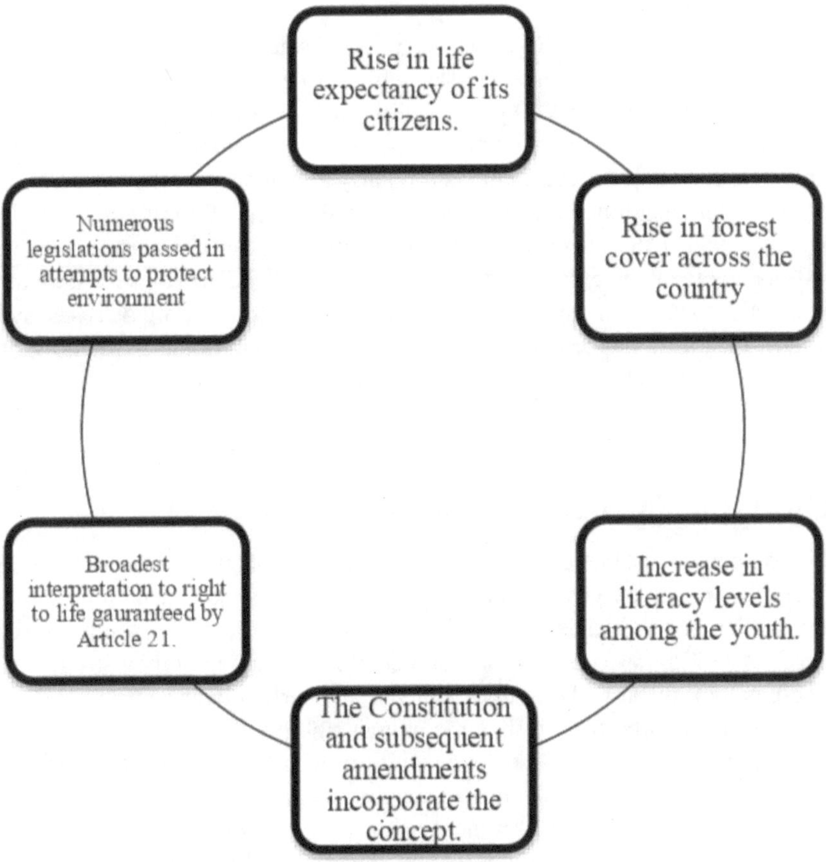

Figure 17.1 Sustainable Development Goals.

Sustainable Development and Right to Clean Water

In 2015, the UN General Assembly adopted an integrated system of undertaking 2030 Agenda for Sustainable Development. This agenda, as decided by UNDP, is centered on multidimensional poverty, inequality of rights, social exclusion, and sustainability.[9] One of the key areas of focus of this agenda is "ensuring availability and sustainable management of water and sanitation for all."[10] By 2030, the UN agencies hope to achieve equitable access to safe and affordable clean water for all.[11]

The WHO/UNICEF Joint Monitoring Program for Water Supply, Sanitation and Hygiene is the primary UN body tasked with monitoring the regional and global progress in achieving the SDG related to equitable access to clean water.

In Rio+20, the member states took cognizance of the fact that "water is at the core of sustainable development as it is closely linked to a number of key global challenges."[12]

According to official UN data,[13] scarcity of safe clean water hinders the sustainability of natural resources, as well as social and economic development, affecting more than 40 percent of the population of the world. Access to clean water is considered a crucial factor by the developing countries, their long-term growth prospects being particularly affected.[14] It is the key solution to poverty eradication, education, gender equality, reduction of child mortality, improved maternal health, combat against major water-borne diseases, and achievement of environmental sustainability.[15] All of these issues are inherently linked with water, as it is a carrier for life-threatening diseases, and its lack of access or inequality in access brings an additional burden on the economy. Sustainable management of water, therefore, plays a central role in realizing the SDGs.[16]

Right to Clean Water as Environmental Justice

Environmental justice is a recently formulated concept that is now being given importance by governments. It is essentially concerned with how certain sections of the society (especially the impoverished, discriminated, or marginalized) are affected by environmental issues and how they struggle to access natural resourced that they actually have a right over.

The UN's efforts to recognize the human right to clean water in addition to the various instances of such recognition in Indian jurisprudence marks significant progress toward achieving environmental justice. The recognition of such a right is a strong argument against the marketization of the water sector, thereby extending water for all, regardless of ability to pay, rather than privileging the most productive uses, or those who are able to afford.[17]

It allows the marginalized section of society to demand improved access to clean water and if denied, it provides a legal remedy for it. In this way, the right to clean water serves the purpose of environmental justice and aids in achievement of environmental justice goals.

Right to Clean Water in India

Public interest litigation (PIL) has played an important role in the enforcement of one's right to safe clean water. This form of litigation has allowed public-spirited individuals or organizations to approach the courts in their individual capacity and fight for the benefit of society and especially for the underprivileged and poor.

In the case of *A. P. Pollution Control Board II v. Prof. M.V. Nayudu*,[18] the Supreme Court held that the central government could not exempt industries and allow them to emit their discharge into water bodies.

In *Subhash Kumar v State of Bihar*,[19] it was held that the right to life included within its ambit the right to enjoy pollution-free water and if anything led to the abridgment of this right, the citizen could seek remedy under Article 32 of the Constitution.

Further, in *M. C. Mehta v Kamalnath*,[20] it was very specifically ruled by the Supreme Court that the state is not only responsible for the regulation of water supply but also for ensuring it is safe for consumption by the citizens.

A landmark judgment by the Bombay High Court from 2014 states that the city municipal corporation was legally bound to extend water supply to the dwellers of notified as well as the non-notified slums of Mumbai.[21] This was a highly favorable order that benefitted more than three million people living in the non-notified slums of Mumbai. The high court upheld that the right to water was an important ingredient of the right to life that was guaranteed by the Constitution. The court further observed that water access should not be denied on grounds regarding property rights, thereby separating the security of tenure from the right to water. In simple terms, the court ordered that until these slums are removed, resettled, or rehabilitated, which could probably take years, inhabitants should be provided with access to the city water supply.

ISSUES AND QUESTIONS RAISED

The paper is primarily concerned with how a widely recognized human right, the right to access clean water, has become a matter of privilege among the urban poor population of Mumbai. The objective of this here is to evaluate the gap in the provision of clean and consumable water to the slum dwellers of Mumbai, and identify the potential legal solutions to fill that gap.

The following questions are sought to be answered by this chapter:

1. What is the current legislative and policy framework/mechanism in place to ensure right to clean water in the slums of Mumbai? How effective has it been?
2. What are some of the challenges faced while implementing the human right to clean water in the slums of Mumbai?
3. What is the impact of the lack of access to clean water on the sustainable development goals of Mumbai?
4. What are some of the ways the gap in the provision of clean and consumable water to the dwellers in slums be reduced?

ANALYSIS AND BACKGROUND

Inadequate access to water is one characteristic that helps to define a "slum," based on the United Nations (UN) definition.[22] Nine percent of the total projected national population of 1.28 billion of India lives in slums.[23] Mumbai is notorious for accommodating the largest slum population of any city in India, with more than half of its population living in informal settlements.[24] More than a million of these slum dwellers lack access to clean water which has led to a severe negative impact on their standard of living, health, employment, education, and right to live with human dignity.[25]

If one were to characterize the nature of water supply in the slums of Mumbai, it would include the following adjectives:

CURRENT LEGISLATIVE POLICY FRAMEWORK

International Level

As early as 1977, a resolution was passed at the UN Water Conference that pledged access to clean drinking water for everybody, to which India is a signatory.

India is also a signatory to the International Covenant on Economic, Social and Cultural Rights (ICESCR) since 1979, and therefore, it is required to ensure protection, fulfilment, and respect to human rights. In 2002, General Comment 15 was held where it was acknowledged that ICESCR was to be interpreted to include the right to water under the right to health guaranteed by Article 12 and the right to an adequate standard of living guaranteed by Article 11.

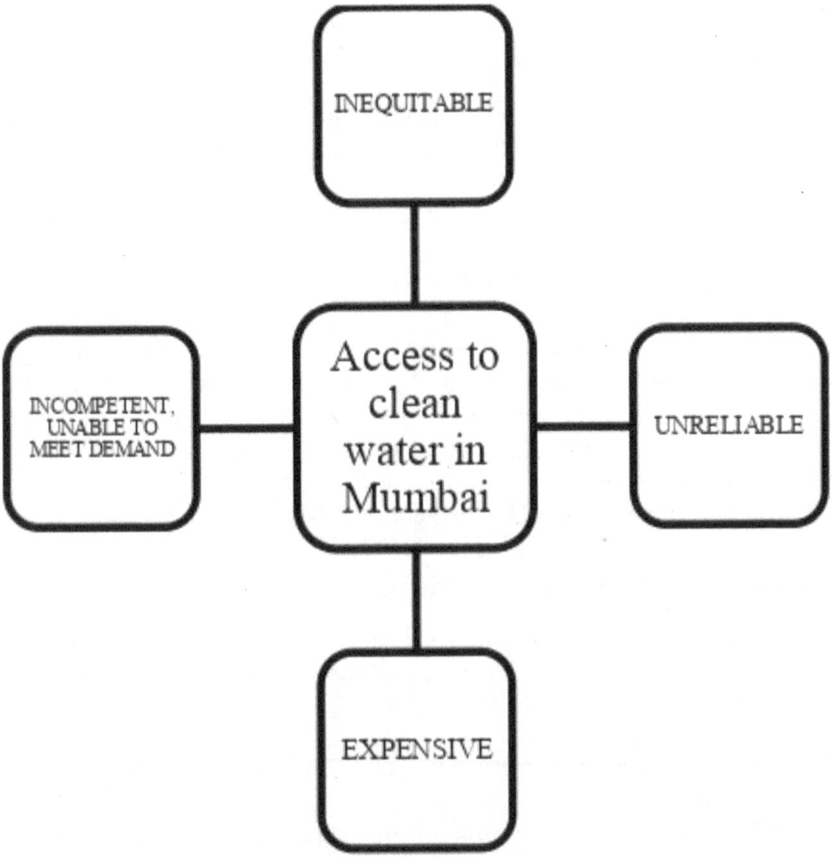

Figure 17.2 Nature of Water Supply.

The right to clean water was recognized as a human right by the UN General Assembly in 2010. India was one of the 120 countries that voted in favor of this motion.[26]

In 2011, the UN Human Rights Council passed a resolution to take up the right to safe clean water as a human right. This resolution requires all states to ensure adequate financing for delivery of water in a sustainable manner.[27]

Other instruments that India is a signatory to regarding the right to water include

- The Convention on the Rights of the Child
- The Convention on the Elimination of All Forms of Discrimination against Women
- The Delhi Declaration

Central Level

The Constitution of India, 1950

Whenever any issue has arisen regarding the shortage of drinking water before the Indian judiciary, it has always been dealt with keeping in mind the human rights angle.[28]

In recent Indian jurisprudence, the denial of the right to clean water has been deemed to be the denial of the right to life under the Constitution.[29] The right to clean water, from a constitutional perspective, is a fundamental right that is read into Article 21 of the Constitution.[30] Numerous other fundamental rights cannot be realized without access to safe clean water, such as the right to life, right to self-determination, right to adequate standard of living, etc. Further, Article 39(b) of the Constitution,[31] which is a Directive Principle of State Policy, mandates the state to ensure equal access to the material resources of the country.

Entry 56 within the Union List includes water as the center's subject.

Statutes by the Parliament

The Indian legislature has attempted to approach the problem of access to water in a two-fold manner. There are essentially two mechanisms that have been deployed to deal with the issue.

1. Legislations focusing on water supply and sanitation by the state governments
2. Policy initiatives by the central government to assist and supplement the states' activities with the overall objective of providing safe drinking water and thereby promoting public health

There exist various enactments by the legislature regarding water and water resources such as the Prevention and Control of Pollution Act, 1974; Provisions of the Environment (Protection) Act, 1986; and the Indian Easements Act, 1882. While these acts do not expressly give a right to water to the citizens, they help in protection and preservation of the resource.

The Water Act[32] is one of the most important central legislations regarding water resources. It aims to preserve the wholesomeness of the natural resources by prohibiting discharge of domestic or industrial waste into the water bodies without proper treatment.

The scope of Environment (Protection) Act, 1986 extends to water quality and prevention of water pollution. This act empowers the central government to establish standards for the quality of water and quantity of emissions into water bodies.

The Indian Easements Act, 1882 grants the right to unpolluted water to all those who own land with an adjoining river or water stream. Such an owner enjoys their right to water of undiminished flow, quantity, and quality and the right to allow the water to go beyond their land without obstruction.[33]

State Level

Water supply and sanitation are a state-government responsibility as per the Constitution of India.

Entry 17 of the State List mandates that water is state subject in addition to entry 56 of the Union List which also mentions water. Thus, water is as much a central subject as it a state subject.

Following the 73rd and 74th constitutional amendments, the state may give the responsibility and powers to Panchayati Raj Institutions (PRIs) and urban local bodies (ULBs), both representing local communities.

Local Level

The Maharashtra State Water Policy was announced in the year 2003 and was framed with the purpose of enabling the preservation of clean drinking water as a scarce natural resource and its equitable distribution throughout the state. To maintain water quality, the Maharashtra State Water Policy also aims to establish a program to control the discharge of pollutants to the surface and subsurface waters of the state, including oceans, bays, and saltwater marshes. In terms of management of water resources, the policy also speaks of building a robust management information system, water audit, and benchmarking of water resource projects.

Mumbai's water service provider is the Brihanmumbai Municipal Corporation (BMC), also known as Municipal Corporation of Greater Mumbai (MCGM). It is responsible for the following functions:

- Providing water
- Managing the water distribution network
- Billing and collection of revenues

The department in charge of these functions is the Hydraulic Engineering Department of MCGM in Greater Mumbai. There is one HE or a hydraulic engineer who is in charge of the water distribution. He is assisted by other DHEs or deputy hydraulic engineers. Under BMC, there is also a Water Supply and Sanitation Department.

CHALLENGES TO ACCESSING CLEAN WATER IN MUMBAI

Despite the elaborate legislative and policy framework, most of Mumbai's slum dwellers are not able to enjoy their right to access quantities of safe,

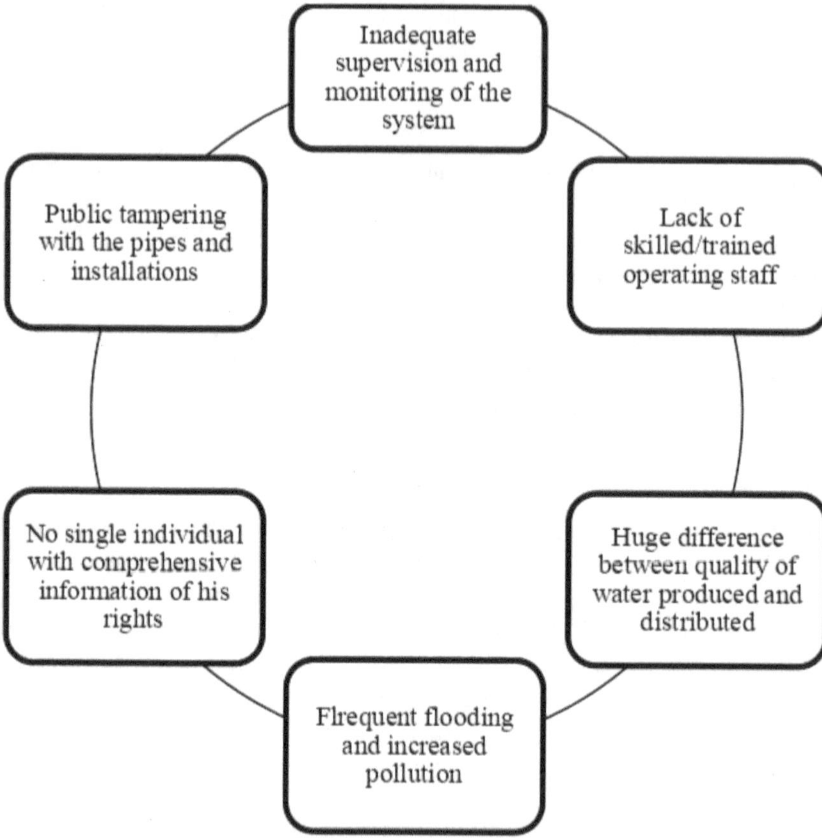

Figure 17.3 Lacunas in the Implementation of the Framework.

accessible, acceptable, and affordable water. The barriers to accessing safe and clean water in Mumbai are not only monetary or technical in nature, but also legal, political, and institutional.[34]

A study was conducted to understand the challenges to the aforementioned legislative and policy framework in Mumbai.[35] This study highlights the following lacunas in the implementation of the framework mentioned above:

IMPACT OF LACK OF ACCESS TO CLEAN WATER ON THE SUSTAINABLE DEVELOPMENT OF THE AREA

Lack of access to clean water has a constellation of negative impacts on the potential for sustainable growth and development in any area. To study the negative impact of this lack of access on the slums of Mumbai, a survey was conducted among the urban poor of Mumbai. The objective was to identify the various indicators of sustainable development that are affected when the people are unable to enjoy their right to clean and consumable water. A sample of fifty residents from the most densely populated slum of Mumbai, the Sangharsh Nagar slum, were selected at random.

The primary data was collected by way of interviews. The target respondents were those slum dwellers who served as domestic helps and other daily wage earners, employed in the same locality as that of the author's residence.

Data Analysis

The first question that was asked was the number of members present in their household. This question was asked to examine the quantity of water required by each household. More the number of people, more is their requirement.

The slums are so densely populated that each household has an average of 4–6 people. Satisfying the needs of each member of a household with the limited amount of water in that household is the main problem that is faced in the slum.

The Sangharsh Nagar slum does not house a corporation-given water connection. The primary source of water is at an approximate distance of 3 kilometers from the slum. There are fixed timings in the day, from 4 p.m. to 8 p.m. when the water is available. The people either use a bicycle to transport barrels of water across the distance or roll the containers all the way. Either way, there is pilferage of water in the middle, leading to wastage. The dwellers may also buy water from the water merchants who bring the water to the slums on vehicles. However, these merchants do not have a fixed price system and enjoy the liberty to charge whatever they please. They are also irregular and unreliable.

With the given sources of water, accessing clean water daily is difficult for the slum dwellers. They face problems such as the following:

i. Water is available for a very short period of time, usually during working hours. Fetching water usually means skipping work.

Table 17.1 Frequency of Quantity of Water Required

Number of People in the Household	*Frequency*
0–2	1
2–4	8
4–6	12
>6	4

Table 17.2 Monthly Cost of Water

Monthly Cost of Water (Rs.)	*Frequency*
0–300	0
300–600	6
600–900	11
900–1200	5
>1200	3

ii. Within the short period of time water is available, they get stuck in long queues only to find that water gets over and they have to go home empty-handed.
iii. Carrying water across 3 kilometers is tiresome and expensive every day.
iv. Buying water every day is too expensive.

On an average, a household spends Rs. 600 to 900 per month on water.

The following table examines the impact the lack of access to clean water has caused on the prospect of sustainable growth and development of these families.

Inferences

A slum household spends a considerable part of their budget on water. This survey is proof that there exists a significant gap between the international ideals of the human right to access clean water and the current state of affairs in Mumbai.

This survey also shows that even though a corporation pipeline is not a viable option to rely on for daily water needs, there are no adequate alternative options available in the slums. If they do exist, they are either costly or unreliable. Such a situation inhibits the prospects of sustainable growth in a region.

CONCLUSIONS AND RECOMMENDATIONS

The right to access clean water in the slums of Mumbai is a serious challenge. With factors such as a rapid increase in population, depletion of water resources, and the ever-increasing consumer demands, the realization of this right is still a distant dream for the slum dwellers.

It has become clear over the years that an uninterrupted supple of piped water from the corporation is a distant dream for the slums in Mumbai. This is because such a plan is extravagant when it comes to its infrastructure requirements. Therefore, it has become important to focus on alternate frameworks for achieving easy and affordable access to water in slums.

Table 17.3 Impact of Lack of Access to Right to Clean Water

Indicator of Sustainable Development	*Impact on the Indicator*
1. Health	• Decrease in life expectancy • Hampering of growth of children • Spread of waterborne diseases such as cholera • Severe effects of dehydration such as ulcers, urinary infections, and infectious skin
2. Education	• Prolonged absence from school owing to health issues • Unaffordability for many to send children to school owing to increased water prices • Children required to fetch water
3. Employment	• Many daily wage earners skipping work and fetching water owing to unpredictable water timings • Many slum dwellers having to forego jobs in the hospitality industry or those that require interacting with other people owing to insufficient water to have a bath every morning and look presentable
4. Standard of Living	• Insufficient water to clean house, wash clothes, wash dishes on a regular basis • Constant stress and tension
5. Household Economy	• Buying water every day putting stress on the earning of daily wage earners • Increase in medical bills
6. Right to Human Dignity	• Have to often depend on autocratic and oppressive water merchants and pay the price they demand owing to lack of other options • Slum dwellers living in non-notified areas of the city getting mistreated when they report the issue to the local authorities

Enabling Environment for Urban Small Water Enterprises (USWEs)

There exists an urgent need for a decentralized and market-oriented machinery. A short-term solution to the abovementioned problems is the promotion of Urban Small Water Enterprises or USWEs. This is a market-oriented solution that looks after the water quality, affordability, standards of compliance, etc. For the time being, USWEs will be able to cater to the drinking and cooking water needs of the slums, providing them with safe and healthy water.

Public Private Partnerships

A best practice from the Netherlands involves water companies incorporated as private companies, with majority shares owned by the local or central government. This has successfully helped in achieving "public ownership with operation according to commercial business principles." While the cost of water is entirely borne by the user, all profits are invested in making the clean water more accessible in terms of quality and quantity.

Social Business Models for Water Supply

Social attempts to protect the right to access clean water have shown highly favorable results around the world, especially in India. Some of these models that can be applied in Mumbai and particularly its slums include:

i. Sarv-jal: Water purification installations with bottling units and water stations
ii. Water ATMs
iii. Nandi community water services: Creating a localized body to enable the use of community cooperation to provide reasonably priced decentralized drinking water
iv. Water guardians: Establishment of local organizations that can fix pipes, advise, and sell the cheapest and best water storage and treatment solutions, and create awareness for water conservation

Increasing Public Awareness

Increasing public awareness amounts to bringing about a change in the behavior of the people concerned. In spite of the fact that there is only a limited amount of water that is available to these slum dwellings, they are guilty of wasting a lot of water. There is limited awareness and interest with respect to important water-related topics, such as water conservation and

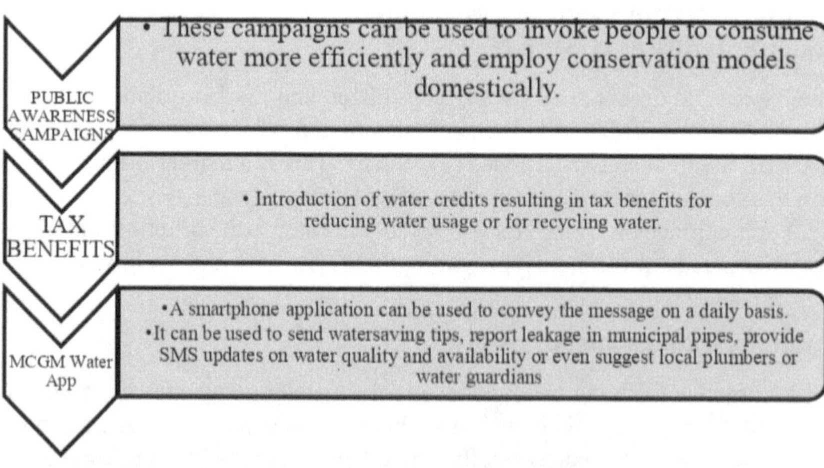

Figure 17.4 Initiatives and Incentives to Sensitize the People of the Slums.

sewage recycling practices, the actual cost of water supply, subsidies and pricing, appropriate storage, and water quality. Following initiatives and incentives can be employed to sensitize the people of the slums toward water conservation:

Recycling Sewage and Gray Water

Treated sewage and gray water might represent a supply of water that is even cheaper than fresh water, especially compared to the prices of water for industrial usage. Further, industries such as the construction industry that have no use for clean water should be made to use gray water instead of clean water.

NOTES

1. United Nations World Commission on Environment and Development, Brundtland Report, 1987. TA \l "United Nations World Commission on Environment and Development, Brundtland Report, 1987." \s "United Nations World Commission on Environment and Development, Brundtland Report, 1987." \c 3.

2. Goodland and Ledec, Neoclassical economics and principles of sustainable development. (1987); 38(1): 19–46. TA \l "Goodland and Ledec, Neoclassical economics and principles of sustainable development. (1987); 38(1): 19–46" \s "Goodland and Ledec, Neoclassical economics and principles of sustainable development. (1987); 38(1): 19–46." \c 4.

3. J. C. Dernbach Sustainable Development as a Framework for National Governance. Case Western Reserve Law Review, 1–103., 1998

4. Stockholm Declaration UN Conference on the Human Environment (16 June 1972) UN Doc A/Conf 48/14/Rev.I,II ILM 1461 (1972). TA \l "Stockholm Declaration UN Conference on the Human Environment (16 June 1972) UN Doc A/Conf 48/14/Rev.I,II ILM 1461 (1972" \s "Stockholm Declaration UN Conference on the Human Environment (16 June 1972) UN Doc A/Conf 48/14/Rev.I,II ILM 1461 (1972" \c 3.

5. Declaration of United Nations Conference on Human Environment 1972. TA \l "Declaration of United Nations Conference on Human Environment 1972" \s "Declaration of United Nations Conference on Human Environment 1972" \c 3.

6. Supra 1.

7. Rio+20 Outcome Document "The Future We Want", United Nations Conference on Sustainable Development, 2012. TA \l "Rio+20 Outcome Document \"The Future We Want\", United Nations Conference on Sustainable Development, 2012" \s "Rio+20 Outcome Document \"The Future We Want\", United Nations Conference on Sustainable Development, 2012" \c 3.

8. UN Department of Economic and Social Affairs, https://sustainabledevelopment.un.org/unsystem. TA \l "UN Department of Economic and Social Affairs,

https://sustainabledevelopment.un.org/unsystem" \s "UN Department of Economic and Social Affairs, https://sustainabledevelopment.un.org/unsystem" \c 8.

9. Ibid.

10. 2015 UN-Water Annual International Zaragoza Conference. Water and Sustainable Development: From Vision to Action. TA \l "2015 UN-Water Annual International Zaragoza Conference. Water and Sustainable Development: From Vision to Action" \s "2015 UN-Water Annual International Zaragoza Conference. Water and Sustainable Development: From Vision to Action" \c 3.

11. A/RES/70/1 - Transforming our world: the 2030 Agenda for Sustainable Development. TA \l "A/RES/70/1 - Transforming our world: the 2030 Agenda for Sustainable Development" \s "A/RES/70/1 - Transforming our world: the 2030 Agenda for Sustainable Development" \c 3.

12. Supra 7.

13. UNITED NATIONS – UN. UN-water global analysis and assessment of sanitation and clean-water 2014 report: investing in water and sanitation: increasing access, reducing inequalities. Geneva: WHO, 2014. 108p. TA \l "UNITED NATIONS – UN. UN-water global analysis and assessment of sanitation and clean-water 2014 report: investing in water and sanitation: increasing access, reducing inequalities. Geneva: WHO, 2014. 108p" \s "UNITED NATIONS – UN. UN-water global analysis and assessment of sanitation and clean-water 2014 report: investing in water and sanitation: increasing access, reducing inequalities. Geneva: WHO, 2014. 108p" \c 3.

14. Christian von Hirschhausen, Maya Flekstad, Georg Meran, and Greta Sundermann, Clean water as a Sustainable Development Goal: fair, universal access with increasing block tariffs, ISSN 2192-7219. TA \l "Christian von Hirschhausen, Maya Flekstad, Georg Meran, and Greta Sundermann, Clean water as a Sustainable Development Goal: fair, universal access with increasing block tariffs, ISSN 2192-7219" \s "Christian von Hirschhausen, Maya Flekstad, Georg Meran, and Greta Sundermann, Clean water as a Sustainable Development Goal: fair, universal access with increasing block tariffs, ISSN 2192-7219" \c 4.

15. UNESCO International Hydrological Programme Paris, France 2014, IHP/SDG-Water/1/2014.

16. Ibid.

17. L. Harris, L. Rodina, C. Morinville (2015) Revisiting the Human Right to Water from and Environmental Justice Lens, Politics, Groups and Identities Journal DOI: 10.1080/21565503.2015.1080619. TA \l "L. Harris, L. Rodina, C. Morinville (2015) Revisiting the Human Right to Water from and Environmental Justice Lens, Politics, Groups and Identities Journal. DOI: 10.1080/21565503.2015.1080619" \s "L. Harris, L. Rodina, C. Morinville (2015) Revisiting the Human Right to Water from and Environmental Justice Lens, Politics, Groups and Identities Journal. DOI: 10.1080/21565503.2015.1080619" \c 4.

18. A.P. Pollution Control Board II v. Prof. M.V. Nayudu [2001 2 SCC 62] TA \l "*A.P. Pollution Control Board II v. Prof. M.V. Nayudu*" \s "A.P. Pollution Control Board II v. Prof. M.V. Nayudu" \c 1.

19. Subhash Kumar v State of Bihar [1991) 1 SCC 598] TA \l "*Subhash Kumar v State of Bihar*" \s "Subhash Kumar v State of Bihar" \c 1.

20. M.C. Mehta v Kamalnath [(1997)1 SCC 388] TA \l "*M.C. Mehta v Kamalnath*" \s "M.C. Mehta v Kamalnath" \c 1.

21. Pani Haq Samiti & Ors v. Brihan Mumbai Municipal Corporation and Ors.[CHAMBER SUMMONS NO. 74 of 2012]. TA \l "Pani Haq Samiti & Ors v. Brihan Mumbai Municipal Corporation and Ors.[CHAMBER SUMMONS NO. 74 of 2012" \s "Pani Haq Samiti & Ors v. Brihan Mumbai Municipal Corporation and Ors.[CHAMBER SUMMONS NO. 74 of 2012" \c 1.

22. UN-HABITAT. Defining slums: towards an operational definition for measuring slums. Nairobi: United Nations Human Settlements Programme; 2002 TA \l "UN-HABITAT. Defining slums: towards an operational definition for measuring slums. Nairobi: United Nations Human Settlements Programme; 2002" \s "UN-HABITAT. Defining slums: towards an operational definition for measuring slums. Nairobi: United Nations Human Settlements Programme; 2002" \c 4.

23. Dipak Kumar, By 2017, India's slum population will rise to 104 million, The Times Of India, Aug 20, 2013, 05:28 IST. TA \l "Dipak Kumar, By 2017, India's slum population will rise to 104 million, The Times Of India, Aug 20, 2013, 05:28 IST." \s "Dipak Kumar, By 2017, India's slum population will rise to 104 million, The Times Of India, Aug 20, 2013, 05:28 IST."\ c 4.

24. National Sample Survey Organization. Key indicators of urban slums in India. National sample survey 69th round. July 2012-December 2012. TA \l "National Sample Survey Organization. Key indicators of urban slums in India. National sample survey 69th round. July 2012-December 2012" \s "National Sample Survey Organization. Key indicators of urban slums in India. National sample survey 69th round. July 2012-December 2012" \c 2.

25. S. Kumar Karn and H. Harada, "Field survey on water supply, sanitation and associated health impacts in urban poor communities - A case from Mumbai City, India," *Water Science and Technology*. (2002); 46/11: 269–275. TA \l "S. Kumar Karn and H. Harada, \"Field survey on water supply, sanitation and associated health impacts in urban poor communities - A case from Mumbai City, India,\" *Water Science and Technology*. (2002); 46/11: 269–275" \s "S. Kumar Karn and H. Harada, \"Field survey on water supply, sanitation and associated health impacts in urban poor communities - A case from Mumbai City, India,\" Water Science and Technology. (2002); 46/11: 269–275" \c 4.

26. United Nations General Assembly Adopts Resolution Recognizing Access to Clean Water, Sanitation as Human Rights, by Recorded Vote of 122 in Favour, None Against, 41 Abstentions, UN Doc. No. GA/10967 (July 28, 2010). TA \l "United Nations General Assembly Adopts Resolution Recognizing Access to Clean Water, Sanitation as Human Rights, by Recorded Vote of 122 in Favour, None Against, 41 Abstentions, UN Doc. No. GA/10967 (July 28, 2010)." \s "United Nations General Assembly Adopts Resolution Recognizing Access to Clean Water, Sanitation as Human Rights, by Recorded Vote of 122 in Favour, None Against, 41 Abstentions, UN Doc. No. GA/10967 (July 28, 2010)." \c 3.

27. Human Rights Council Resolution A/HRC/RES/18/1. TA \l "Human Rights Council Resolution A/HRC/RES/18/1" \s "Human Rights Council Resolution A/HRC/RES/18/1" \c 3.

28. Delhi Water Supply & Sewage Undertaking and Another v State of Haryana and Others (1996) 2 SCC 572. TA \l "Delhi Water Supply & Sewage Undertaking and Another v State of Haryana and Others (1996) 2 SCC 572" \s "Delhi Water Supply & Sewage Undertaking and Another v State of Haryana and Others (1996) 2 SCC 572" \c 1.

29. Bandhua Mukti Morcha vs. Union of India [(1997) 10 SCC 549]. TA \l "Bandhua Mukti Morcha vs. Union of India" \s "Bandhua Mukti Morcha vs. Union of India" \c 1.

30. The Constitution of India, 1950. TA \l "The Constitution of India, 1950" \s "The Constitution of India, 1950" \c 2.

31. Ibid.

32. Water (Prevention and Control of Pollution) Act, 1974. TA \l "Water (Prevention and Control of Pollution) Act, 1974" \s "Water (Prevention and Control of Pollution) Act, 1974" \c 2.

33. Section 7, Indian Easements Act, 1882. TA \l "Section 7, Indian Easements Act, 1882" \s "Section 7, Indian Easements Act, 1882" \c 2.

34. Murthy SL. Land security and the challenges of realizing the human right to water and sanitation in the slums of Mumbai, India. Health Hum Rights. 2012; 14(2):61–73. PMID: 23568948. TA \l "Murthy SL. Land security and the challenges of realizing the human right to water and sanitation in the slums of Mumbai, India. Health Hum Rights. 2012; 14(2): 61–73. PMID: 23568948" \s "Murthy SL. Land security and the challenges of realizing the human right to water and sanitation in the slums of Mumbai, India. Health Hum Rights. 2012; 14(2):61–73. PMID: 23568948" \c 4.

35. S Ramakrishnan, K N Chandran and P Gopalakrishnan, Improving the Efficiency and Functioning of Operation and Maintenance of CWSS Including Preventive Maintenance Upgradation of Existing Water Conveyance Systems. TA \l "S Ramakrishnan, K N Chandran and P Gopalakrishnan, Improving the Efficiency and Functioning of Operation and Maintenance of CWSS Including Preventive Maintenance Upgradation of Existing Water Conveyance Systems" \s "S Ramakrishnan, K N Chandran and P Gopalakrishnan, Improving the Efficiency and Functioning of Operation and Maintenance of CWSS Including Preventive Maintenance Upgradation of Existing Water Conveyance Systems" \c 4.

Chapter 18

The Supreme Court and the Ban on Firecrackers

An Intrusion Looking Intervention

Anisha Singh and Ankit Singh

INTRODUCTION

New Delhi, the capital of India, has struggled with pollution for long. In 2014, the World Health Organization (WHO) declared Delhi as the most polluted city from a list of 1,600 cities of the world.[1] The pollution level in the same year increased to its maximum on the eve of Diwali, the festival of lights. Not much later, in 2017, Delhi was again declared the most polluted city in the world. The statistics available from the US State Department show the level of particulate matter in the air reached a reading of 1,000, much beyond the hazardous limit.[2]

With the air quality in Delhi declining perceptibly, hospitals such as AIIMS reported a 20 percent hike in the number of patients with respiratory issues.[3] The doctors in the city also stated that breathing in Delhi's air for one day was equivalent to smoking fifty cigarettes.[4] Though the situation of bad air quality in Delhi has become perennial, conditions seem to reach their worst extreme around the time of Diwali.

Keeping in mind the deteriorating air quality in Delhi and the expected worst situation around Diwali, the Supreme Court of India, considering a petition filed by three kids—Arjun Gopal and others—through a bench headed by Justice A. K. Sikri declared a ban on sale of firecrackers in Delhi (NCR) till November 1, 2017, that is, till ten days after Diwali. The court declared that since the quality of air fell abysmally every year after Diwali, crossing hazardous limits, it wanted to test the effect of the firecracker ban after Diwali, which left the city covered in smoke each year. The ban resulted in Delhi observing the cleanest environment, though still in poor condition, after Diwali in the past three years. This clearly indicated that the decision of the Supreme Court to intervene in the harmful practices observed during Diwali was completely justified on its part.

Moreover, among all crackers, Chinese firecrackers are the most used in the country. They not just offer greater overall revenue to the vendors; they attract customers and also burn brighter and far longer. However, they are unusually unstable and have an increased oxidizing capacity. These costly crackers contain hazardous and perilous levels of potassium chlorate because of which the central government issued a notice that informed the venders, shippers, and overall population of the critical outcomes involved with the utilization of foreign crackers. The level of pollution caused by such firecrackers is considerably higher.[5]

However, this choice of the Supreme Court has again brought into light the Hindutva hypocrisy wherein religious gatherings denounce the choice of the Supreme Court as one singling out the Hindu demography and against the Hindu sentiments since it influences the custom of burning firecrackers. In the light of the above, the Supreme Court, which should be lauded for its decision for taking with seriousness the health of the Delhi people, is being labeled as an anti-Hindu entity, even though the court had only banned the sale of firecrackers and not criminalized their bursting. Therefore, the question whether the decision of the Supreme Court be condemned assumes great importance.

This brings out the necessity to defend the decision of the Supreme Court on grounds such as the court's authority to intervene in matters of public importance, its writ jurisdiction, the duty of state to ensure a healthy environment under Article 48A of the Constitution of India, a greater emphasis on public health over the economic losses, and the fact that a ban on firecrackers does not mean a ban on Diwali.

THE BAN, THE NECESSITY FOR INTERVENTION, AND DELHI'S POST-DIWALI ENVIRONMENT—AN ANALYSIS

A bench headed by Justice A. K. Sikri, while delivering the verdict on a plea filed by three children in *Arjun Gopal and others*,[6] declared that the licenses to sell firecrackers in the Delhi NCR region be suspended till November 1, 2017 and that no new licenses be issued for the said period. Thereby, the court restrained the sale of firecrackers in the Delhi region till 10 days after the festival of Diwali.

The court justified its verdict by stating that the level of pollution in the air of Delhi reached dangerous levels on the day of Diwali as it had crossed the limit prescribed by the WHO a whopping twenty-nine times.[7] This justification of the court also stands in concurrence with the judgment in the Sagun Kaushik case[8] wherein the Central Pollution Control Board (CPCB), the authority for air quality monitoring under the Air (Prevention and Control of Pollution) Act, 1981, had stated that on Diwali, between 9 p.m. and midnight, the air quality in Delhi reached dangerous levels. This, when considered in the light of the instant judgment in questions, favors the decision of the court, given that the air in Delhi, even without the firecracker pollution, was already unfit for living and thereby called for an intervention for the greater good of the society.

The Need for Intervention by the Court

What needs to be analyzed to justify the act of banning the sale of firecrackers by the Supreme Court as merely an intervention and not an intrusion are facts such as the UNICEF report of 2016 that placed India in the category of the world's most polluted countries.[9] Further, a WHO report of 2016 stated that 88 percent of all the deaths because of illnesses related to air pollution occur in low-income countries and that India is a major contributor to the number of deaths caused by air pollution.[10] This information too needs to be considered before condemning the much-required act of intervention by the Supreme Court aimed at preserving public health by preventing further release of toxic pollutants in the atmosphere.

Raising questions on the ban on firecrackers by the Supreme Court also brings into the ambit of questioning measures such as the odd–even scheme introduced in Delhi to put a check on pollution and the banning of registration of diesel vehicles with engine capacities above 2000 cubic centimeters in the Delhi region.

The government of Delhi had for the third time, during November 13–17, 2017, initiated the odd–even scheme[11] in which vehicles were allowed to ply on the road according to the last number of their registration number plates. This practice in Delhi came as a desperate measure of the government in an attempt to put a curb on the constantly spiking pollution levels. Similarly, the National Green Tribunal had banned diesel vehicles older than 10 years from plying on Delhi roads. Also, the registration of new diesel vehicles with engine capacities above 2,000 cubic centimeters was denied on grounds of high carcinogenic pollutant–emitting properties.

These recent developments in the Delhi administration with relation to air pollution when considered with the Supreme Court's decision clearly indicates that desperate measures were needed before Diwali to protect human and environmental life. This also justifies the necessity of intervention on part of the court, in the light of which tainting of the ban as an act of intrusion only appears as an attempt to besmirch the dignity of the Indian judiciary.

Result of the Ban

The ban on firecrackers resulted in Delhi waking up to the cleanest atmosphere post-Diwali in the previous three years.[12] Though the level of pollution did not fall down to exceptional levels, it has to be understood that firecrackers were only one of the reasons for the high pollution in Delhi. However, various facts such as 40 percent reduction in the level of pollution as compared to Diwali 2016[13] clearly showed the positive impact of the intervention by the Supreme Court. It is also notable that in the absence of the ban, the pollution in Delhi on Diwali could have reached an unprecedented level.

THE BAN ON FIRECRACKERS BY SUPREME COURT—A LEGAL JUSTIFICATION

To justify the Supreme Court's banning of firecrackers as only an act of intervention makes imperative the analysis of judicial grounds on which the order stands valid. In this regard, the order of the Supreme Court stands valid on constitutional grounds such as Article 48A, Article 51A(g), Article 142, and the doctrine of precautionary principle.

In delivering its judgment in *Arjun Gopal and others*,[14] the court considered Article 48A of the Indian Constitution, which states that the state shall make attempts to improve the quality of the country's environment.[15] Relating Article 48 with the theory of three pillars of the state,[16] wherein the judiciary is an integral pillar, it becomes clear that the court is authorized to decide and intervene in matters concerning the protection of the environment of the state.

Further, the court also laid emphasis on Article 51A(g) of the Constitution, whereby it is a fundamental duty of the citizens of India to protect the environment of the country. However, the most important of these is the doctrine of precautionary principle, which the court considered while declaring its order. The precautionary principle states that a substance or activity posing a threat to the environment shall be prevented from adversely affecting the environment, even if there is no conclusive scientific proof linking that particular substance or activity to environmental damage. It also states that while it is the task of lawmakers at the international, regional, national, and local levels to enable economic progress, a richly diverse and viable environment shall be protected and nurtured.[17] In this regard, the judgment of the Supreme Court stands valid wherein going by the principle the court could, by merely considering firecrackers as a threat to already deteriorating air quality in Delhi, have been authorized to deliver the judgment.

In the Arjun Gopal case, Article 142 did not come into the picture; however, the petition brought before the Supreme Court gave it the authority to adjudicate on the matter. Article 142 of the Indian Constitution lays down the principle of complete justice. It states that the court, in exercise of its jurisdiction, may pass any order or decree as it considers necessary to perform complete justice.[18] Thereby, Article 142 gives the Supreme Court immense and unlimited authority to decide upon the matters brought before it, without any restrictions.[19]

Further, that the National Green Tribunal was the appropriate authority to decide upon matters related to environment also needs to be considered in the current scenario. Though clauses (1) and (2) of Section 14 of the National Green Tribunal Act (NGT Act), 2010 give it jurisdiction over environment-related issues,[20]a closer look at the NGT Act, 2010 indicates that the act nowhere expressly prohibits the Supreme Court from exercising its jurisdiction over matters of such accord.

Further, the absence of any separate act to regulate the manufacture, sale, and possession of firecrackers in India only increases the court's jurisdiction in this matter. Presently, matters related to firecrackers are governed by the Explosives Act, 1884, which along with the Explosives Rules 2008 governs the display and storage of firecrackers. Apart from this, there is no statute in India to govern the nature, number, or method of bursting firecrackers. Only the bursting of firecrackers at a distance less than 4 meters from the point of sale is prohibited.[21]

Moreover, the Explosives Rules 2008 (Rule 14) mandates that "every manufacturer shall on the box of each firecrackers shall mention details of its chemical content, sound level and that it satisfies requirements laid down by the chief controller." In order to curb the trading of imported firecrackers, the Department of Industrial Policy and Promotion, Ministry of Commerce and Industry, has banned the making and selling of crackers consisting of sulfur or sulfurate with any chlorate.[22]

Therefore, in light of the above, it becomes evident that the Supreme Court while declaring the ban on firecrackers clearly did not exceed its authority, thereby making the judgment a bona fide act of intervention, well within the scope of its power, for the greater good of the residents of Delhi and its environment.

THE BAN VS THE HINDUTVA HYPOCRISY

The festival of Diwali has been celebrated in the Hindu religion since time immemorial. According to Hindu mythology, when Lord Ram returned to Ayodhya after killing Ravana and ending his fourteen years of exile, the citizens of Ayodhya lit thousands of lamps, drowning the city into an ocean of light celebrating Ram's return. Thus, the festival of Diwali was born. In the

Hindu religion, Diwali has the philosophical connotation of celebrating the victory of good over evil and the victory of light over dark.

However, the decision of the Supreme Court banning the sale of firecrackers has been condemned by religious leaders as well as celebrities, and is being painted as an attack on the Hindu religion and religious sentiments of Hindus. The attackers stated that firecrackers form an essential part of Diwali celebrations and are therefore a part of Hindu culture being intruded upon by the Supreme Court.

In this regard, what needs to be understood is that the festival of Diwali is symbolized by lights and not firecrackers. Further, there has been no mention of burning of firecrackers as a method of celebrating Ram's return to Ayodhya in the Hindu mythology. Therefore, the question of the act of ban being an attack on the Hindu religion stands fallacious in itself. In addition, what needs to be considered is the fact that firecrackers did not find their origin until seventh century AD in the Tang Dynasty of Medieval China.[23] Therefore, the statement of firecrackers forming an integral part of Diwali celebrations stands invalid, considering that firecrackers did not even originate in India and are a much later addition to the celebrations of Diwali.

Second, it needs to be reiterated that the ban imposed by the Supreme Court was only on the sale of firecrackers in the Delhi NCR region, and the lighting of firecrackers was neither banned nor criminalized the order of the court.[24] Therefore, there was only an implied prohibition on the use of firecrackers by suspending the license of the sellers, thereby reducing the ease of access to firecrackers. Thus, the condemnation of the Supreme Court's order on the grounds of the Hindu ideology needs to be measured on the parameters of firecrackers not being an integral part of Diwali celebrations and the requirement of radical steps to curb pollution in Delhi.

Further, the changing societal consensus on the topic of a firecracker-free Diwali, wherein the approach of the modern society has been shifting toward the celebration of a cracker-free Diwali for the protection of the environment, adds a new dimension to the issue. This clearly indicates that the modern society will not have much difficulty in observing any such act of ban with a progressive and positive outlook.

ECONOMIC IMPLICATIONS VS PUBLIC HEALTH— THE QUESTION OF GREATER IMPORTANCE

The Supreme Court's decision of banning firecrackers is definite to have certain economic implications on the firecrackers industry. In this regard, it is to be noted that the Delhi metropolitan area makes up 25 percent of the total market of firecrackers in India.[25]Also, it was predicted that the ban would result in the firecrackers industry suffering a loss of approximately Rs. 1,000 crores[26] as the sellers in the area already stocked firecrackers for selling well before the arrival of the festival.

Thus, it becomes necessary to mention that the ban on firecrackers in Delhi as imposed by the Supreme Court was only temporary in nature,[27] where the situation of the permanent license holders to sell firecrackers in Delhi was considered by the court, and thus, only a temporary ban was imposed. In this regard, Article 19(1)(g) of the Constitution of India needs to be brought into the picture. Though the article provides the citizens of India a fundamental right to carry out their profession, it is not absolute and can be made subject to reasonable restrictions in the interest of the general public as per Article 19(6). In the current scenario, it was expedient on the part of the Supreme Court to ban firecrackers considering the health of Delhi's public. Therefore, the ban cannot be questioned as an act of judicial overreach.

Likewise in *Prevention of Environment & Sound Pollution v. Union of India*,[28] the court held that "Diwali is primarily associated with Pooja and is considered as a festival of lights, not of noises and that shelter in the name of religion cannot be sought for, for bursting firecrackers." It further ruled that the "excessive use of firecrackers has assumed the nature of a public hazard and is a violation of one's fundamental rights to a clean and healthy environment as enshrined in the Constitution of India." The plea to relax restrictions on the burning of firecrackers during Diwali was declined, and the court reasoned that "if relaxation is allowed to one community, there will be no justification for not permitting relaxation to others and if we do, so the relaxation will become the rule."

Furthermore, Article 47 of the Indian Constitution under the Directive Principles of State Policy makes it the duty of the state to ensure the improvement of public health, which cannot be ensured without putting a check on issues like pollution. This was also considered by the Supreme Court in *Arjun Gopal and others*, wherein it stated that the health of the people of Delhi and NCR takes precedence over any commercial interest or the benefit of the permanent licensees. Thereby, the court made it clear that in a question involving public health and economy, the former carries more importance. This demonstrates the court's point of view as the guardian of the people of Delhi and its environment, whereby it attempted to protect public health by making a slight intervention in the city's Diwali-celebrating practices.

DIFFERENTIATING INTERVENTION FROM INTRUSION

The Constitution of India has assigned for judicial review under Articles 32 and 226 the Supreme Court and high courts, respectively. This allocation serves dual goals. On the one hand, it seeks to check the power of the government and safeguard individual rights and liberties; on the other hand, it serves the vision of the framers who believed that the country needed a judiciary with the capacity of massively intervening in the society to overcome injustices that threaten liberal democracy. Thus, the scope of judicial intervention can include everything from civil liberty to urban planning.[29]

Though the Supreme Court has widened its scope of interference in public administration, such interference remains an intervention till the time the court is aware of its limitations. In *P. Ramachandran Rao v. State of Karnataka*,[30] the Supreme Court observed that it did not consider itself as a despotic branch of the state. In *A Lakshman Kutty*,[31] the court observed that special responsibility devolves upon the judges to ensure that they do not trespass into the spheres earmarked for the other two branches of the state. The judges should avoid entering fields earmarked for the legislature and the executive. Judges cannot act as legislators, as they have neither been elected by the mandate of the people nor do they possess practical wisdom to understand the needs of different sections of society. The Supreme Court of India remains well aware of its limitations and till the time it works within the sphere constitutionally allotted to it by the state, all such acts of the court will come within the limit of positive judicial intervention.

While the act of the judiciary to call upon the legislature to perform its obligations remains desirable, any act of the judiciary to usurp the position of the legislature or the executive goes against the will of the Constitution, leading to a situation of judicial overreach, or in simpler terms, judicial intrusion. For example, while the intervention of the judiciary in matters involving minimum wage and ecological issues would be perceived as an act of judicial activism, its interference in matters such as fiscal policy of the state would be one of judicial intrusion.[32]

Some other examples of judicial overreach can be the judgment of the Supreme Court in *S. R. Bommai v. Union of India*[33] wherein it declared that the presidential proclamation of dissolving a state legislative assembly is subject to judicial review. The court laying down judicial legislations in *Vishakha v. State of Rajasthan*[34] regarding the prevention of sexual harassment of women at workplaces can be another such example of the court overstepping the thin constitutional line between judicial intervention and judicial intrusion, that is, activism and overreach.

Though there is no constitutionally decided framework to prevent the Supreme Court from performing an act of judicial overreach, the only solution of the issue can be a self-restriction imposed by the Supreme Court itself. This has been noted by the Supreme Court itself in the Indian Pharmaceutical Ltd case,[35] wherein it noted that there is a broad separation of power under the Indian Constitution, and the judiciary must know its limits.

CONCLUSIONS AND SUGGESTIONS

Amid the entire clamor against the ban that the Supreme Court imposed on the sale of firecrackers in the Delhi NCR region, the ban in its entirety stands valid from a legal point of view. The Supreme Court in exercising its writ jurisdiction comes out to be justified in delivering the judgment considering the fact that Article 142 of the Constitution has provided it with unconditional powers to decide upon such matters. Further, Articles 48A and 51 as considered by the court in delivering the judgment also corroborate supportively the ban imposed, considering they make it the duty of the state as well as its citizens to improve the quality of the environment and ensure the protection the environment.

The ban remains justified considering the fact that it led to the cleanest Diwali in three years in Delhi. Moreover, the ban led to a 40 percent drop in the level of pollution amid a situation that had seen an increase in the number of patients suffering from ailments caused by air pollution in hospitals, clearly showing the necessity of taking radical steps on the part of the court to protect the health of public of Delhi. The court did exactly this by giving importance to public health over issues such as economic implications of the ban, and thereby performed its duty of protecting public health as mentioned under Article 47 of the Constitution.

Further, since the ban was only on the sale of firecrackers and firecrackers do not form an integral part of Diwali celebrations. This too affirms the action as not being one of judicial overreach. In addition, the difference between judicial intervention and intrusion as discussed herein makes it clear that in the matter of banning the sale of firecrackers, the Supreme Court did not exceed its scope of authority. Though there have been multiple examples of the Supreme Court performing an act of judicial overreach, this decision cannot be treated in that category.

The authors would like to state a few suggestions in order to curb the pollution caused by the burning of firecrackers:

- For curbing the issue of pollution due to firecrackers in the region of Delhi NCR, the introduction of e-crackers, as seen in the Philippines, can be a viable option considering that the e-crackers cause no environmental degradation.
- Though the ban by the court has reduced the level of pollution due to firecrackers, an act of judicial intervention cannot be considered as a long-term solution. Therefore, there is a need for the creation of a better and effective legislative statute to govern the usage of firecrackers in already heavily polluted areas such as Delhi NCR.

- In the absence of statutory provisions differentiating judicial activism from judicial overreach, it becomes necessary for the courts to not exceed the defined constitutional sphere of their jurisdiction through self-restriction. For this, new judges need to be sensitized about the limit of their authority.
- There is a need for a statute governing the usage of firecrackers and limiting their quantity to put a check on the pollution caused by them.

NOTES

1. Payal Dey, Diwali: A Smog-mare for the Indian Capital, Indian Journal of Immunology and Respiratory Medicine, 2016, pp 78–79.

2. U.S. Mission India Now Cast Air Quality Index, https://in.usembassy.gov/embassy-consulates/new-delhi/air-quality-data/ (last visited on Nov 05, 2018, 3:30 pm).

3. Soutik Biswas, Delhi's Air Pollution is Triggering a Health Crisis. 2017 http://www.bbc.com/news/world-asia-india-41925067, 2017

4. Sanjeev Miglani, New Delhi Pollution Hits Dangerous Level, Putting Runners at Risk, https://in.reuters.com/article/us-india-pollution/new-delhi-pollution-hits-dangerous-level-putting-runners-at-risk-idINKBN1D70QN, November 07, 2017

5. Lawyered, What Delhi Government's Ban on Chinese Firecrackers means for the environment, http://www.thebetterindia.com/73456/ban-chinese-firecrackers-enforced-delhi-govt/, October 29, 2016.

6. Arjun Gopal and Ors. Vs Union of India, WRIT PETITION (CIVIL) NO. 728 OF 2015.

7. Ibid.

8. Sagun Kaushik vs Lt. Governor of Delhi and Others, ORDER C.W.P. Nos. 3364/97.

9. UNICEF, Clear the air for children, The Impact of Air Pollution on Children, October 2016, available at https://www.unicef.org/publications/files/UNICEF_Clear_the_Air_for_Children_30_Oct_2016.pdf.

10. World Health Organization, 'Household Air Pollution and Health', 2016.

11. Odd-even 3.0 to Combat Delhi Smog: All you need to know about the previous drives, Hindustan Times, Nov 9, 2017.

12. Ritam Haider, Delhi has Cleanest Diwali in 3 years after Cracker Sale Ban, But don't Celebrate, Hindustan Times, 20 Oct, 2017.

13. Delhi Air Pollution: 40% Dp in Emissions from Firecrackers this Diwali, Hindustan Times, 30 Oct, 2017.

14. Ibid. at 5.

15. Indian Constitution, Article 48A.

16. Dr M N Buch, Centre for Governance and Political Studies, VIF A Relook at the Three Pillars of the State: Wisdom by Hindsight, (Sept. 11, 2012).

17. Vol XIV, James Cameron , Juli Abouchar, The Precautionary Principle: A Fundamental Principle of Law and Policy for the Protection of the Global Environment (1st ed. 1991).

18. Ind. Const. art. 142.

19. Delhi Judicial Service vs. State of Gujarat and Others, 1991 AIR 2176.

20. National Green Tribunal Act, § 14 (2010).

21. Rule 89, Environment Protection Rule, 1986.

22. Notification GSR No.64 (E) dated 27.1.1992.

23. Robert K.G. Temple , The Genius of China: 3,000 Years of Science, Discovery, and Invention 256–265 (2007).

24. Ibid. at 5.

25. Ritu Prasad, Is Delhi's Diwali Firework Ban an Attack on Hinduism? (Oct. 19, 2017), available at http://www.bbc.com/news/blogs-trending-41670543.

26. Sanjeev Singh, Five Reasons why Ban on Sale of Firecrackers won't Curb Pollution in Delhi, Economic Times, Oct. 10, 2017).

27. Ibid., at 5.

28. Prevention of Environment & Sound Pollution v. Union of India SC/1717/2005.

29. Pratap Bhanu Mehta, The Rise of Judicial Sovereignty, Journal of Democracy (April 2007).

30. P. Ramachandran Rao v State of Karnataka, (2002) 4 SCC 578.

31. State of Kerala vs. Alakshman Kutty, (1986) 4SCC 632.

32. R. Shunmuga Sundaram, Judicial activism and overreach in India , Amicus Curiae, 2007.

33. S.R. Bommai vs UNION OF INDIA 1994 SCC (3) 1.

34. Vishakha and Others. vs. State of Rajasthan (6) SCC 241, 1997

35. Indian Drugs & Pharmaceuticals Ltd v Workmen, 1 SCC 408, 2007

Chapter 19

The Impact of Judicial Pronouncement in Promoting Environmental Concerns

Sakshi Sabharwal

INTRODUCTION

Environment is the wellspring of life on earth. Like one cannot live without water, air, and so on, similarly life without a green environment cannot be imagined. Environment has been intrinsic to many ancient civilizations. The Atharva Veda states, "What of thee I dig out let that quickly grow over."[1] There are a lot of threats to the environment in the form of new innovations such as thermal power, atomic energy, and so on that result in global warming and climate change. The pattern of Indian legislation to make new legislations and passing new bills is akin to old wine in a new bottle. In the recent years, the Indian judiciary has played an important role in devising and monitoring the implementation of measures for protecting our environment.

THE CONCEPT OF ENVIRONMENT

The word "environment" relates to surroundings. It has been not defined specifically. Sec. 2(a) of the Environment Protection Act, 1986 states that environment "includes water, air and land and inter-relationship which exists among and between water, air and land and human beings, other living creatures, plants, micro-organisms and property."[2]

Need for Environmental Laws

We are in the twenty-first century where everything has changed. We live in a nuclear arena and technology world. The environment is being continuously harmed by human activities. The dropping of nuclear bombs by the United States on Hiroshima and Nagasaki caused a lot of harm to the environment. The incident of Bhopal gas tragedy is one of the biggest disasters for humanity that not only caused tremendous loss to the environment but also greatly affected people, many of whom are still suffering. There is an acute need to have laws that keep pace with the developmental need as well as ecological balance.

EFFORTS BY INTERNATIONAL COMMUNITY TO PROTECT ENVIRONMENT

The Chernobyl nuclear accident deposited radio nuclides throughout the northern hemisphere. Since then, the concern of world is on the future health.[3]

The landmark toward the protection of environment was set by the United Nations Conference on Human Environment. The conference was held in Stockholm in 1972 and is popularly known as the Stockholm Conference.

After twenty years, the next conference was held in Rio de Janeiro, which is known as the Rio Declaration. The conference in Johannesburg—the World Summit on Sustainable Development—committed to build a humane, equitable, and caring society.

SIGNIFICANT CONVENTIONS/AGREEMENTS FOR PROTECTING ENVIRONMENT

Stockholm Conference, 1972

It was the first conference on the human environment held in Stockholm from June 5 to 16, 1972. More than 107 states participated in it. The then Indian Prime Minister Indira Gandhi was the first head of the state who addressed the conference. The Stockholm Conference can be seen as the first holistic approach to tackle the environmental problems.

Some important nonbinding instruments that were adopted are as follows:

- A declaration containing seven home truths
- Twenty-six principles
- Resolution on institutional and financial arrangements
- An action plan containing 109 recommendations

Convention on International Trade in Endangered Species of Wild Fauna and Flora, 1973

The aim of this convention was to recognize the growing value of wild flora and fauna from different points of view such as aesthetic, scientific, cultural, recreational, and economic. It was also seen that to protect the species from overexploitation through international trade, international cooperation was essential. It came as a result of a resolution adopted in the 1963 IUCN Meeting. It was aimed at controlling or preventing the commercial trade of endangered species or of products derived from them. India became a signatory to the convention in 1976.

Bonn Convention on Conversation of Migratory Species of Wild Animals, 1979

Wild animals are an irreplaceable part of the Earth. The convention was aimed at protecting migratory species and their habitats.

Nairobi Declaration, 1982

The Stockholm Conference's tenth anniversary was celebrated and a declaration known as Nairobi Declaration was adopted. It reinstated the principles of the Stockholm Conference.

World Charter for Nature, 1982

It was adopted by the UN General Assembly. It has twenty-four principles. It recognized that mankind is part of nature. Human civilizations have been shaped and nurtured by nature. It is, thus, our duty to protect and preserve it instead of harming it. We need to follow sustainable development if we want mankind to exist in the future. States have to adopt measures, disseminate environment education, formulate policies, encourage research, and so on.

Vienna Convention on Protection of Ozone Layer and Montreal Protocol, 1987

The Vienna Convention was signed with the objective of further developing scientific knowledge about the ozone layer and checking the possible adverse effects that may result from its modification. This was done to protect the ozone layer, which acts as a shield around the earth and protects it from ultraviolet rays. The convention made provisions for exchange of socioeconomic, commercial, and legal information.

PROVISIONS IN THE CONSTITUTION OF INDIA

After the Stockholm Conference, the 42nd amendment to the Constitution of India was brought. Provisions such as Article 48A and 51(a)(g) were added to it.

A new directive principle was added in the form of Article 48A. It states that the state shall endeavor to protect and improve the environment and to safeguard the forest and wildlife of the country.

A fundamental duty in the form of Article 51(A)(g) was added. It states that every citizen has a duty to protect wildlife and improve the natural environment, including forests, lakes, rivers, and life, and to have compassion for living creatures.

The Water (and Control of Pollution) Act, 1974 was added under Article 252 of the Constitution. It empowers the Parliament to enact on a state subject if two or more states make such a request.

The Air (Prevention and Control of Pollution) Act, 1981 and the Environment Protection Act, 1986 were enacted under Article 253 of the Constitution.[4]

ROLE OF JUDICIARY IN PROTECTING THE ENVIRONMENT

The Indian legal system in the 1980s underwent a sea change. It charted out new horizons of social justice. The judiciary has played a major role in protecting the environment and making laws to protect it.

There have been many cases in which judiciary has played its role toward protecting the environment, though there was reluctance in the beginning.

The question whether the right to life extends to the right to health and other hygienic conditions was answered in a simple manner by the Supreme Court in *Rural Litigation and Entitlement Kendra v. State of Uttar Pradesh.*[5] The petitioners were a voluntary organization. They feared that mining activities of the lessees caused ecological disturbance.

The Supreme Court ordered the closing of mining operations. The court considered the hardship but was of the view that 'it is a price that has to be paid for protecting and safeguarding the right of the people to live in healthy setting with borderline disturbance to ecological balance.'[6]

Another landmark decision was given by the Andhra Pradesh high court in *T Damodhar Rao v. Special Officer, Municipal Corporation of Hyderabad.*[7] A development plan earmarked an area as an open space for recreational purposes. The municipal corporation of Hyderabad had approved the plan. The state government subsequently acquired a part of the area for building residential quarters for LIC. The people living in the area challenged it as it was converting an open space in their vicinity into another residential complex.

The court noted that the attempt to build houses in such an open space was contrary to law.

The court held:

> Environmental law has succeeded in unshackling man's right to life and private liberty from the clutches of common law theory of individual possession. Examining the matter from the above constitutional points of view, it would be reasonable to hold that the enjoyment of life and its attainments and fulfillment guaranteed by Article 21 of the constitution embraces the protection and reservation of nature's gift without (which) life cannot be enjoyed. There can be no reason why practice of violent extinguishment of life alone would be regarded as violative of Article 21. The slow poisoning by the polluted atmosphere caused by environmental pollution and spoliation should also be regarded as amounting to violation of Article 21.

In *V Lakshmipathy v. State of Karnataka*,[8]it was held that once a development plan had earmarked an area for residential purpose, the land is to be used for that purpose only.

The court lay down:

> The right to life inherent in Art 21 of the Constitution of India does not fall short of the requirement of quality of life which is possible only in an environment of quality where, on account of human agencies, the quality of air and quality of environment are threatened or affected, the court would not hesitate to use its innovative power . . . to enforce and safeguard the right to life to promote public interest.

In *F. K. Hussain v. Union of India*,[9] the right to clean water was held to be attributing of the right to life.

Article 21 along with Article 51(A)(g) was emphasized in *L. K. Koolwal v. State of Rajasthan*[10] in which the court decided that citizens had a right to ask municipal authorities to clean the city as the right to clean city comes under the right to life under Article 21.

In *Subhash Kumar v. State of Bihar*,[11] it was observed that the right to live includes the right to enjoyment of pollution-free water and air for full enjoyment of life.

EXTENSION OF RIGHT TO LIFE

In *Consumer Education and Research Centre v. Union of India,*[12] the right to life was expanded to include the right to social security, human conditions of work, and leisure of workmen. According to the court, the fundamental right to health and medical care continues even after retirement. The court issued appropriate directions for filling the gaps in law relating to the compensation to the victims of asbestos industries.[13]

THE MISERY OF A VILLAGE

Indian Council for Environ-Legal Action v. Union of India[14] tells us how destroying our environment can become a misery for a village.

Remedial action was sought for a malady where industries manufacturing toxic H acid were located. The respondents stopped producing the toxic material. But they did not comply with the court's order of completely removing the sludge that flowed into the irrigation canal and affected the crops.

The Supreme Court fixed the responsibility on the errant company. It asked the Central Government to recover damages, in case the company fails to do so. It is the duty of the court to protect the fundamental right and liberty of citizens.[15]

COMBINED EFFECT OF ECO-PROVISIONS

In *M. C. Mehta v. Union of India,*[16] Articles 39(e), 47, and 48 were referenced to collectively cast a duty on the state to secure and improve public health and protect the environment. The court issued several directions to phase out grossly polluting old vehicles and non-CNG buses.

In *Hench Lal Tiara v. Kamala Devi,*[17] emphasis was laid on Articles 48A and 51(A)(g) of the Constitution.

In *Indian Handicrafts Emporium v. Union of India,*[18] it was ruled that under Article 19(1)(g), a trade dangerous to ecology could be either regulated or totally prohibited.

BHOPAL GAS TRAGEDY: AN INCIDENT THAT COMPLETELY SHOOK THE NATION

The Bhopal Gas Tragedy is a very familiar one. The incident not only destroyed the environment but also dangerously affected human beings, some of whom are still facing its repercussions. There has not been such a big incident till today. It shook people all over the world.

Compensation to the victims of the Bhopal disaster raised a dilemma in the Indian law of torts, which has originated from the English Common Law. It disclosed stark realities of a developing nation. A challenge was thrown to the Indian legal system.

The Bhopal Gas Leak Disaster (Processing of Claims) Act, 1985 was passed that conferred responsibility on the Union of India of suing *parent's patria* on behalf of victims.

Many criticized the decision saying that the court missed the opportunity of making a new law for such cases.

IMPORTANT PRINCIPLES FORMULATED BY INDIAN JUDICIARY

Supreme Court Formulates the Absolute Liability

The Supreme Court, in view of cases of carelessness and ensuing tragedy, formulated the Doctrine of Absolute Liability. It is a strict absolute liability without exceptions.

Polluter Pays Principle

> "If anyone advisedly spoils the water of another . . . let him not solely pay damages, but purify the stream or cistern which contains the water."—Plato

Over time, the polluter pays principle has become popular. If we create a mess, it is our duty to clean it. The Rio Declaration had the origin of this principle.

In *Vellore Citizen's Forum v. Union of India*,[19] it was declared by the Supreme Court that this principle is an essential feature of sustainable development.

Precautionary Principle

This principle has its origins in the Rio Declaration. The Supreme Court developed three principles in the Vellore citizen forum case:

1. Environmental principles must prevent, anticipate, and attack the causes of environmental degradation.
2. For postponing measures, lack of certainty should not be used.
3. The onus of proof is on the actor to show that their action is benign.

Public Trust Doctrine

This doctrine has its origins in Rome. It was adopted by the English Common Law and later came in India. It rests on the principle that certain resources like air, water, sea, and forests have great importance to people.

In *M. C. Mehta v. Kamal Nath and Others*,[20] the court ruled that the public trust doctrine is a part of the law of the land.

Doctrine of Sustainable Development

The World Commission on Environment and Development created the Brundtland Report. The report signifies sustainable development as that which meets the needs of the present without compromising the ability of future generations to meet their own needs.

Mahatma Gandhi justifiably said, "The earth has enough for everybody's need but not for everybody's greed."

In *Rural Litigation and Entitlement Kendra v. State of UP*,[21] the court for first time took into cognizance issues relating to the environment and development.

In the Vellore citizen's forum case,[22] the Supreme Court held that sustainable development is a viable concept to improve the quality of human life.

CONCLUSIONS

Environment plays a major role in our lives. Our life depends on the environment. As one cannot live without water, air, and so on, a heathy life without a green environment cannot be imagined. Environment has been intrinsic to many ancient civilizations. We harm the environment for our greed without realizing its importance. But now the time has come to protect the environment to sustain ourselves and our future generations on this Earth. The judiciary has played a major role in this regard. It has tried to bring the right to a healthy environment as the right to life under Article 21 of the Constitution of India. It has also formulated many important principles. Judiciary is trying to fill the gaps where there is laziness on part of the legislature. Media, which is the fourth pillar of democracy, also plays a major role in creating awareness among people. The need of the hour is for the legislature to join hands with judiciary and make and follow rules to protect the Earth. This can be done by creating awareness among people and joining hands together.

"The power of one is that the power of the many, the ability of modification."

NOTES

1. MC Mehta, Growth of Environmental Jurisprudence in India, p. 71, 1999.
2. Sec2(a) of EPA, 1986.
3. Lynn R Anspaugh, 'The Global Impact of Chernobyl Reactor Accident', Science, 16 December 1988, p 1513.
4. AIR 1981 SC.
5. AIR 1985 SC 652.
6. AIR 1985SC, pp 656, 657.
7. AIR 1987AP171.
8. AIR 1992 Kant57, p 62.
9. AIR1990Ker321.
10. AIR1988Raj2.
11. AIR 1991 SC 421, p 424.
12. AIR 1995 SC 922.
13. Ibid.
14. AIR 1996SC1446.
15. Ibid.
16. AIR2002SC1696.
17. (2001)6scc496.
18. AIR2003SC3240.
19. AIR 1996 5 SCC 647.
20. 1997 SCC 388.
21. AIR 1987SC1037.
22. AIR 1996 5 SCC 647.

Chapter 20

Air Pollution in India

A Critical Challenge and Its Solutions

Mani Bhushan Kumar Jha

INTRODUCTION: AIR POLLUTION—THE CHALLENGE

A healthy environment and clean air are the basic requirements for the well-being of human beings. Industrialization and an increase in the urban landscape have been happening at a swift rate throughout the world. This may be required to meet the requirements of the human population with the limited resources of the Earth. However, the increasing industrial growth and the rapid growth of urban landscape have badly affected the level of clean air in cities.[1] The increasing level of air pollution has caused many problems that affect the lives of people, putting them at various risks. One such risk is the health risk caused by the exposure to increasing levels of air pollution. Throughout the world, over seven million premature deaths occur annually, as per the estimates by the World Health Organization in 2018. Again as per WHO in the same year, more than 80% of people living in urban areas that monitor air pollution are exposed to air quality levels that exceed WHO guideline limits, with low- and middle-income countries suffering from the highest exposures, both indoors and outdoors.

India's population of 1.3 billion, which accounts for almost 17 percent of the world's population, has created enormous pressure on India's environment. The rapid industrialization and economic growth are also causing many hazards to India's environment. India's capital, New Delhi, features at the top in the list of world's most polluted capital cities by different global studies and ambient air quality databases, as per Reuters, in 2019.[2] As per a report by WHO, New Delhi's average annual ambient concentration of particulate matter (PM) 2.5 (particulate matter with diameters less than 2.5 microns) in a cubic meter of air was 113.5 micrograms in 2018, almost 13 times the WHO air quality guideline (10 micrograms per cubic meter) and three times the Central Pollution Control Board (CPCB) annual air quality standard (40 micrograms per cubic meter).[3] As per the world air quality report of 2018 by IQ AirVisual, thirteen out of the fifteen most polluted regional cities in the world are in India.[4] According to Global Burden of Disease, a comprehensive regional and global research program including 500 researchers representing over 300 institutions and 50 countries, has estimated that 3283 Indians died per day due to outdoor air pollution in India in 2015, making the potential number of deaths due to outdoor air pollution in India in 2015 to 11.98 lakh".[5]

HEALTH RISKS OF AIR POLLUTION

There are many undesirable elements present in the air, causing an increased level of air pollution. Elements such as PM 2.5, PM 10, sulfur dioxide, and nitrogen oxides are very dangerous for human health. The high level of pollution present in the urban areas has affected human health to a great extent.[6] As mentioned in the previous section, this process is ever-growing, and thus, the risk level is also increasing with the increase in the level of air pollution. With every breath that a person inhales, the health risks increase. The risk is not just injurious but also deadly for human life. As a result, air pollution has been infamously recognized as a threat to public health in different parts of the world. The State of Global Air report released in 2017 has highlighted the risk of death caused by air pollution owing to the increasing level of pollutants.[7] The report also states that exposure to PM 2.5 is ranked fifth in the world when compared to all the risks worldwide. Thus, people who are exposed to different levels of air pollution are also exposed to the adverse effects of air pollution on their health and other aspects of living standards.

Apart from the risk to human beings, the increasing level of pollution also causes a great risk to the environment as it leads to climate change and global warming. The increased level of ozone in the lower levels of the Earth's atmosphere is decreasing the agricultural productivity, thus directly affecting the people who are dependent on agriculture for their livelihoods.

CAUSES OF AIR POLLUTION

From 36 crores in 1951 to 121 crores in 2011, the population of India has grown multifold. Driven by the rural to urban migration, the urbanization level has grown from 17 percent in 1951 to 31 percent in 2011, as evident in the Census of 2011. The increasing population has a direct relation with the fuel consumption. Even after the successful implementation of the Ujjwala Scheme where rural households have been provided with free liquefied petroleum gas (LPG) connections, the households in slums and some rural areas still depend on biomass for cooking. The population growth, along with the rise in economic growth in cities, has increased transportation requirements. From 5.3 million registered vehicles in 1981, India had over 159 million registered vehicles in 2012. This has caused increased usage of fuel consumed by the transportation sector, which has in turn caused a great amount of resuspension of dust particles in the atmosphere, further adding to the concentration of PM.

There has been exponential industrial growth over the past few decades. A comprehensive study by the CPCB formulated an environmental pollution index in 2009, and it found that over half of the industrial areas/clusters present in the country were critically polluted.[8] To fulfill the energy requirements of the growing population and the industries, electricity generation has also increased in India from 5 billion kilowatt-hour in 1951 to 811 billion kilowatt-hour in 2011.[9] India had mainly coal-based power plants until the recent past, and they are major sources of air pollution. The growth of the construction sector has also contributed greatly to the level of emissions in the atmosphere.

The open burning of agricultural crop residue is one of the major causes of a serious level of air pollution in cities like Delhi. States like Punjab, Haryana, and Uttar Pradesh witness a large amount of crop burning, which causes emissions of pollutants.

Overall, the huge population growth, development of urban landscapes, industrial growth, energy growth, agricultural crop burning, and so on are some of the major drivers that lead to air pollution by releasing a great amount of emissions of different kinds.

AIR POLLUTION CONTROL POLICIES AT PRESENT

India's environment protection philosophy dates back to its ancient times. In modern times, the legislations that affect air pollution either directly or indirectly started in British India. Post-Independence, Part IV of the Indian Constitution consisted of several articles that underlined the philosophy for environment protection. But the 42nd constitutional amendment provided stronger laws. In response to the Stockholm International Conference on the Human Environment (1972), Article 48A in the chapter of Directive Principles of State Policy and Article 51(A)(g) in the chapter of Fundamental Duties of the Indian Constitution was inserted. It expressed India's commitment to protect and improve the environment and preserve air quality. The Stockholm International Conference also promoted the development of environmental legislation in India. Water Act, which led to the formation of CPCB and state pollution control boards (SPCBs), Air Act, Environment Conservation Act, Motor Vehicles Act, and so on are some of the landmark acts enacted in that period. In India, the need to integrate environmental concerns into the process of economic development was voiced as far back as the late 1960s, during the formulation of the Fourth Five Year Plan (1969–1974), which stated that "Planning for harmonious development is possible only on the basis of a comprehensive appraisal of environmental problems." The integration of environmental resource management with national economic planning started with the Sixth Five Year Plan (1980–1985). The Seventh and Eighth Five Year Plans recognized the issues of environmental resource preservation and sustainability as being as important as many other developmental objectives. The policies, enunciated in the National Conservation Strategy and Policy Statement on Environment and Development, and the Policy Statement on Control of Pollution, both established in 1992, were pursued in the Ninth Five Year Plan. Assigning conservation a high priority both at the central and state levels, the Tenth Five Year Plan (2002–2007) also sought to tackle environmental degradation in a holistic manner in order to ensure both economic and environmental sustainability. These all proved to have played a very significant role in controlling India's environmental pollution, especially air pollution.

The Supreme Court has also been instrumental in leading the charge to curb air pollution. The Supreme Court Action Plans (SCAPs) have been very instrumental in reducing the industrial as well as vehicular pollution. Starting from Delhi, SCAPs have been implemented in over 15 cities.

The CPCB and SPCBs, responsible for data collection and policy implementation, have been created by the Water Act and the Air Act, respectively. A national environmental monitoring program soon became a reality under their governance structure. A monitoring network for the assessment of ambient air quality has been set successfully. Under the National Air Quality Monitoring Programme (NAMP), air quality is being monitored at 770 places, which consists of 339 cities in 28 states, and presently, ambient air quality is being monitored at 779 locations throughout the country. Further, real-time monitoring is taking place at 170 locations in 102 cities in 18 states/UTs.[10]

Numerous sectoral interventions to curb air pollution have also taken place over the years. Be it industry or biomass, many sector-specific actions have produced results. All these schemes of things have their own pros and cons. The environmental jurisprudence in India has developed over a period of time, but the level of pollution has not reduced so far. Different governments and executive authorities have introduced different policies at different times to counter the same problem of the increasing level of air pollution. The policies introduced to tackle, manage, and reduce the risks of air pollution have not been able to provide any long-term solution, resulting in the increased concentrations of emissions causing air pollution. The air quality touches new low every year, and declaration of public health emergencies has become a routine now. The government's own data validates the increasing level of air pollution. It is high time that we learn from the failures of the past and introduce a holistic and comprehensive plan to control the emissions. The National Clean Air Programme (2019) is a step in the right direction, and if followed religiously along with the following set of recommendations, it can show immediate results.

RECOMMENDATIONS OF THE STUDY

Urban Planning and Administration

Apart from controlling the emissions, the pollution level can be affected by the design of cities, its geographical distribution, and other administrative factors. Policymakers can effectively plan the structural distribution of pollution sources. For example, traffic routes, open areas, landfills, industries, electricity generation plants, and so on can be relocated strategically.

Expanding the Ujjwala Scheme to Provide Subsidies to Below Poverty Line (BPL) Households

Under the Ujjwala scheme, the Indian government has distributed more than 80 million LPG cylinders to poor households in rural areas. This has increased access to green fuels, thus reducing the risk of exposure to indoor pollution. However, the problem is refilling those cylinders. The poverty level is not allowing the poor households to get their LPG cylinders refilled. The government should step in and provide subsidies to poor households for the refilling process.

Increased Use of Solar and Other Renewable Energy Forms to Meet Rising Energy Demands

The reliance on thermal power plants and fossil fuels is not sustainable. The process of shifting from traditional nonrenewable forms of energy to new renewable forms of energy should be fastened. India is facing difficulties in financing the energy transition, but it should use its diplomatic clout for importing better technology from the developed nations, which have much enhanced green energy processes. Solar energy should also be used for areas where people are still using kerosene oil for lighting purposes. Solar lanterns are not only sustainable but also help in the reduction of emissions.

Creating Awareness and a Citizen Movement to Control Air Pollution

In the past few years, awareness regarding air pollution has increased, but it has not reached every part of society. The awareness is limited to educated people living in urban clusters. The experience of Swachh Bharat Abhiyan (Clean India Program) should be put to use by the administration. Citizen-driven governance and movement is the need of the hour.

Efficient Collection and Segregation Mechanism

Waste management in India's urban landscape is not efficient and creates a lot of emissions. The PCBs should collaborate with city corporations and use the available technology to engage citizens in a better way.

Ban on Waste Burning

Despite there being a law banning waste burning, it is a regular incidence in big cities. Strict adherence should be maintained by imposing a huge fine on nonadherence. Technology can be used to engage with citizens in getting information about waste burning. Developing an app may also help.

Harnessing Technology to Create Energy from Waste

The proper segregation of wastes can be incentivized so that people start doing it in their homes. With proper segregation, modern technological solutions should be harnessed to create energy from waste materials. Strict implementation of India's biomass policy can yield good results. Public–private partnership models can also be used for this.

Controlling Vehicular Emissions

Strategies should be adopted to reduce private transportation demands. Private motorized modes should be shifted to public nonmotorized mediums. There can be a reduction of 90–95 percent in the level of carbon monoxide and volatile organic compounds (VOCs) by the use of public transportation. It can also lead to a reduction in the level of carbon dioxide and nitrogen oxides by 50 percent.[11] Enhanced quality of fuels, technology, and infrastructure should be put in place to improve the overall performance of the sector.

Following International Best Practices to Implement Vehicle Ownership Controls

Vehicle quota systems, taxes, and insurance are great tools for vehicle ownership control. These measures are already in place in Singapore, Japan, and Hong Kong. The control measures increase the cost of owning a car and thus restrict car ownership.[12]

WAY FORWARD

To sum up, India can benefit from the National Clean Air Programme, which the government launched in January 2019. The process of open burning of garbage is a very crucial problem that increases the risk of air pollution in the winters. Public participation is crucial to solve the problem of air pollution as people play a major role in facilitating social capital and enforce effective solutions. Without the interest and cooperation of the general public, the control policies for air pollution cannot succeed.

Apart from recommendations in this brief, the government should increase its reach to the public at large. Awareness campaigns should be launched, workshops conducted, media engaged constructively, and schools, colleges, and so on used to compel a behavioral change to control air pollution. The long-term success of these processes will depend on the stringent implementation of the policies and regulations. Therefore, the government should harness technological solutions and engage the private sector as well in its campaign. "Cities like Delhi could follow the examples of Mexico City, and use its recently launched early warning system to generate health advisories for the people, especially children, senior citizens, and other sensitive groups".[13]

For decades now, the people living in cities of India have not seen blue skies in winters. The world's largest democracy cannot delay any further the citizens' right to clean air. It is high time that the Government of India takes the lead with. After all, democracy is of the people, by the people, and for the people.

NOTES

1. Veron, R. (2006). Remaking Urban Environments:The Political Ecology of Air Pollution in Delhi. *Environment and Planning*, 93–109.

2. Reuters. (2019, March 5). *New Delhi is World's Most Polluted Capital, Beijing Eighth.* Retrieved from Reuters: https://in.reuters.com/article/us-india-pollution/new-delhi-is-worlds-most-polluted-capital-beijing-eighth-idINKCN1QM1FH.

3. WHO. (2018). *Air Pollution.* Retrieved from World Health Organization: https://www.who.int/health-topics/air-pollution#tab=tab_1.

4. IQAirVisual. (2018). *World Most Polluted Cities 2018 (PM2.5).* (2018). Retrieved from Air Visual: https://www.airvisual.com/world-most-polluted-cities.

5. IQAirVisual. (2017). *Airpocalypse : Assessment of Air Polluiton in Indian Cities.* Greenpeace India.

6. CPCB. (2011–2015). *Non-attained Cities with Respect to Ambient Air Quality India.* New Delhi: Central Pollution Control Board.

7. HEI. (2017). *State of Global Air.* Health Effects Institute.

8. Central Pollution Control Board (CPCB). (2009). *Comprehensive Environmental Assessment of Industrial Clusters.* New Delhi: Central Pollution Control Board.

9. CSO. (2011). *Energy Statistics Report.* New Delhi: Central Statistics Office.

10. MoEFCC, G.O.I. (2019, July 26). *Advance Question Search, Starred question number 486.* Retrieved from Parliament of India, Loksabha: http://164.100.24.220/loksabhaquestions/annex/171/AS486.pdf.

11. Shapiro, R. J. (2002). *Conserving and Preserving the Environment -The Role of Public Transportation.* Washington: American Public Transportation Association.

12. Sharma, S. (2018). *Certain Measures for Air Pollution Control in Urban Centres of India.* New Delhi: The Energy and Resources Institute.

13. Jha et al. (2019, October 26). *To Clean Its Air, There Are Miles to Go Before Delhi Can Sleep.* Retrieved from The Wire: https://thewire.in/environment/to-clean-its-air-there-are-miles-to-go-before-delhi-can-sleep.

BIBLIOGRAPHY

CPCB. (2014). *National Ambient Air Quality Status.* New Delhi: Central Pollution Control Board.

Thorton, A. (2019, March). *7 of the World's 10 Most Polluted Cities are in India.* Retrieved from World Economic Forum: https://www.weforum.org/agenda/2019/03/7-of-the-world-s-10-most-polluted-cities-are-in-india/.

Index

About the Contributors

Amit Dhall is assistant professor at Amity Law School, Amity University, Noida, Uttar Pradesh. He holds BCom, LLB, LLM, MBA, PGDFM, PGDCLM, and PhD degrees. He has fifteen years of experience working in legal departments, courts, and academic institutions. He has authored various research articles in national and international journals, as well as book chapters. Furthermore, he has guided LLM and LLB students in carrying out their legal research.

Amit M. Bhattacharya is director at Research, Innovation & Development Associates (RIDA), New Delhi. He earned his doctoral degree from Banaras Hindu University, Varanasi, Uttar Pradesh, and worked as an executive in the banking sector for around three decades. He then worked as professor of economics and financial management in two universities for a few years. He has authored research papers on various socioeconomic issues that are published in various national and international journals. As an independent researcher, he participated in a good number of national and international conferences and delivered thought-provoking lectures widely appreciated by academia. Dr. Bhattacharya has authored around thirty-nine research papers, innumerable write-ups published in dailies and periodicals, chapter contributions in five edited books, and one book on industrial relations. He was the CEO of a company in the infrastructure sector in Madhya Pradesh. Since 2014, Dr. Bhattacharya is honorary director of RIDA that comprises a team of intellectuals undertaking various research studies and regularly contributing to shaping up of national policies. He is also senior advisor at Think India Council that supports and promotes government initiatives for uplifting marginalized people.

Abdul Jabbar Haque is assistant professor in law at Haldia Law College, Haldia, West Bengal, affiliated to Vidyasagar University, since November 2014. He obtained his BA, LLB (Hons.), and LLM (with specialization in environmental law) degrees from Haldia Law College in 2009 and 2012, respectively. He practiced law as an advocate at the High Court of Judicature, Kolkata, in 2009–2010 and again in 2012–2013. Haque served as assistant professor in law at Mohammad Abdul Bari Institute of Juridical Science (affiliated to University of Kalyani), Domkal, Murshidabad, West Bengal, from December 2013 to November 2014. His areas of interests are environmental law, information technology law, intellectual property law, human rights law, constitutional law, banking law, insurance law, and women and children laws. He has published numerous papers in various law journals of national and international repute, and has also edited books. In addition, he has attended and presented at several national and international seminars and conferences.

Alok Gupta is assistant professor at Amity Law School (Delhi), Noida, Uttar Pradesh, affiliated to GGSIP University, since September 2011. His areas of interests are micro- and macroeconomics, development planning, environmental studies, and disaster management. He has published several articles in research journals, authored books, and presented papers at various national and international conferences and seminars on various aspects of disaster management, such as Asian Conference of Remote Sensing, Taiwan, and International Mapping Forum, Okinawa, Japan. For the latter, he was awarded the "Young Authors Award." He has also attended various international training courses on disaster management at Asian Disaster Preparedness Centre (ADPC), Bangkok, and GFZ, Potsdam, Germany.

Urmil Vats is assistant professor in the Department of Political Science, Shyama Prasad Mukherji College, University of Delhi, New Delhi. She has been teaching at Delhi University since 2006 and has published numerous articles and research papers in national and international journals. She has been awarded National Women's Empowerment and Development Award by the International Association of Educators for World Peace. She has keen interest in Indian politics, political theory, and human rights.

Kriti Parashar is a PhD research scholar and visiting faculty at Lucknow University, Lucknow, Uttar Pradesh. Before this, she was assistant professor at Amity University, Lucknow. She authored a book on "Triple Talaq" published in 2018. Her article titled "Globalisation vis-à-vis Human Rights: Critical Perspectives" was published in the *International Journal of Human Rights and Constitutional Law*. Her article on Uttar Pradesh Crime Control

Act was published in the *GLC Law Review*. She has also written pieces for several newspapers and blogs.

Vatsala Sood is a law student pursuing BA, LLB (Hons.) at Symbiosis Law School, Pune, Maharashtra. When she is not studying or attending classes, she likes to travel, listen to music, and go for long walks.

Priti Chahal is assistant professor at Shyama Prasad Mukherji College, University of Delhi, New Delhi. She is conducting research on refugees in South Asia and the Saharawi refugees of Western Sahara, Africa. She has authored two books—titled *Refugees* and *Host State* and *Sahrawi Refugees: Western Sahara Conflict*—and contributed to one edited book titled *Your Laws and Your Rights*. She has written many articles for Delhi University syllabus books on political science, as well as papers for journals.

Amrit Kaur Pannu is an advocate, registered with the Bar Council of India. She holds a BA, LLB (Hons.) degree from RGNUL, Patiala, Punjab, and an LLM degree in international law from the University of Edinburgh, Edinburgh, UK. Her master's thesis was based on the violation of the principle of non-refoulement by India in the wake of the Rohingya refugee crisis. She is currently working at the Delhi High Court as judicial law clerk.

Ashwani Pant is assistant professor, Amity Law School, Amity University, Noida, Uttar Pradesh, and has a teaching experience of ten years. He earned his LLM degree in from Banaras Hindu University, Varanasi, Uttar Pradesh. He also holds a PG Diploma in international environmental law and is currently pursuing PhD in environmental law. His areas of interest include constitutional law, criminal law and procedural laws, environment laws, and comparative laws. He specializes in international environmental laws and procedural laws. He has written research paper and articles for various international and national journals. He has a keen interest in environmental law and its enforcement policies, and is working on a book on environmental law.

Ashutosh Tripathi is assistant professor at the School of Law, University of Petroleum and Energy Studies, Dehradun, Uttarakhand, and has six years of teaching experience. He has published articles in several reputed law journals.

Jayshree Sharma is lecturer at Tinsukia Law College, Tinsukia, Assam, since 2015. She teaches subjects such as human rights, intellectual property law, and legal research methodology. She has participated in and presented papers at seminars hosted by Indian Law Institute (in collaboration with International Council of Jurists, London) and Wildlife Trust of India (in collaboration with IMES, University of Cologne, Germany and Institute of Biodiversity Law, Stetson University, USA). Some of her publications include a piece titled "The Hidden Holocaust of Chechnya" in the book *Legal Status of Sexual Minorities: National and International Perspective* (2018). She has also written articles on 3D printing, detrimental impact of gold mining, and the harmful effects of plastics for a legal website.

Aadarsh Anand is a law scholar at the School of Law, University of Petroleum and Energy Studies, Dehradun, Uttarakhand. The environment and energy sector has always interested him. He has several publications to his name, including "Impact of Global Warming and Changes: Environmental Refugees" published in *Journal for Socio-Economic Issues*, published by Vidhi Aagaz; "Stalking in India: A Critical Analysis," which was adjudged the best paper at Madhya Pradesh Law Conclave; "Cyber Crimes: A Step towards Modern Harassment" published in the *Legal Mirror Journal*; and an article on "Challenging the Strict Liability Rule" published in *International Journal of Socio-Legal Research*. Mr. Anand has worked and researched on various aspects of law by way of internships, but the main focus has always been on energy and environmental law.

Dalima Arora is a law student at the School of Law, University of Petroleum and Energy Studies, Dehradun, Uttarakhand. When it comes to research, she is interested in a very wide range of topics. Although her inclination is toward the law of taxation, she tries to gain knowledge about different subjects of law through research papers. Environmental law is another area that attracts her interest. She has also researched on matters related to the Arbitration and Conciliation Act, 1996; Companies Act, 2013; Code of Civil Procedure, 1908; and Insolvency and Bankruptcy Act, 2016.

Vedant Dikshit is a law scholar who earned his BA, LLB (Hons.) degree from NALSAR University of Law, Hyderabad, Telangana. He has actively participated in various conferences and has published a number of papers on various topics. He is the recipient of the Anantha Narasimha Reddy Gold Medal for securing the top rank in constitutional law. He has written as article titled "British Creation/Codification of Hindu Law" published in the *GNLU Journal of Law, Development, and Politics*. He served as the managing editor of the journal *Indian Journal of Contemporary Legal Issues* from November 2015 to November 2016 and received a Letter of Appreciation for academic performance from Mr. Kapil Sibal in 2012, then Minister of Human Resource Development in the Government of India. Mr. Dikshit also received a certificate of appreciation in State-Level Environmental Awareness Examination 2009 held by Environmental Care and Sustainable Development Society, Madhya Pradesh.

Sharaban Tahura Zaman is an environmental lawyer and academic based in Bangladesh, working to promote environmental and climate justice. Currently, she is serving as lecturer in the Department of Law, North South University, Bangladesh, and as senior research fellow with the Centre for Climate Justice-Bangladesh (CCJ-B). Ms. Zaman is a Chevening Scholar and competed her specialized LLM in global environment and climate change law from the University of Edinburgh, UK. She is also a member of Legal Research Group (LRG), Centre for International Sustainable Development Law (CISDL) of the Faculty of Law at McGill University, Montreal, Canada, with particular research interest in climate change and development. She is also involved in the UN climate change negotiations to support the least developed countries (LDCs) negotiations team on compliance and nationally determined contributions (NDCs). She has written a large number of research papers and also presented papers at various conferences.

M. Hafijul Islam Khan is an environmental lawyer, working on legal issues related to environment, natural resource management, and climate change for the past sixteen years. Mr. Khan is a climate change negotiator and currently acting as co-coordinator of the LDCs group for loss and damage negotiation stream at the UN Framework Convention on Climate Change. He is leading the CCJ-B as its director. Mr. Khan is research fellow at the Centre for Sustainable Development Law (CISDL), Canada, and senior fellow at the Centre for International Governance Innovation (CIGI), Canada. He is a member of IUCN World Commission on Environmental Law and also involved with Environmental Law Alliance Worldwide (E-LAW). Mr. Khan has LLM degrees from the University of Dhaka and Central European University (CEU). He has also completed a number of diplomas and short courses from a number of reputed universities, including the University of Oxford, and has published a number of articles and book chapters on climate law and policy.

Riya Gulati is paralegal at the law offices of Caro Kinsella & Youth Ambassador for the ONE Campaign, Ireland. She has completed LLM (intellectual property and information technology) from University College Dublin and BA, LLB from Bharati Vidyapeeth Deemed University, Pune. She has published a number of papers and articles in various national and international journals.

Ritika Chauhan is a BBA-LLB student at the Symbiosis Law School, Pune. She is currently focusing on making a career in taxation law and taxation litigation. She has interned with some top-tier law firms in this field. She has authored three research publications in reputed journals on topics such as lifting and reverse lifting of the corporate veil and critique on the concept of rule of law and its applicability in Indian polity. Despite her chosen field being tax law, Ms. Ritika is extremely passionate about environment law and litigation. She has founded a nonprofit organization dedicated to saving the environment by taking up local projects in Pune and Mumbai.

Anisha Singh and Ankit Singh are law students at Chanakya National Law University, Patna. They are dedicated to researching the various aspects of law. They were the joint runners-up at the 2nd Justice H.R. Khanna Memorial essay writing competition and the Novo Juris Legal essay writing competition on data privacy laws. They have even represented their college at the renowned Philip C. Jessup International Moot Court Competition."

Sakshi Sabharwal is a lawyer in New Delhi. She has participated in various moot courts, Model United Nations, and law conferences and has published papers in Nyay Disha, a UGC-recognized newsletter by Indore Institute of Law; in a book titled *Ameya*; and in a magazine, known as Kaleidoscope, Dubai, UAE.

Mani Bhushan Kumar Jha is a master's student at Willy Brandt School of Public Policy, Erfurt, Germany. He is currently specializing in international political economy, and public and nonprofit management. He is a lawyer by background and has worked previously at Public Policy Research Centre and World Resources Institute, New Delhi. He is also the founder of a youth-led nonprofit in India, Chanakya Policy Foundation, which works at the intersection of law and public policy to engage young people in policy-making processes.

www.ingramcontent.com/pod-product-compliance
Lightning Source LLC
LaVergne TN
LVHW091533200926
848483LV00002B/386

* 9 7 8 1 7 9 3 6 1 4 5 4 4 *